The Child's World

of related interest:

Approaches to Needs Assessment in Children's Services
Edited by Harriet Ward and Wendy Rose
ISBN 1 85302 780 4

Child Development for Child Care and Protection Workers
Brigid Daniel, Sally Wassell and Robbie Gilligan
ISBN 1 85302 633 6

Making an Impact – Children and Domestic Violence
A Reader
Marianne Hester, Chris Pearson and Nicola Harwin
ISBN 1 85302 844 4

Parental Substance Misuse and Child Welfare
Brynna Kroll and Andy Taylor
ISBN 1 85302 791 X

Effective Ways of Working with Children and Families
Edited by Malcolm Hill
ISBN 1 85302 619 0

Disabled Children and the Law
Research and Good Practice
Janet Read and Luke Clements
ISBN 1 85302 793 6

The Early Years
Assessing and Promoting Resilience in Vulnerable Children 1
Brigid Daniel and Sally Wassell
ISBN 1 84310 013 4

The School Years
Assessing and Promoting Resilience in Vulnerable Children 2
Brigid Daniel and Sally Wassell
ISBN 1 84310 018 5

Adolescence
Assessing and Promoting Resilience in Vulnerable Children 3
Brigid Daniel and Sally Wassell
ISBN 1 84310 019 3

The Child's World

Assessing Children in Need

Edited by Jan Horwath

Jessica Kingsley Publishers
London and New York

First published in the United Kingdom in 2001
by Jessica Kingsley Publishers Ltd
116 Pentonville Road
London N1 9JB, England
and
29 West 35th Street, 10th fl.
New York, NY 10001–2299, USA

www.jkp.com

Copyright © the NSPCC and the University of Sheffield 2001

Second Impression 2001
Third Impression 2002
Fourth impression 2003
Fifth impression 2003

Library of Congress Cataloging in Publication Data
A CIP catalog record for this book is available from the Library of Congress

British Library Cataloguing in Publication Data
A CIP catalogue record for this book is available from the British Library

ISBN 1 85302 957 2

Printed and Bound in Great Britain by
Athenaeum Press, Gateshead, Tyne and Wear

Contents

Part III Assessing the developmental needs of children

The chapters in this section are designed to:
- provide an overview of the developmental needs of children
- consider the specific issues relating to the needs of particular groups of children
- explore research and current practice and provide practical guidance related to specific assessment tasks.

Part IV Assessing parental capacity to respond to the developmental needs of the child

The chapters in this section are designed to:
- enable the reader to begin to identify ways in which parenting issues may impact on parenting capacity
- raise awareness of specific parenting issues and factors which should be considered as part of the assessment process
- provide some practical guidance to assessing parenting capacity.

Foreword

Securing the wellbeing of children, protecting them from all forms of harm and ensuring their developmental needs are responded to appropriately are primary aims of Government policy. Local authority social services departments, working with other local authority departments and health authorities, have a duty to safeguard and promote the welfare of children in their area who are in need and to promote the upbringing of such children, wherever possible by their families, through providing an appropriate range of services. A critical task is to find out with the family whether a child is in need and how that child might best be helped. The effectiveness with which a child's needs are assessed will be key to the effectiveness of subsequent actions and services, and ultimately to the outcomes for the child.

A framework for assessing children in need

The *Framework for the Assessment of Children in Need and their Families* (Department of Health *et al.* 2000), developed as an integral part of the 'Quality Protects' programme, provides a systematic way of understanding, analysing and recording what is happening to children and young people within their families and the wider context of the community in which they live. From such an understanding of what are inevitably complex issues and interrelationships, clear professional judgements can be made. These judgements include whether this is a child in need, whether the child is suffering or likely to suffer significant harm, what actions must be taken and which services would best meet the needs of this particular child and family. The evidence-based knowledge which has informed the development of the framework has been drawn from a wide range of research studies and theories across a number of disciplines and from the accumulated experience of policy and practice.

The guidance, to which *The Child's World: Assessing Children in Need* relates, describes the Assessment Framework and government expectations of how it will be used. The framework has been incorporated into the Government's guidance on safeguarding children from harm, *Working*

Together to Safeguard Children (Department of Health *et al.* 1999). Both documents were issued under Section 7 of the Local Authority Social Services Act 1970 which requires local authorities in their social services functions to act under the general guidance of the Secretary of State. As such, the documents do not have the full force of statute, but should be complied with unless local circumstances indicate exceptional reasons which justify a variation.

The policy context

The Government is committed to ending child poverty, tackling social exclusion and promoting the welfare of all children – so that they can thrive and fulfil their potential as citizens throughout their lives. Programmes such as 'Sure Start', 'Connexions' and 'Quality Protects' are designed to support families, promote educational attainment, reduce truancy and school exclusion and secure a future for young people in education, employment or training. All aim to ensure that children and families most at risk of social exclusion have every opportunity to build successful, independent lives.

At the same time, the Government is committed to improving the quality and management of those services responsible for supporting children and families particularly through the modernisation of social services, through the promotion of cooperation between all statutory agencies and through building effective partnerships with voluntary and private agencies.

Promoting the wellbeing of children to ensure their optimal outcomes requires integration at both national and local levels: joined-up government – in respect both of policy making and of service delivery – is central to the current extensive policy agenda. A ministerial group on the family, supported by a family policy unit in the Home Office, encourages this approach at Government level. Its aim is to provide a new emphasis on looking more widely at the needs of vulnerable children and families in the community.

Effective practice

The development of the *Framework for the Assessment of Children in Need and their Families* will contribute to integrated working. Its primary purpose is to improve outcomes for children in need. The effectiveness with which this aim can be achieved is, in part, dependent on the capacity of the workforce to implement the Assessment Framework. This means having sufficient staff in place, who have the requisite knowledge, skills and confidence to undertake assessments. They must be able to make sound judgements about the needs of each child and how best to enable those caring for them to respond appropriately to their needs.

Work with children and families can be complex, difficult and stressful. It is crucial that all staff keep up to date with developments in practice, research and policy. This includes being provided with opportunities for developing appropriate competencies commensurate with their responsibilities, including further and post-qualifying training. Staff who are at the front line must be well supported. Their managers and supervisors also require professional experience and knowledge to enable them to undertake their critical tasks. Their need for opportunities for learning is of equal importance to practitioners who carry out assessments. A culture of individual staff learning can only exist successfully within an organisational context which values this activity. Thus the whole organisation should be involved in a learning process.

This book complements the range of publications produced by the Department of Health to inform practitioners and their managers about the most up-to-date knowledge from research and practice, and makes an important contribution to enabling practitioners, managers and policy-makers to have an evidence-based approach to their work with children and families.

Jenny Gray
Children's Services Branch
Department of Health

Acknowledgements

I would like to offer my sincere thanks to the many people who gave generously of their time and energy in assisting in the production of this book. First, thanks to the authors for their thoughtful contributions, enthusiasm and commitment to the project. Second, I appreciated the expertise and advice offered by members of the Learning Materials Development Group, the Reader Development Group and individual critical readers who advised on the overall content and provided invaluable guidance regarding the individual chapters. Third, and not least, thanks to the many typists and secretaries who provided such an efficient service to both the authors and myself.

Members of the Learning Materials Development Group

Chair

Jenny Gray	Social Services Inspector, Department of Health

Members

Margaret Adcock	Social work consultant and trainer
Dr Nick Banks	Lecturer in social work, University of Birmingham
Sarah Bateman	Section Head (Child Protection), Department of Health (until August 1999)
Professor Tim Booth	Professor of Social Policy, University of Sheffield
Bruce Clark	Section Head (Child Protection), Department of Health (from August 1999)
Dr Hedy Cleaver	Senior research fellow, Royal Holloway, University of London
Professor Anthony Cox	Professor of Child and Adolescent Psychiatry, Guys Hospital
Dave Edwards	Family Rights Group
Bryan Gocke	Child Protection Coordinator, Doncaster Social Services Department
Rosemary Gordon	National Training Manager, NSPCC

Ann Gross	Section Head (Child Protection Policy) Department of Health (until September 1999)
Di Hart	Children's development officer, London Borough of Camden Social Services
Enid Hendry	Head of Child Protection Training, NSPCC
David Hill	Head of Children's Services, London Borough of Havering
Jan Horwath	Lecturer in social work, University of Sheffield
Professor David Howe	Professor of Social Work, University of East Anglia
Dr Bob Jezzard	Department of Health
David Johnstone	National Assembly for Wales
Dr David P.H. Jones	Consultant paediatrician, The Park Hospital for Children, Oxford
Helen Jones	Social Services Inspector, Department of Health
Ilan Katz	Head of Practice Development, NSPCC
Ruth Marchant	Triangle Services
Professor Peter Marsh	Professor of Child and Family Welfare, University of Sheffield
Katrina McNamara	Nursing officer, Department of Health
Wendy Rose	Senior research fellow, The Open University
David Shemmings	Senior lecturer in social work, University of East Anglia
Steve Walker	London Borough of Kingston
Dave Ward	NSPCC
Dr Harriet Ward	Senior research fellow, Loughborough University

Members of the Reader Development Group

Pat Buckley	Training and development officer, Northumbria Social Services Department
Rosemary Gordon	National Training Manager, NSPCC
Andy Hampson	Principal Officer, Children's Services, Salford Social Services Department
Dave Hill	Head of Children's Services, London Borough of Havering

Ilan Katz	Head of Practice Development, NSPCC
Judith Milner	Trainer and consultant, brief therapy and assessment practice
Pete Nelson	Senior practitioner and practice teacher, Sheffield Social Services Department
Jayne Stokes	Project manager, Family Centre, NCH action for children

In addition to the above, the following acted as critical readers:

Kevin Ashby	Team manager, Sheffield Social Services Department
Dr. Arnon Bentovim	Consultant child and adolescent psychiatrist, The London Child and Family Consultation Centre
Martin Calder	Child protection reviewing officer, Salford Social Services Department
Tony Morrison	Independent social care consultant and trainer
Kate Rose	Child protection reviewing officer, Salford Social Services Department
Catherine Spencer	Senior practitioner, Sheffield Social Services Department

Members of staff at Havering Social Services Department

Jan Horwath, University of Sheffield

Introduction

Jan Horwath

Aims

This book aims to promote assessment practice that leads to informed decision-making, planning and intervention, which in turn results in better outcomes for children and families. One of the key principles underpinning the *Framework for the Assessment of Children in Need and their Families* (Department of Health *et al.* 2000) is that assessment practice should be grounded in evidence-based knowledge. The book, which appeared originally as part of the training and development pack *The Child's World: Assessing Children in Need* (NSPCC and University of Sheffield 2000) has been written with the objective of providing trainers, practitioners and managers with up-to-date, relevant knowledge to inform assessments of children and families. The contributors, who are all experts in their fields, provide an overview of current research, theory and best practice related to the assessment of children in need and their families, combined with that which is well grounded and has stood the test of time.

Readership

The chapters have been written for a wide readership. Trainers and educators will find the book useful for the underpinning knowledge required for using the accompanying training resources. It also provides a valuable source of reference for individual practitioners and managers who wish to develop their own assessment practice in terms of understanding, analysing and evaluating the needs of children and their families.

It has been produced primarily for social work personnel. Yet assessments of children's needs, as outlined in the *Framework for the Assessment of Children and Families*, should be interdisciplinary and involve a range of personnel both across agencies and in the community. Contributors to the book have therefore considered issues from a variety of different professional and user perspectives, so that it provides an important resource for practitioners who are likely to be involved in the assessment of a child's needs because of their knowledge of the child, the parent/carer or the family and community network.

Professional practice builds on knowledge from theory and research, gained during qualifying and post-qualifying training. With this in mind, the book includes material that is of relevance to students completing qualifying as well as post-qualifying awards in social work and related health and social care professions. The Department of Health and the Central Council for Education and Training in Social Work have developed a Post-Qualifying Child Care Award (PQCCA) that is designed to consolidate and develop the knowledge and skills of qualified social workers in child care practice (CCETSW 1999). *The Framework for the Assessment of Children in Need and their Families* is integral to the conceptual framework and curriculum guidance for this award. *The Child's World* is a particularly useful resource for candidates working towards the PQCCA. Each chapter includes a summary of key research findings and theory relevant to a specific topic, and the authors discuss issues and dilemmas that can influence effective practice; key texts are also included for further reading.

Effective use of the Assessment Framework by practitioners depends on organisational structures and systems that proactively encourage analysis and decision-making through the use of professional judgement within a broad framework of policies and procedures. While the book is primarily a resource for practitioners and front line managers, the contributing authors make recommendations regarding best practice that have implications for both policymakers and senior managers. It will therefore assist senior managers to identify the needs of staff expected to undertake effective assessments of children in need and their families.

Contents

The book is divided into four sections; each section builds on the learning from the previous section. However, chapters can be read in their own right. The foreword and the first two chapters consider the context and content of the *Framework for the Assessment of Children in Need and their Families*. The foreword and Chapter 1 provide the reader with an overview of the policy, research and practice which influenced the development of the framework.

Chapter 2 is an introduction to the guidance, describing the principles underpinning the framework and offering an overview of the way in which the framework should be used in practice to promote effective outcomes for children and families.

The second section is concerned with the assessment process. In Chapter 3 Gordon Jack explores ecological perspectives. He aims to increase the reader's understanding of the theoretical model underpinning the Assessment Framework and the implications for assessment of family and environmental factors. The rest of this section addresses different aspects of the assessment task. In Chapter 4 Margaret Adcock identifies the nature and purpose of the core assessment process. She considers the key components for an effective core assessment based on the use of the framework, and highlights how practitioners should apply the assessment guidance in order to safeguard children and promote their welfare. Within her chapter Adcock stresses the importance of the use of professional judgement at all stages of the assessment process. Assessment is an ongoing dynamic process. In Chapter 5 Jan Horwath and Tony Morrison explore the meaning of this in terms of the assessment of parental motivation to change. The following two chapters consider assessment from the child and family perspective. Yvonne Shemmimgs and David Shemmings provide an overview of current research to indicate ways in which practitioners can work with both children and families to engage them positively in the assessment process. Consideration is given to issues related to disengagement, and strategies are included for working with children and carers in these situations. Anne Bannister in Chapter 7 focuses on ways of communicating with children to ensure that their views are taken into account when assessing the child's needs and the parents', family's and community's ability to respond to these needs. The last two chapters in this section consider the role of the practitioner undertaking assessments using the framework. The authors consider ways in which practitioners can both positively and negatively influence the assessment process. Nick Banks explores these issues in terms of power and oppression related to the assessment of families from minority ethnic groups and Rosemary Gordon and Enid Hendry discuss the role of the supervisor regarding the identification of factors that can distort an assessment.

The second half of the reader focuses more specifically on the knowledge that is required to complete an assessment of a child in need, taking into account the developmental needs of children and the parent's or carer's capacity to respond to these needs. The third section of the book centres on the developmental needs of children. Harriet Ward in Chapter 10 sets the dimensions of developmental needs used in the *Framework for the Assessment of*

Children and their Families in context. She identifies how the different dimensions utilised in the framework build on the dimensions already used to assess the developmental needs of children looked after by the local authority. The following two chapters, written by Robbie Gilligan and David Howe respectively, explore two key issues that practitioners should bear in mind when assessing the developmental needs of children. That is, the protective factors that influence the individual child's resilience, and the attachment patterns the child has experienced. In this section consideration is given to the needs of three particular groups of children, and the authors explore research and current practice in order to provide practical guidance related to the specific assessment tasks. In Chapter 13 Ruth Marchant considers the Assessment Framework and its application to children with complex needs; Chris Deardon and Saul Becker go on to discuss the needs of young carers, and Di Hart explores the tensions and dilemmas encountered by professionals completing pre-birth assessments.

The final section of *The Child's World* addresses issues related to assessing parental capacity to respond to the developmental needs of children. In Chapter 16 David Jones explores the meaning of parental capacity and identifies the assessment issues underpinning the dimensions of parenting capacity that are used in the framework. The final three chapters focus on specific parenting issues: Hedy Cleaver considers the impact of mental health, alcohol and drug misuse and domestic violence on the parent's or carer's capacity to meet the needs of the children in their care; Cotson, Friend, Hollins and James in Chapter 18 consider ways in which the *Framework for the Assessment of Children in Need and their Families* should be applied to assessing parental capacity when the parent has a learning disability. The final two chapters, written by Marcus Erooga and Bobbie Print, identify ways in which parental capacity can be assessed in order to meet the developmental needs of children when intrafamilial sexual abuse is a concern. In Chapter 19 the focus is assessment when sexual abuse by an adult is a concern. In Chapter 20 the authors consider the particular assessment issues related to assessing a young person who sexually abuses, in terms of their own developmental needs.

As can be seen from the description of the contents, the book is intended to be far more than a guide to the use of the *Framework for the Assessment of Children in Need and their Families*. The chapters are written to inform the evidence base of practitioners, trainers and managers, enabling them to develop effective assessment practice that results in appropriate provision of services to safeguard and promote the welfare of children in need and their families.

References

Aldgate, J. and Coleman, R. (1999) *Post Qualifying Award in Child Care: Conceptual Framework*. A project for the Department of Health and CCETSW, Leicester: University of Leicester.

Department of Health, Department for Education and Employment and Home Office (2000) *Framework for the Assessment of Children in Need and their Families*. London: The Stationery Office.

The NSPCC and The University of Sheffield (2000) *The Child's World. Assessing Children in Need*. Training and development pack. London: NSPCC.

Part I

The Framework

CHAPTER 1

Assessing the World of the Child in Need
Background and Context
Jan Horwath

[The *Framework for the Assessment of Children in Need and their Families*] is underpinned by a set of principles which seek to remedy some of the misunderstandings about the task of working with children and families to find out what is happening to them and how they might best be helped.

(Preface to the *Framework for the Assessment of Children in Need and their Families*, p.xii)

In this chapter the following are considered:

- the Children Act 1989 in practice
- messages from child protection research
- assessment practice in the 1990s
- lessons learnt from social work policy and practice in the 1990s
- assessing the child's world using the *Framework for the Assessment of Children in Need and their Families*.

Introduction

In 1964 D.W. Winnicott published a book entitled *The Child, The Family and The Outside World*. This title captures the essence of child care practice: the needs of the child cannot be met without considering the family and the world in which the child lives. As we embark on a new millennium, the Government has introduced a conceptual framework for assessing children in need and their families. This framework is based on an ecological model that provides a systematic way of analysing, understanding and recording what is happening to children and young people within their families and the wider context of the community in which they live (Department of Health *et al.* 2000). Although the Children Act 1989 takes a broad view of child welfare, until the mid-1990s child protection work had tended to dominate child care practice, with a focus on an incident of abuse rather than on the developmental needs of the child (Department of Health 1995). This chapter will provide an overview of the way in which practice developments in the 1970s and 1980s were influenced by public inquiries into child deaths, which in turn resulted in an emphasis on child protection issues. Consideration will be given to research findings regarding the impact this narrow focus on child abuse had in terms of social workers' understanding of the assessment task and outcomes for children and families. The chapter concludes by identifying ways in which these research findings have informed the development of the *Framework for the Assessment of Children in Need and their Families.*

The Children Act 1989 in practice

Key legislation for children and family social work practice is the Children Act 1989. The Act takes a broad view of child welfare provision, emphasising the local authority's duty to safeguard and promote the welfare of children. The concept of a 'child in need' was introduced in Part III Section 17 of the Act. Part III of the Act stresses the importance of family support services that are designed to safeguard and promote the welfare of the child and to assist parents to bring up their children. Parts IV and V of the Act relate to the local authority's duty to provide protection for children suffering from or likely to suffer from significant harm. Part V provides the legal steps which may be taken to protect a child at risk of or suffering significant harm. The Act recognises that for the majority of children the family is the most appropriate place for a child to be brought up, and that parents should retain responsibility for their children's upbringing. In this legislation, local authorities are required to balance their support and work with parents with a duty to safeguard children from harm.

The implementation of the Children Act 1989 at a local level was, however, influenced by the public inquiries into child deaths and into sexual abuse which were held in the 1970s and 1980s. These inquiries raised concerns among professionals and the general public with regard to ways in which children who have been, or were likely to be, maltreated could best be protected from harm (Parton 1997). A number of reports have been completed since the inception of the Act which indicate the influence that child maltreatment has had on the way in which the Children Act 1989 has been implemented by local authorities. The Children Act Report 1993 (Department of Health 1994) noted that section 17 was not being fully implemented according to the spirit of the Children Act 1989. In practice the emphasis seemed to be on a reactive social policing role, with services targeted at children at risk of significant harm. The report recommended a shift to a more positive partnership between families and services, with services aimed at preventing family breakdown. The Audit Commission in 1994 supported this recommendation and suggested that 'social services departments must develop a more proactive rather than reactive approach, paying particular attention to Part III section 17 of the Children Act which covers authorities' responsibilities to children in need' (Audit Commission 1994, p.3), and 'local authorities will need to broaden their remit to promote a wider range of initiatives that provide families with support' (*ibid.* p.2).

The recognition that priority for support services was given by social services departments to children at risk of significant harm was noted in a study undertaken by Aldgate and Tunstill (1995). They found a hierarchy of access, with children in need given less priority in terms of service provision than children perceived to be at risk of significant harm. Aldgate and Tunstill also found that some local authorities had no clear criteria for service provision for disabled children. Some authorities tended to provide services if these children were also perceived to be at risk of significant harm.

Meeting the needs of children suffering from or likely to suffer from significant harm

If, as indicated above, social services departments tend to target services at children suffering from or likely to suffer significant harm, it is important to establish whether these services promote positive outcomes for this group of children. *Child Protection: Messages from Research* (Department of Health 1995) summarises the main findings of twenty research studies on child protection. The studies highlighted the following points:

- The child protection system was operating with the greatest emphasis on section 47 inquiries rather than planning and intervention to meet the needs of children (see Farmer and Owen (1995) and Hallett (1995)).

- The investigation tended to be incident-focused, yet Gibbons, Gallaher *et al.* (1995) found that a single abusive incident rarely caused long-term difficulties for children. They found a negative environment, particularly one of low warmth and high criticism, was far more damaging in the long term than an isolated incident of physical abuse.

- More than half of the families who were filtered out of the system prior to the child's name being placed on the child protection register received no services. Gibbons, Conroy *et al.* (1995) tracked child protection referrals from eight local authorities for a 26-week period. They found that 26 per cent of the referrals were filtered out by social work staff without any direct contact with the child or family, although other professionals may have been consulted. They noted that 50 per cent were filtered out before an initial child protection conference, but after section 47 inquiry and involvement with the family. This left 24 per cent who went to child protection conference, with only 15 per cent being placed on the child protection register and 4 per cent of children being removed from home.

- The section 47 inquiry process can alienate and anger parents. The emphasis on identifying whether or not abuse took place can be at the cost of interventions to meet the needs of children and families. This practice leaves parents feeling stigmatised and frustrated because they have gained little in terms of assistance and support. (See Farmer and Owen 1995; Thoburn, Lewis and Shemmings 1995)

An inconsistent response to safeguarding and promoting the welfare of different groups of children from minority groups also emerged from other studies completed during the mid-1990s. Westcott highlighted the fact that disabled children were particularly vulnerable to maltreatment and yet formed a disproportionately small number of children placed on the child protection register (Westcott 1993). There is under-representation of children from Asian communities whose names are on child protection registers and in local authority care (Luthera 1997) compared to over-representation of African-Caribbean children on child protection registers (Armstrong 1995) and in local authority care (Luthera 1997).

Lack of attention to parenting issues that influence parenting capacity

The emphasis on protection and safety issues in child care practice in the late 1980s and early 1990s also meant that insufficient attention was given to the needs of parents, which in turn can influence their parenting capacity and outcomes for children. Farmer and Owen (1995) studied 44 children for a period of 20 months after child protection registration. They found that in only 30 per cent of cases had the needs of the parent or carer been reasonably met. This was cause for concern because the researchers found that for children who remained at home there were limits to the extent to which the welfare of the child could be improved if the parents' needs were not addressed. They concluded that a system had developed that was fairly effective at keeping children safe in the short term but failed to meet the wider welfare needs of children and their parents. This means that where the needs of parents are ignored the longer-term protection of children from abuse cannot be assured.

Farmer and Owen completed their data-gathering in 1991. Thoburn *et al.* (1995) began a further study commencing in 1993, two years after the implementation of the Children Act 1989. Their findings were similar to Farmer and Owen's. They noted that of the 105 parents involved in the study there were concerns about 98 per cent of the parents' ability to fulfil the main parenting role. They also noted a high incidence of violence between adults in the home. Their findings were similar to Farmer and Owen's in as much as in only 17 per cent of cases were the parents' problems addressed, and in 29 per cent of cases parents still had serious problems and unmet needs which influenced their parenting capacity. Thoburn *et al.* also noted that earlier intervention with some of these families could have addressed issues which resulted in later events leading to significant harm for children.

The child, their family and the community

As highlighted above, by the mid-1990s the focus of assessment and intervention has become narrow. This has been described by Stevenson as 'protecting children from "dangerous" adults, usually their parents, and on the assessment of risk in individual cases [which] seems to reinforce an "individualistic" model for understanding, indeed for constructing the very problem, rather than an emphasis on external factors' (Stevenson 1998, p.10).

This narrow focus has influenced the perception of the social work task and has resulted in the positive and negative influences of the family network and the community being marginal to the core business of child care social work practice (Jack 1997). The result is that broader issues, such as poverty, racism and unemployment, have been ignored. The report from the Commission on Social Justice recognised that poverty, unemployment and poor housing make positive parenting difficult, although they do not necessarily result in poor parenting (Hewitt and Leach 1993).

Inter-agency child care practice

Working Together under the Children Act (Department of Health 1991) was designed to provide a framework to enable a coordinated response from professionals to meet the needs of those children who are suffering or are likely to suffer significant harm. The research studies that were commissioned by the Department of Health and which focused on inter-agency child protection practice are summarised in *Child Protection: Messages from Research* (Department of Health 1995). The research (Hallett 1995; Hallett and Birchall 1995) indicates:

- there was a general acknowledgement amongst practitioners that inter-agency working and adherence to procedures promoted good practice

- the system operated as a communication network rather than one of close collaboration and support

- agencies in general worked well together during the Section 47 inquiry phase of an allegation of significant harm or likely significant harm, with collaboration peaking at the initial child protection conference

- commitment to inter-agency practice fell off dramatically after the initial child protection conference

- professionals had different threshold criteria for making decisions regarding significant harm

- levels of commitment to inter-agency practice varied amongst groups of professionals.

What is apparent from the research studies, particularly in terms of post-registration practice, is that social workers tend to take responsibility for assessment, decision-making and interventions, while other professionals take on 'monitoring' and information-gathering roles (Calder and Horwath 1999).

Assessment practice in the 1990s

The primary source for assessment guidance that has been available for social workers to date has been *Protecting Children. A Guide For Social Workers Undertaking a Comprehensive Assessment*, which became known as the 'Orange Book' (Department of Health 1988). This guide was designed to provide a framework for long-term planning in child protection cases. As stated in the guide itself, it was not intended for initial assessment. The practice guidance was produced in response to concerns that were identified in inquiry reports regarding individual social work assessments, following the deaths of Jasmine Beckford, Kimberley Carlisle and others. At the time of publication it was recognised that the guide 'will need revision in due course in the light of experience of its use' (Department of Health 1988 p.5).

Katz (1997) in his critique of the 'Orange Book' noted that the guidance provided a much needed, structured assessment framework when it was first introduced in the late 1980s; however, concerns had arisen amongst those involved in child care practice regarding the way in which the 'Orange Book' was being used. For example, Katz noted that some practitioners used the 'Orange Book' as a checklist, which was not its original intention. In addition the Social Services Inspectorate (SSI) in an overview report of child protection inspection findings (1997a) noted the following points regarding comprehensive assessments:

- practice varied within teams in social service departments
- some assessments were unfocused
- the comprehensive assessment is not always used to determine the content of the child protection plan.

As indicated above, the 'Orange Book' was intended as a guide for assessing and planning interventions in cases of child abuse; to date there has never been a national, standardised framework for assessing children in need. This would seem to have had an impact on practice. For example, the Social Services Inspectorate overview report *Assessment, Planning and Decision-Making, Family Support Services* (SSI 1997b) found the following:

- inadequate early responses resulted in no further action as the assessment of need was often cursory

- no structure for the assessment of risk of significant harm or the developmental needs of the child

- lack of a systematic framework for information-gathering.

This overview report highlighted a lack of standardisation and consistency within and between social service departments in terms of assessment practice for children in need. This may result in some children receiving a minimal assessment of their needs while other children, particularly those suffering or likely to suffer significant harm, are over-assessed, with the assessment focusing on information-gathering at the expense of hypothesising, reaching decisions, planning and delivering effective interventions (Samra-Tibbetts and Raynes 1999). A summary of the findings on assessment from child care inspections by the Social Services Inspectorate during the period from 1993 to 1997 completed by Pont (Department of Health 2000b) highlights the above and makes the following recommendations:

- policies and procedures should state that services are provided on the basis of an assessment of need

- policies and procedures on assessment should be inclusive of racial and cultural factors

- guidance should contain clear time-scales

- sufficient information should be taken at point of referral to enable effective decision-making

- a range of professional involvement is necessary for the completion of effective assessments. There should be careful integration of information from other agencies into the assessment, planning and decision-making process

- clear and accurate recording is essential. Assessment reports should demonstrate the decision-making process which led to the specific plan

- the views of children, families and carers should be sought and clearly identified in reports

- supervision, monitoring and training are essential for high-quality assessments.

Lessons learnt from social work policy and practice in the 1990s

What has emerged from the reports and the associated research studies can be summarised by this statement in *Child Protection: Messages from Research*: 'If policy and practice changes are to follow from this round of research, it should be to reconsider the balance of services and alter the way in which professionals are perceived by parents accused of abusing or neglecting their offspring' (Department of Health 1995, p.55).

Cumulatively, recommendations from the reports, inspections and findings of the research studies informed the Government's thinking with regard to ways in which the systems should be altered and modernised. A number of key themes emerged as follows.

Inclusive family support services

The Government recognises that in the twenty-first century a more integrated approach to children in need is required. This was first proposed by Rose (1994) who raised concerns that family support and child protection were perceived as mutually exclusive, as the emphasis on a particular incident of alleged abuse tended to preclude full consideration of the needs of the child and his or her parents. Rose advocated less emphasis on the alleged incident and a greater emphasis on enquiring and analysing whether family support services are needed. The message was clear: do not ignore issues of maltreatment; rather, be mindful that family support includes the need to provide services that protect and keep safe children at risk of significant harm.

Assessments based on need

The early to mid-1990s was a time when work with children and families tended to be service-led rather than based on the needs of the child (NCH 1996). In addition, as identified above, initial inquiries and assessments tended to focus on the incident of abuse rather than the developmental needs of the child. The Department of Health was clear that the developmental needs of children should determine the services provided by local authorities. This was reflected in 1996 by the introduction of a legal requirement that local councils should produce Children's Services Plans (Children's Service Planning Order 1996). The purpose of Children's Services Plans is to identify and assess the needs of children within the area, consult with those requiring and providing services as to the way in which needs will be met and finally to publish the resulting plans (Department of Health 1996).

Working with children and families: building on strengths as well as identifying difficulties

As described above, what emerged from the research findings reported in *Child Protection: Messages from Research* (Department of Health 1995) was that children and families felt that they had little control regarding their involvement with social service departments and the services they received. The system tended to focus on family weaknesses and problems, which resulted in stigmatising families. Rose (1994) stated that a task for social workers is to identify ways in which they can provide acceptable, non-stigmatising services which safeguard children and promote their welfare by:

- working alongside families rather than disempowering them
- raising the self-esteem of parents rather than provoking a defensive or angry response
- promoting family relationships enabling parents to safeguard and promote the wellbeing of their children whenever possible
- focusing on the overall developmental needs of children rather than concentrating narrowly on the alleged incident of abuse.

In addition, the Association of Directors of Social Services and National Children's Homes emphasised that responses to concerns about children can result in better outcomes if professionals are sensitive to the needs of children and listen to their voices (NCH 1996).

The *Framework for the Assessment of Children in Need and their Families*

The government recognised that guidance on assessment should be further developed in light of research findings, practice wisdom and experience, to reflect the needs of children and families at the turn of the century. The new guidance sets out a framework for assessing children in need under the Children Act 1989. The framework has also been incorporated into *Working Together to Safeguard Children* (Department of Health *et al.* 1999) and will be used for all assessments undertaken under this inter-agency guidance.

The Assessment Framework and the underpinning principles are described in detail in Chapter 2.

Summary

A legal framework and accompanying guidance cannot on their own guarantee effective services for children and families. Children's services will only be truly effective if the implementation of the legislation, the guidance and the use of resources reflect and respond to the changing needs of the children and families who use these services.

One of the major lessons learned in the last decade was that 'decisions about children in need are, to some extent, socially constructed and that the same need may require different inputs in different historical eras. Post-Cleveland the need was for an ordered protection service; in ten years' time the need might well be for family support and protection' (Department of Health 1995, p.55).

The *Framework for the Assessment of Children in Need and their Families* provides a conceptual map for undertaking assessments of children in need and their families, which should ensure that practitioners, managers and policymakers maintain a child focus, irrespective of how the world of the child changes and develops over time.

Recommended reading

Brandon, M., Schofield, G., and Trinder, L. with Stone, N. (1998) *Social Work with Children.* London: Macmillan.

Parton, N. (ed.) (1997) *Child Protection and Family Support. Tensions, Contradictions and Possibilities.* London: Routledge.

Stevenson, O. (ed.) (1998) *Child Welfare in the UK.* Oxford: Blackwell.

References

Aldgate, J. and Tunstill, J. (1995) *Making Sense of Section 17.* London: HMSO.

Armstrong, H. (1995) *Annual Report of Area Child Protection Committees 1994–5.* London: HMSO.

Audit Commission (1994) *Seen But Not Heard. Coordinating Community Health and Social Services for Children in Need.* London: HMSO.

Calder, M. C. and Horwath, J. (eds.) (1999) *Working for Children on the Child Protection Register: An Inter-Agency Guide.* Aldershot: Arena.

Department of Health (1988) *Protecting Children. A Guide for Social Workers Undertaking a Comprehensive Assessment.* London: HMSO.

Department of Health (1991) *Working Together under the Children Act 1989: A Guide to Arrangements of Inter-agency Co-operation for the Protection of Children from Abuse.* London: HMSO.

Department of Health (1994) *Children Act Report 1993.* London: HMSO.

Department of Health (1995) *Child Protection: Messages From Research, Studies in Child Protection.* London: HMSO.

Department of Health (1996) *Children's Services Planning.* London: HMSO.

Department of Health, Home Office, Department of Education and Employment (1999) *Working Together to Safeguard Children.* London: The Stationery Office.

Department of Health, Department for Education and Employment and the Home Office (2000) *Framework for the Assessment of Children in Need and their Families.* London: The Stationery Office.

Department of Health (2000b) *Studies Informing the Development of the Framework for the Assessment of Children in Need and their Families.* London: The Stationery Office.

Farmer, E. and Owen, M. (1995) *Child Protection Practice. Private Risks and Public Remedies.* London: HMSO.

Gibbons, J., Conroy, S. and Bell, C. (1995) *Operating the Child Protection System: A Study of Child Protection Practices in English Local Authorities.* London: HMSO.

Gibbons, J., Gallaher, B., Bell, C. and Gordon, D. (1995) *Development After Physical Abuse in Early Childhood.* London: HMSO.

Hallett, C. and Birchhall, E. (1995) *Coordination and Child Protection.* London: HMSO.

Hallett, C. (1995) *Interagency Coordination in Child Protection.* London: HMSO.

Hewitt, P. and Leach, P. (1993) *Social Justice, Children and Families.* London: The Commission on Social Justice, IPPR.

Jack, G. (1997) 'Discourses of child protection and child welfare'. In *British Journal of Social Work 27*, p.659–78.

Katz, I. (1997) *Current Issues in Comprehensive Assessment.* London: NSPCC.

Luthera, M. (1997) *Britain's Black Population: Social Change, Public Policy and Agenda.* Aldershot: Arena.

NCH Action for Children (1996) *Children Still in Need. Refocusing Child Protection in the Context of Children in Need.* London: ADSS and NCH.

Parton, N. (1997) *Child Protection and Family Support. Tensions, Contradictions and Possibilities.* London: Routledge.

Rose, W. (1994) 'An overview of the developments of services – the relationship between protection and family support and the intentions of the Children Act 1989', Sief Conference, September 1994.

Samra-Tibbetts, C. and Raynes, B. (1999) 'Assessment and planning'. In M. Calder and J. Horwath (eds.) *Working for Children on the Child Protection Register.* Aldershot: Arena.

Social Services Inspectorate (1997a) *Messages from Inspections; Child Protection Inspections 1992/1996.* London: HMSO.

Social Services Inspectorate (1997b) *Assessment, Planning and Decision-making. Family Support Services.* London: Department of Health.

Stevenson, O. (1998) *Neglected Children: Issues and Dilemmas.* Oxford: Blackwell.

Thoburn, J., Lewis, A. and Shemmings, D. (1995) *Paternalism or Partnership? Family Involvement in the Child Protection Process.* London: HMSO.

Westcott, H. (1993) *Abuse of Children and Adults with Disabilities.* London: NSPCC.

Winnicott, D. W. (1964) *The Child, the Family, and the Outside World.* Harmondsworth: Penguin.

CHAPTER 2

Assessing Children in Need and Their Families

An Overview of the Framework

Wendy Rose

A framework has been developed which provides a systematic way of analysing, understanding and recording what is happening to children and young people within their families and the wider context of the community in which they live. From such an understanding of what are inevitably complex issues and inter- relationships, clear professional judgements can be made.

> (Preface to the *Framework for the Assessment of Children in Need and their Families,* p.viii)

Within this chapter the following are considered:

- the legislative context

- improving outcomes for children: developments through the 1990s

- an exploration of the three domains of the Assessment Framework

- using the framework: principles and practice.

Introduction

> 'Developing a detailed understanding of a child's needs, identity and best interests enables us to take the action required to meet and fulfil them' (Utting 1989, p.iii).

This chapter outlines the statutory responsibility of local authorities laid down in the Children Act 1989 both to identify children in need in their area and to promote and safeguard their welfare. In order to establish whether a child is in need, careful assessment is required in which all the relevant information has been evaluated and recorded as the basis for professional consideration, planning and action. To assist good practice across this broad spectrum of need, a framework has been developed for understanding what is happening to a child in relation to his or her parents (or carers) and the wider context of the family and community. The framework is built on a body of knowledge derived from theories, research, policy and practice, well tested over several decades. The critical issue is how this knowledge is understood and used by child welfare agencies in order to achieve better outcomes for children in need and their families. The process for using the framework in assessing children is underpinned by a clear set of principles which are discussed.

The legislative context

The Children Act 1989 lays a duty on every local authority to identify children who are in need in their area (schedule 2 paragraph 1) and 'to safeguard and promote the welfare of children who are in need; and so far as is consistent with that duty, to promote the upbringing of such children by their families, by providing a range and level of services appropriate to those children's needs' (section 17 subsection 1). A specific duty is laid on other agencies, including health, education and housing, to assist local authority social services in the exercise of these responsibilities for children in need (section 27), in so far as this is compatible with their own duties and obligations. Two of the major principles of modern child welfare are thus enshrined in this Act: first, the duty of the state through local authorities to safeguard and promote the welfare of vulnerable children; second, that children are best brought up in their own families wherever possible and that families may need to call on services to support them when they need help.

But who are children in need? The Children Act 1989 defines need broadly and in developmental terms as children unlikely to achieve or maintain a reasonable standard of health and development without services, whose health and development will be significantly impaired without services, or who are disabled (section 17 subsection 10). As discussed in Chapter 1, applying this broad definition in practice has not proved easy for social services departments. An early Children Act Report 1993 (Department of Health 1994), drawing on work later published by Aldgate and Tunstill in 1995, commented on the generally slow progress towards full implementation of section 17: 'Further work is still needed to provide across the country a range of family services aimed at preventing families reaching the point of breakdown. Some authorities are still finding it difficult to move from a reactive policing role to a more proactive partnership role with families' (para 2.39). As a result of the focus on child protection, assessment of children and families had become characterised as assessment of risk of abuse. Seden (Department of Health 2000b) comments that: 'Highly publicised "failures" to protect children from danger have led the professions to develop checklists of indicators and predictors which claim to measure the safety of a child within a family.'

The findings from research studies and inspections explored in detail in Chapter 1 (Audit Commission 1994, Department of Health 1995, and others) indicated the need to review the process of assessment, which has informed the revision of *Working Together to Safeguard Children* (Department of Health *et al.* 1999), and the development of the *Framework for the Assessment of Children in Need and their Families* (Department of Health *et al.* 2000).

Improving outcomes for children: developments during the 1990s

In parallel with the growing demands of child protection work during the last fifteen years, there has been a remarkable piece of work undertaken by leading childcare researchers and practitioners, led by Parker and Ward, to find ways of improving the outcomes for children who are growing up in public care (Parker *et al.* 1991). They identified seven dimensions of children's development which should be actively reviewed and progressed by their care-givers, as any reasonable parent would do in the course of family life. These became the foundation for a major programme of work by the Department of Health, 'Looking After Children: Assessing Outcomes in Child Care' (launched in 1995). For the first time social work practitioners had a framework for understanding and monitoring children's needs which was relevant from infancy to young adulthood.

Failure to recognise parents' needs and their impact on parental capacity, as described by Horwath in Chapter 1, has led to researchers from a range of disciplines exploring how adults' own difficulties or problems can impair their capacity to respond appropriately to the needs of children (Cleaver and Freeman 1995; Reder and Lucey 1995; Falkov 1996; Buchanan 1996; Cleaver, Unell and Aldgate 1999, and many others). A study by Falkov (1996) for the Department of Health under section 8 of *Working Together to Safeguard Children* (Department of Health *et al.* 1999), 'Reviews of fatal child abuse and serious injuries to children', revealed that, in a hundred reviews, nearly a third had evidence of parental psychiatric disorder. As child welfare agencies generally recognised the need to refocus their work with children and families (ADSS/NCH 1996), so more broadly based assessment models were being developed in partnership with parents, in family centres and health units such as at the Park Hospital, Oxford and the Marlborough Day Unit, London (described by Robbins in Department of Health 2000b).

The third stream of development affecting children's outcomes, referred to in Chapter 1, has been the increasing recognition of the influence of circumstances in which families are bringing up children and the impact of environmental factors. Writers such as Jack (1997) and Stevenson (1998) have been concerned at the exclusion of environmental considerations from the social work process. Research studies have shown the strong association between economic disadvantage and living conditions and the chances that children will fail to thrive (Brown and Harris 1978; Utting 1995; Social Exclusion Unit 1998). Differences are clearly apparent in the health and educational development of children growing up in areas of deprivation. This has its impact both on adults' abilities to succeed as effective parents and directly on children themselves, through the standards of schools available to them, the subculture of peer groups with whom they relate and the community facilities provided. As Utting (1995) comments: 'Living on low income in a run-down neighbourhood does not make it impossible to be an affectionate, authoritative parent of healthy, sociable children. But it does, undeniably, make it more difficult' (p.40). Holman, at a conference in 1998, put it more starkly, commenting that 'Poverty undermines parenting'.

Bebbington and Miles (1989) have demonstrated how the cumulative effect of disadvantage can dramatically increase a child's chances of coming into the care system:

Child 'A' Aged 5 – 9	Child 'B' Aged 5 – 9
No dependence on social security benefits Two parent family Three or fewer children White Owner occupied home More rooms than people	Household head receives income support Single adult household Four or more children Mixed ethnic origin Privately rented home One or more persons per room
Odds are 1 in 7,000	Odds are 1 in 10

Figure 2.1 The effect of disadvantage. Adapted from Bebbington and Miles 1989.

The association between living in areas high in factors contributing to disadvantage and long-term adverse consequences for children is now acknowledged. As a result, these issues have been the subject of concerted government attention through the Social Exclusion Unit, Health Action Zones, Education Action Zones, Sure Start and other initiatives.

The relationship between disability and disadvantage has not always been well understood, although disabled children are defined as children in need. Ball (1998) and a number of other writers have recently emphasised this. A compelling example is the study by Lawton (1998) of families with more than one disabled child (of which there are some 17,000 in the United Kingdom). Such families are:

- more likely to be single parents
- less likely to be in work
- more likely to be in semi-skilled or unskilled jobs
- more likely to be dependent on income support
- less likely to own their own home
- likely to report housing as unsuitable
- more likely to have extra costs.

This study serves to reinforce the importance of considering the wider context in which families are caring for and bringing up disabled children. These considerations of context and environment also apply to children from minority ethnic families. The Social Exclusion Unit (1998) reported that 'ethnic minority groups are more likely to live in poor areas, be unemployed, have low incomes, live in poor housing, have poor health and be victims of crimes'. These issues and their implications for assessment are explored in detail in *Assessing Children in Need and their Families: Practice Guidance* (Department of Health 2000a).

A framework for assessment

Any assessment of a child and his or her family which aims to understand what is happening to a child has to take account, therefore, of a child's developmental needs, the parenting capacity to respond to those needs, and the wider family and environmental factors. Together these form three systems or domains whose interactions have a direct impact on the current and long-term wellbeing of a child. They constitute a framework for assessment in order to understand what is happening to a child (Figure 2.2). The Assessment Framework represents a way of trying to capture the complexity of a child's world and beginning to construct a coherent approach to collecting and analysing information about each child. As such, it provides a conceptual map which will help professionals in their work with children and families.

Figure 2.2 The Assessment Framework

Children's developmental needs

At heart, child and family social work is a practice concerned with the developmental wellbeing of children. (Howe 1998, p.6)

AGE PERIOD	TASK
Infancy	• attachment to caregiver(s) • language • differentiation of self from environment • self control and compliance
Middle childhood	• school adjustment (attendance, appropriate conduct) • academic achievement (e.g. learning reading, writing and mathematics) • getting along with peers (acceptance, making friends) • rule-governed conduct (following rules of society for moral behaviour and prosocial conduct)
Adolescence	• successful transition to secondary schooling • academic achievement (learning skills needed for higher education and work) • involvement in extra-curricular activities (e.g. sport, music, clubs) • forming close friendships within and across gender • forming a cohesive sense of self-identity

Figure 2.3 Examples of developmental tasks. Adapted from Masten and Coatsworth 1998.

Children develop along several dimensions, often simultaneously, and a series of developmental tasks must be completed successfully if optimal outcomes are to be achieved. The dimensions of children's development incorporated into the Assessment Framework are:

- health
- education

- emotional and behavioural development

- identity

- family and social relationships

- social presentation

- self-care skills.

These dimensions are discussed more fully by Ward in Chapter 10. As well as understanding the importance of each dimension individually and collectively, their significance over time in a child's life must be taken into account. Jones, Newbold and Byrne explain this point: 'The developmental perspective emphasises that as the child grows he/she becomes increasingly organised and integrated, each stage laying the foundation for increasingly complex development' (Jones *et al.* 1999, p.33).

Masten and Coatsworth (1998) usefully summarise some of the key developmental tasks at different periods (Figure 2.3). Successful attachment to a parent or caregiver in early infancy is fundamental to future wellbeing, for example, while forming a cohesive sense of self-identity is an important task for the adolescent.

Parenting capacity to respond to a child's needs

There is a number of key parenting tasks which are prerequisites for a child's wellbeing and development. These are not unfamiliar to social services practitioners. They have been at the heart of family placement services and used in the processes for recruiting and selecting foster carers and approving prospective adoptive parents. They have not always been so clearly differentiated and used in work with children and families in the community. The dimensions of parenting have been identified as:

- basic care

- ensuring safety

- emotional warmth

- stimulation

- guidance and boundaries

- stability.

In Chapter 16 Jones explores why each dimension is important, and the key parenting tasks involved. Again, these tasks will apply differently to children according to the stage of their development. The basic care a newborn baby requires will be very different from the care of an adolescent (but no less demanding). A key feature of parenting is, therefore, the capacity to adapt parenting behaviour appropriately to the age and stage of development of the individual child. If parents are experiencing difficulties in their parenting tasks, then knowing the parents' own family history, assessing their understanding of the impact of what is happening to them on their children, and their capacity to adapt and change becomes crucial.

Family and environmental factors

The care and upbringing of children does not take place in a vacuum, and the Assessment Framework takes account of this. The domain 'family and environmental factors' recognises the importance of the following dimensions in terms of what is happening to a child and the family:

- family history and functioning
- wider family
- housing
- employment
- income
- family's social integration
- community resources (including universal services of health and education).

The interaction between a family and the environment involves a complex set of processes. Stevenson (1998) draws attention to the way in which 'individuals and families internalise social and cultural norms so that the world outside lives in the minds and feelings of those within the family' (p.17).

The influences on family members include the immediate environment of the family, such as accommodation, work and income, as well as the networks of wider family, neighbours and friends and the community, with its facilities of shops, transport, playgrounds, schools, clinics and other services. The presence or absence of these factors and the extent to which they support or undermine the family's functioning are all relevant in the assessment of what is happening to a child and the family. Nelson (1997), in arguing from an American perspective for the need to build strong, supportive communities, identifies some of the key requirements for parents to succeed in bringing up their children. They can be summarised as follows:

- opportunity to earn enough for children's basic needs
- chance to fulfil constructive and culturally valued roles
- ability to protect children from danger
- access to education for children
- access to a network of supportive adults
- access to hope or faith or fellowship.

Jack explores the significance of environmental factors and the cumulative effect of more than one area of stress and disadvantage in Chapter 3.

Safeguarding and promoting welfare

The three domains constitute a framework for assessing children which is the foundation for safeguarding and promoting children's welfare and identifying whether their health and development is being or is likely to be impaired by their present circumstances. An overriding concern for child welfare agencies must be whether a child is experiencing significant harm or impairment. Bentovim's valuable definition of significant harm can be clearly located in the framework: 'A compilation of significant events, both acute and long-standing, which interact with the child's ongoing development and interrupt, alter or impair physical and psychological development… Significant harm represents a major symptom of failure of adaptation by parents to their role, and also involves both the family and society' (Bentovim 1998, p.57).

Jones *et al.* (1999) similarly relate child maltreatment to a developmental perspective, arguing that it can lead to disruption of the 'progressive build up of competence'. The extent to which the child is affected by this maltreatment, or recovers, is dependent upon a wide range of influences which may be either compensatory or ameliorative, as discussed by Gilligan in Chapter 11.

Using the framework: principles and practice

Assessment, planning, intervention and review are fundamental activities which lead the processes of working with children and families. The Assessment Framework, and its use in practice, is underpinned by key principles:

- it is child-centred, ensuring the child is always kept in focus
- it is rooted in child development (which includes recognition of the significance of timing in a child's life)
- it takes an ecological approach of locating the child within the family and the wider community
- it is based on ensuring equality of opportunity for all
- it involves working with families, children and young people
- it builds on strengths in each of the three domains with the aim of encouraging growth, as well as identifying difficulties
- it requires an inter-agency approach in which it is not just social services departments which are the assessors and providers of service
- assessment is seen as a process, not just a single event
- action and services are provided in parallel with assessment, according to the needs of the child and family, and do not await completion of assessment
- it is grounded in evidence-based knowledge derived from theory, research, policy and practice.

Both the *Framework for the Assessment of Children in Need and their Families* (Department of Health *et al.* 2000) and *Working Together to Safeguard Children* (Department of Health *et al.* 1999) set out government expectations of how assessments are to be undertaken. There are key features common to both sets of complementary guidance:

- there must be clarity of purpose about the questions to be answered by the assessment process
- evidence, and not unsubstantiated opinion, of what is seen, heard and read must be carefully collected and recorded
- attaching meaning to the information collected must distinguish the child's and family's understanding from that of professionals
- there must be clarity about the sources of knowledge which inform professional judgement
- severity, immediacy and complexity of the child's situation will have important influences on the pace, scope and procedural formality of assessment

- coordinated and holistic assessments must be followed by judgement leading to clear decisions and coordinated and holistic planning and intervention/action

- there has to be clarity about what has to change, how it will be achieved, in what time-scale and how it will be measured and reviewed.

Some of the important questions which will determine the process of assessment are, for example:

- what are the strengths to be built on?

- what are the difficulties which need addressing?

- what are the best options for this child?

- how will this child cope with services/interventions?

- how well is this child doing (following interventions/services/placement)?

- what is the impact on the child and family?

- does the plan need amending?

Each question may require further collection and analysis of information, coordination between agencies, such as schools or primary health care services, or commissioning specialist contributions from, for example, a speech therapist or child psychiatrist. The result of assessment activity may bring the practitioner into other formal agency processes, such as agreeing a child protection plan at a child protection conference, preparing a care plan for court, working with education to develop a statement of special educational needs, finding a foster care placement for a child (or more than one child) and reviewing progress, or considering whether family reunification is an option to be pursued. All these processes, however, are underpinned by the same set of principles discussed earlier. Critical is the importance of not repeating assessments unnecessarily but, rather, thoroughly reviewing information already gathered and carefully planning any further assessment and intervention with the family and between agencies.

Throughout the process, there will be diminishing numbers of children whose needs are so severe, complex or enduring that they require more comprehensive and detailed assessment. Understanding what is happening in such circumstances is, however, likely to require the specialist contributions of a range of professionals and community-based services, in order to secure the best possible information, analysis, judgement and planning to respond to the needs of the child and the family. Effective collaborative work between professionals is built on purposive and planned activity, understanding and respect for each other's roles and responsibilities, and clarity about tasks of leadership and coordination. Familiarity with the Assessment Framework on the part of all local agencies working with children and young people will, therefore, assist staff in making their contribution to assessing children in need and their families. The test will be whether use of the Assessment Framework will lead to more effective intervention and provision of services, and ultimately to better outcomes for children in need.

Summary

Identifying whether children are in need under the Children Act 1989 and how best to help them requires careful consideration of children's developmental progress within the context of what is happening in their families and the environment in which they are growing up. It is understanding the interaction between these factors and their impact on the child which is important. The Assessment Framework provides a way of structuring the gathering of information and analysis which makes sense to families and to the wide range of agencies which work to safeguard and promote the welfare of children.

Recommended reading

Department of Health et al. (2000) *Framework for the Assessment of Children in Need and their Families*. London: The Stationery Office.

Department of Health (2000a) *Assessing Children in Need and their Families: Practice Guidance*. London: The Stationery Office.

Department of Health (2000b) *Studies Informing the Framework for the Assessment of Children in Need and their Families*. London: The Stationery Office.

References

Association of Directors of Social Services (ADSS) and NCH Action for Children (1996) *Children Still in Need. Refocusing Child Protection in the Context of Children in Need*. London: NCH Action for Children.

Aldgate, J. and Tunstill, J. (1995) *Making Sense of Section 17: Implementing Services for Children in Need Within the Children Act 1989*. London: HMSO.

Audit Commission (1994) *Seen but not Heard*. London: HMSO.

Ball, M. (1998) *Disabled Children: Directions for Their Future Care*. London: Department of Health.

Bebbington, A. and Miles, J. (1989) 'The background of children who enter local authority care.' In *British Journal of Social Work 19*, 5, 349–368.

Bentovim, A. (1998) 'Significant Harm in Context.' In Adcock, M. and White, R. (eds.) *Significant Harm*. Croydon: Significant Publications.

Brown, G.W. and Harris, S.T. (1978) *Social Origins of Depression. A Study of Psychiatric Disorders in Women*. London: Tavistock.

Buchanan, A. (1996) *Cycles of Child Maltreatment*. Chichester: Wiley.

Cleaver, H. and Freeman, P. (1995) *Parental Perspectives in Cases of Suspected Child Abuse. Studies in Child Protection*. London: HMSO.

Cleaver, H., Unell, I. and Aldgate, J. (1999) *Children's Needs – Parenting Capacity. The impact of parental mental illness, problem alcohol and drug use and domestic violence on children's development*. London: The Stationery Office.

Department of Health (1994) *The Children Act Report 1993*. London: HMSO.

Department of Health (1995) *Child Protection: Messages from Research*. London: HMSO.

Department of Health, the Home Office and the Department for Education and Employment (1999) *Working Together to Safeguard Children. A Guide to Inter-agency Working to Safeguard and Promote the Welfare of Children*. London: The Stationery Office.

Department of Health, the Department for Education and Employment and the Home Office (2000) *Framework for the Assessment of Children in Need and their Families*. London: The Stationery Office.

Department of Health (2000a) *Assessing Children in Need and their Families: Practice Guidance*. London: The Stationery Office.

Department of Health (2000b) *Studies Informing the Development of the Framework for the Assessment of Children in Need and their Families*. London: The Stationery Office.

Falkov, A. (1996) *A Study of Working Together Part 8 Reports. Fatal Child Abuse and Parental Psychiatric Disorder*. London: The Stationery Office.

Howe, D. (1998) 'Assessment in Child and Family Social Work.' In J. Connolly and D. Shemmings (eds.) *Undertaking Assessments of Children and Families*. Norwich: University of East Anglia.

Jack, G. (1997) 'An Ecological Approach to Social Work with Children and Families.' In *Child and Family Social Work*, 1997, 2, 109–120.

Jones, D. P. H. (1997) 'The Effectiveness of Intervention.' In M. Adcock and R. White (eds.) (1998) *Significant Harm*. Croydon: Significant Publications.

Jones, D. P. H., Newbold, C. and Byrne, G. (1999) 'Management, Treatment and Outcomes.' In M. Eminson and R. Posslethwaite (eds.) *Munchausen Syndrome by Proxy Handbook*. London: Butterworth/Heinemann.

Lawton, D. (1998) *The Number and Characteristics of Families with More than One Disabled Child*. University of York: Social Policy Research Unit.

Masten, A. and Coatsworth, D. (1998) 'Development of Competence in Favorable and Unfavorable Environments.' In *American Psychologist*, February 1998.

Nelson, D. (1997) *The Building Blocks of Neighbourhoods that Support Families*. Baltimore: Casey Foundation.

Parker, R. , Ward, H., Jackson, S., Aldgate, J. and Wedge, P. (eds.) (1991) *Looking after Children: Assessing Outcomes in Child Care*. London: HMSO.

Reder, P. and Lucey, C. (1995) *Assessment of Parenting. Psychiatric and Psychological Contributions*. London: Routledge.

Social Exclusion Unit (1998) *Bringing Britain Together: A National Strategy for Neighbourhood Renewal.* London: The Stationery Office.

Stevenson, O. (1998) *Neglected Children: Issues and Dilemmas.* Oxford: Blackwell Science.

Utting, D. (1995) *Family and Parenthood: Supporting Families, Preventing Breakdown.* York: Joseph Rowntree Foundation.

Utting, W. (1989) Foreword in Department of Health: *The Care of Children: Principles and Practice in Regulations and Guidance.* London: HMSO.

Part II

The Assessment Process

CHAPTER 3

Ecological Perspectives in Assessing Children and Families

Gordon Jack

An understanding of a child must be located within the context of the child's family (parents or caregivers and the wider family) and of the community and culture in which he or she is growing up.

(From the *Framework for the Assessment of Children in Need and their Families,* p.11, 1.39)

This chapter will consider:

- what is an ecological approach to assessment?

- the influences of family history and functioning on the ability of the carer to meet the needs of the child

- the part played by the wider family and social support systems in meeting the developmental needs of children

- the influence of communities and neighbourhoods on parenting capacity and the development of children

- the impact of income and employment on children and families.

Introduction

Against the background of a series of high-profile 'child abuse scandals', the main focus of social work with children and families in Britain over the last two decades has been the development of systems to identify and protect children from 'significant harm' (Department of Health 1995). More recently, in the light of legislative changes and research findings, an effort has been made to refocus services, to locate child protection in the wider context of family support provision. In order to provide appropriate support to families it is necessary to complete an ecological assessment based on an understanding of the processes of mutual influence among individuals, their families and their social and economic environments.

Ecological approaches to assessment are based on the premise that the development and behaviour of individuals can be fully understood only in the context of the environments in which they live (Brooks-Gunn *et al.* 1993). A systems framework is used to examine the mutual influences that the child, family, friends, neighbours, community and wider society have upon one another. It is a holistic model which focuses on the ways in which children's developmental needs, the capacity of their parents to respond appropriately to those needs, and wider environmental factors interact with one another over time. It is this model which underpins the *Framework for the Assessment of Children in Need and their Families* (Department of Health, Department for Education and Employment and The Home Office 2000)

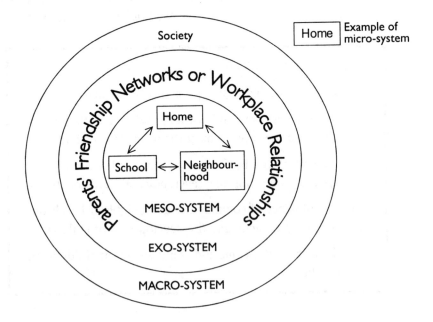

Figure 3.1 Bronfenbrenner's ecological system of human development.

While ecological approaches to crime have a relatively long history (see, for example, Shaw and McKay 1942), similar approaches to the study of children's development are of more recent origin. Uri Bronfenbrenner (1979) was the first to conceive of an 'ecology of human development', that would consist of a 'nested' arrangement of systems, with each system embedded within the one following it.

Settings in which the child is directly involved, such as his or her home, school and neighbourhood, are referred to as micro-systems and inter-actions between them constitute the meso-system. Settings in which the child does not actively participate, such as his or her parents' network of friends or parents' workplace, are referred to as exo-systems, and the wider environment or society, in which everything else is embedded, is the macro-system (Bronfenbrenner 1979, pp.22–6). It can be seen that this approach is reflected in the three domains of the *Framework for the Assessment of Children in Need and their Families*, with the welfare of the child depending on the interactions between the child's developmental needs, the parenting capacity available to the child, and the existing family and environmental factors.

Important features of the ecological model include an assessment of the balance between stresses and supports in a family's environment and an emphasis on an individual's own subjective experience of his or her circumstances:

> Whether parents can perform effectively in child-rearing roles within the family depends on the role demands, stresses and supports emanating from other settings. Parents' evaluations of their own capacity to function, as well as their view of the child, are related to such external factors as flexibility of job schedules, adequacy of child care arrangements, the presence of friends or neighbours who can help out in large or small emergencies, the quality of health and social services and neighbourhood safety. (Bronfenbrenner 1979, p.7)

Researchers have investigated the ways in which parenting capacity and children's development interact with social relationships outside the family (Belsky 1984; Cochran and Brassard 1979) and various aspects of the wider environment (Garbarino and Kostelny 1992; Rutter and Giller 1983). Taking the Assessment Framework as a guide, the influences of the dimensions of the family and environment domain on the developmental needs of children will be examined in more detail.

Family history and functioning

Professionals need to consider the following aspects of family history and functioning:

who is living in the household and how are they related to the child?

significant changes in family/household composition

history of childhood experiences of parents

chronology of significant life events and their meaning to family members

nature of family functioning, including sibling relationships, and its impact on the child

parental strengths and difficulties, including those of an absent parent

the relationship between separated parents.

(From the *Framework for the Assessment of Children in Need and their Families*)

The family environment into which a child is born will exert the most powerful and long-lasting influence over his or her development and future life chances. The early family environment will not only influence the kinds of later environments children are likely to encounter, but also the skills, behaviour and attitudes with which they will meet these environments (Rutter 1984). From various research studies it is clear that, given the right opportunities, many children are capable both of overcoming early adverse family circumstances and of effectively 'escaping from disadvantage' (Pilling 1990). However, faced with a combination of several adverse circumstances in early life, which interact and reinforce one another, children's development is liable to be significantly impaired and their life chances seriously undermined (Garmezy 1994; Werner and Smith 1992).

This cumulative effect of adverse family circumstances is demonstrated by the well-known studies undertaken by Michael Rutter and his colleagues on the different rates of mental disorders found among children in the Isle of Wight and Inner London (Rutter *et al.* 1975; Rutter and Madge 1976; Rutter and Quinton 1977). They found that a constellation of family problems which were associated with the stresses of inner-city life and included marital discord, family breakdown, parental psychiatric history or criminal record and large family size, was largely responsible for the significantly higher rates of disorder found among inner-city children. However, while the presence of one adverse circumstance did not increase the chance of disorder, the presence of two adverse circumstances increased the possibilities by a factor of four. This multiplicative effect obviously carries important implications for social work assessments of children and their family environment.

Similar findings have emerged from studies investigating family circumstances associated with the development of chronic offending. A combination of low socio-economic status, parental history of offending, poor parent child-rearing (for example, lax supervision, harsh or inconsistent discipline, hostile or rejecting interactions) and early onset of anti-social behaviour in the child was predictive of later chronic patterns of offending (see Yoshikawa 1994, for a review).

The specific effects of socio-economic status on later life chances have been illustrated in a long-term national study of a cohort of children born in the UK in 1958. As much as 70 per cent of an adult's earning power has been found to be dependent on their parents' (and even their grandparents') level of earnings (HM Treasury 1999). The same study has also revealed how early these effects begin to operate in a child's life. By the age of only 22 months, children in families in social classes I and II were already 14 per cent higher up an educational development scale than those in social classes IV and V. In general, early experience of 'family disadvantage', including poverty, lone parenting, paternal unemployment and separation from parents, is associated with lower earnings and poorer employment prospects as an adult. Educational disadvantage is a significant factor, but poverty exerts the most powerful influence (Gregg, Harkness and Machin 1999). This is a topic that will be considered in more detail in the later section on income and employment.

However, before leaving the subject of family history and functioning it is also important to consider the way in which childhood experiences influence the sort of parent that a child is likely to become. Studies in the USA of mothers found to have maltreated or neglected their children reveal consistent links with their early attachments. Norman Polansky and his colleagues studied 'neglecting' mothers, finding evidence of a personality trait that derived from early childhood experiences which involved 'social distancing' as a form of psychological defence mechanism. Not only did this directly affect their ability to provide adequate care for their children, but it also tended to isolate them from potential sources of social support outside the family (Polansky et al. 1985). This issue is considered in more depth in the next section, which focuses on the role of social support in parenting capacity and child development.

Further evidence of the links between childhood attachments and subsequent parenting capacity is provided by Crittenden's study of socio-economically matched groups of 'neglecting', 'abusing' and 'adequate' mothers. She found that mothers developed 'internalised working models' of relationships that were based on their early childhood experiences. The 'neglecting' mothers typically avoided relationships out of a sense of despair and hopelessness, whilst the 'abusing' mothers tended to engage in coercive relationships to meet their own needs alone. Only the 'adequate' mothers engaged in cooperative and reciprocal relationships, involving satisfaction for themselves and empathy for others (Crittenden 1985). Other researchers have pointed to the inter-generational transmission of maltreatment within family networks (See, for examples, Monk 1996; Oliver 1993).

Styles of parenting which have been found to be of benefit to children, even in the face of adverse family and environmental circumstances, have also been investigated by researchers. Vigilant supervision of children's activities and friendships in high-crime inner-city areas has been found to be protective (Baldwin, Baldwin and Cole 1990), and appropriate parental expectations, positive parent–child interactions, and the provision of toys and a safe play space can also enhance child development in otherwise high-risk family environments (Bradley *et al.* 1994).

Key messages for assessment

There are several messages here for assessments of children in need:

- adverse family circumstances interact with one another to increase the likelihood of the child's health and development becoming impaired

- certain features in parents' histories and circumstances, including a history of psychiatric problems or offending, low socio-economic status, marital discord and poor parenting (perhaps associated with a history of attachment problems with their own parents), when found in combination, should alert social workers undertaking assessments to the potential for the children's requiring the provision of services to safeguard and promote their welfare

- many children can successfully overcome early disadvantage, as described in Chapter 11. The way in which parents interact with their children, and the micro-system family environment they create, can help to protect children from otherwise potentially harmful surroundings.

Some of the ways in which parents can be assisted in their parenting role will be considered in the following sections.

Wider family and social support

- Who are considered by the child and the parents to be members of the wider family? This includes related and non-related persons and absent wider family. What is their role and importance to the child and parents and in precisely what way?

- What is the degree of the family's integration or isolation, its peer groups, friendship and social networks and the importance attached to them?

(From the *Framework for the Assessment of Children in Need and their Families*)

Personal social support networks are the webs of relationships that develop between individuals and a wide range of people that might include relatives, friends, neighbours, work colleagues and professional and lay helpers. The composition and structure of these networks vary according to factors such as size, proximity, stability, and frequency of contact. Network relationships can be sources of both support and stress, so it is important that assessments consider the content and quality of relationships within networks to understand the influence they are likely to have on parenting capacity and child development.

Network relationships that provide social support have consistently been found to exert positive influences on family functioning, parenting capacity and developmental outcomes for children (Dunst, Snyder and Mankinen 1988). These beneficial effects can be either direct, helping to improve quality of life in general (Mitchell, Billings and Moos 1982), or indirect, protecting individuals from the potentially negative impact of stressful life events and circumstances (Brownell and Shumaker 1984). The most important functions of social support are the provision of practical help, emotional support and information and advice (Cochran and Brassard 1979; Sarason, Sarason and Pierce 1990; Crockenburg 1988).

The main influences of social support on child development tend to be indirect, through more direct influences on parental health and wellbeing and overall family functioning (Dunst and Trivette 1990). Typically, the support networks for women tend to be more stable and confiding than those for men (Leavy 1983; Wills 1985), and higher levels of education and income tend to be associated with larger networks of more intimate relationships, which would include more non-kin and be spread over a wider geographical area for both sexes (Fischer 1982; Werner 1995). Other variables, including marital status, social class and culture also influence network characteristics. For instance, middle-class mothers report larger networks than working-class mothers, while single mothers generally have smaller networks than those in two-parent families. Mothers in the USA have been shown to maintain larger networks than do comparable mothers in Sweden, Germany and Wales (Bell and Ribbens 1994; Gunnarsson and Cochran 1990). Minority ethnic families also appear to rely on more restricted networks, with more local kin and less dispersed kin or friends in their networks (Cross 1990).

Numerous studies have demonstrated the central importance of a close, confiding adult relationship for mothers raising young children (Brown and Harris 1978; Kotch *et al.* 1997; Lacharit, Ethier and Couture 1996), although much less is known about either fathers or older children. Mothers with a reliable source of 'core support' provided by either the partner or a close friend were found to be protected against depression, whereas mothers with either a conflictual or an unreliable intimate relationship were at the greatest risk (Brown *et al.* 1986). Relatives outside the household, friends, neighbours and lay or professional helpers (usually in that order) may also be valuable sources of social support to families (Bronfenbrenner 1986; Gibbons 1990). Informal sources of social support, rather than those which are either professionally arranged or provided, tend to be most effective in enhancing parenting capacity (Beckman 1991). The actual provision of practical and emotional support is of benefit to all parents, but even the perception that support will be available if needed has beneficial effects, particularly for mothers living in impoverished circumstances (Hashima and Amato 1994; Sheppard 1994).

In general social integration, through supportive relationships with network members, has positive benefits, and is associated with better health and psycho-social wellbeing. On the other hand, social isolation is a clear risk factor for poor health (Blaxter 1990) and is found to be associated with families in which child neglect occurs, and in which mothers tend to have smaller social networks and fewer social contacts than non-neglecting control-group mothers (Coohey 1996; Thompson 1995). However, not all social network relationships are consistent sources of support to parents (Gibbons 1990; Smale *et al.* 1994). For example, both single mothers and parents of children with disabilities have been found to experience considerable stress, often in the form of criticism, from their social networks (Brassard 1982; Dunst, Trivette and Jodry 1997).

It is also important to consider the role that children's social support networks can play in their development, including their relationships with siblings, relatives outside the household, friends and neighbours (Belle 1989; Dunn 1993). One of the most consistent findings of research in this area is the value for those children who live in adverse family circumstances of an enduring relationship with a special person outside the household, such as a teacher or a grandparent (Cohen and Wills 1985; Jenkins and Smith 1990). Sources of recognition and achievement outside the home, perhaps through educational or sporting success or involvement in a church or youth group, can also enhance self-esteem and lead to improved future life chances (Werner and Smith 1992). For example, the adult outcomes for children raised in institutional care were significantly enhanced by positive school experiences, and led to better planning and choice of career and marital partner (Rutter, Quinton and Hill 1990). Schools can also exert a direct influence on outcomes for children, not only on educational attainment but also on levels of offending among their pupils (Maughan 1994; Sylva 1994).

Key messages for assessment

In summary, then, social workers undertaking ecologically based assessments with families need to focus on the social support which is available to them. In particular:

- the central role in the support of mothers played by a reliable, confiding relationship with a partner or close friend and the additional support which can be provided by relatives, friends and neighbours outside the household should inform any attempts to improve the development of children living in adverse circumstances

- the value to children of having a reliable and enduring relationship outside of the family, when parenting is failing properly to meet their developmental needs, should be recognised, as described in detail in Chapter 11

- interventions based on a clear assessment of the social support available to families and which seek to increase the supportive potential (and reduce the stressful content) of these networks are likely to be most effective

- there are a number of useful guides available, to assist social workers in the assessment of social support networks and the capacity of community resources to provide support to families with children, which can be utilised (see, for example, Dunst and Trivette 1990; Hawtin, Hughes and Percy-Smith 1994; Kretzman and McKnight 1993; McKnight 1987; Nelson 1997; Trivette, Dunst and Deal 1997; Warren and Warren 1977).

Social integration, housing and community resources

Professionals need to consider:

- an exploration of the wider context of the local neighbourhood and community and its impact on the child and parents

- whether the accommodation has basic amenities and facilities appropriate to the age and development of the child and other resident members. Is the housing accessible and suitable to the needs of disabled family members? Includes the interior and exterior of the accommodation and immediate surroundings. Basic amenities include water, heating, sanitation, cooking facilities, sleeping arrangements and cleanliness, hygiene and safety and their impact on the child's upbringing

- the range of facilities and services in a neighbourhood, including universal services of primary health care, day care and schools, places of worship, transport, shops and leisure activities. Includes availability, accessibility and standard of resources and impact on the family, including disabled members.

(From the *Framework for the Assessment of Children in Need and their Families*)

The communities and neighbourhoods in which families live can have a major influence on both parenting capacity and children's development. This is illustrated by the research undertaken by Rutter (1984), where the stresses of inner-city life were found to be the cause of a constellation of family problems that in turn produced negative consequences for child development.

Numerous research studies have demonstrated clear geographical variations in rates of juvenile crime (Sampson, Randenbush and Earls 1997; Yoshikawa 1994), child abuse and neglect (Coulton *et al.* 1995), health (Blaxter 1990), mortality rates (Phillimore, Beattie and Townsend 1994) and educational and developmental outcomes (Brooks-Gunn *et al.* 1993). Most of these variations can be explained by differences in the socio-economic and demographic composition of different communities.

For example, nearly four-fifths of the variation in rates of child maltreatment among different areas in Chicago was accounted for by nine such measures, which included poverty, unemployment, family structure (ratio of children to adults; percentage of female-headed households), overcrowding, ethnic origin, educational level and stability of residence (Garbarino and Kostelny, 1992). The central role played by poverty, unemployment and income inequality in communities will be examined in detail in the next section. The rest of this section focuses on the nature of the relationships and behaviours that emerge in different communities and the effects that they can have upon children's development.

The community-level interactions among members of a particular population generate different levels of social cohesion. The day-to-day interactions between friends, relatives, neighbours, work colleagues, church members, political and social groups, schools, employers and professional services, at both formal and informal levels in a community, are often referred to collectively, as 'social capital'. The 'capital' is developed and maintained by repeated and varied exchanges among relatively equal members of a community, fostering a collective sense of trust and belonging. However, social capital can be fatally undermined by poverty, inequalities, divisions and exclusions, which act as barriers to the open and reciprocal interactions on which social cohesion thrives (Jack and Jordan 1999). This is perhaps one of the reasons why poor urban communities have been found to demonstrate more restricted ties between neighbours (Coulton et al. 1995), fewer neighbourhood organisations (Furstenberg 1993) and lower levels of participation in social, political and community activities (Howarth et al. 1998). It has already been noted that minority ethnic families tend to rely on more geographically restricted and kin-based social networks than others. This is particularly true for those groups with the lowest levels of educational achievement and income, who are vulnerable to exclusion. Other minority ethnic groups with better levels of attainment in education, employment and home-ownership tend to have access to wider social networks (Barker 1999).

Aspects of the physical environment may also influence social interactions and behaviour. Some locations, such as local shops, are rich 'behaviour settings' for facilitating social exchanges amongst diverse members of a community (Barker 1978), whilst other aspects of the physical environment, such as lack of leisure facilities or the design of housing estates, can increase levels of crime and disorder (Perkins et al. 1993; Bottoms and Wiles 1997). The availability of well-designed and well-maintained homes and safe outside play areas for children are other important features of the physical environment, especially as accidents remain the major cause of death amongst children (Spencer 1996).

Communities with higher levels of social capital, with more democratic and egalitarian structures and higher levels of citizen participation in community life tend to show lower levels of crime and child maltreatment and better levels of child health (Sampson *et al.* 1997; Vinson, Baldry and Hargreaves 1996; Putnam, Leonardi and Nanetti 1993). In relation to reported child maltreatment, this is illustrated by the work of James Garbarino and his colleagues in the USA. In an early study of two socio-economically matched neighbourhoods with markedly different levels of child maltreatment, families in the higher-risk area reported a lack of mutually supportive relationships and informal social networks in their neighbourhood, compared with families in the lower risk area (Garbarino and Sherman 1980). Subsequent work tracked four socio-economically matched neighbourhoods with different rates of child maltreatment over a six-year period. One neighbourhood, which experienced rising levels of child maltreatment during the study, showed low levels of community participation and interactions among neighbours, whereas another area, with falling levels of maltreatment, was perceived to have strong informal and formal social support systems and was described as a 'poor but decent place to live' (Garbarino and Kostelny 1992).

The social demography of a community, the social and economic circumstances of its residents, clearly carries important implications for the development of children and the life chances of adults. Inequality and social exclusion undermine social capital and reduce the willingness or ability of residents to create the supportive environments in which families can raise their children successfully. Often, the groups or individuals in the greatest need of reliable assistance and support outside of the family are those least likely to have access to these. This is where social workers and other welfare professionals have a role to play in supporting and developing social capital in deprived communities.

Key messages for assessment

Assessments and interventions need to bear in mind that:

- informal sources of support that involve opportunities for family members to reciprocate the help offered, and leave in their hands as much choice and control as possible over what help is accepted and offered, tend to be most effective in enhancing personal functioning (Dunst *et al.* 1997)

- priority should be given to strengthening natural support systems wherever possible, and where more formal services need to be used, they should mirror those aspects of informal support systems that are most helpful to families

- several community-based early intervention programmes, using ecological principles, have been developed to support parents and enhance child development. The aspects of these programmes that are most beneficial are beginning to emerge from evaluations carried out on both sides of the Atlantic. They often involve combinations of parenting programmes, home-visiting schemes, centre-based services and wider, community-building components (see, for example, Beresford *et al.* 1996; Crnic and Stormshak 1997; Grimshaw and McGuire 1998; Jack 1997 1998; Johnson, Howell and Molloy 1993; Macdonald and Roberts 1995; Macmillan *et al.* 1994; McLaughlin, Irby and Langman 1994; Olds, Henderson and Kitzman 1994).

Income and employment

Professionals need to consider:

- the income available over a sustained period of time
- the sufficiency of income to meet the family's needs. Is the family in receipt of all its benefit entitlements? Are there financial difficulties which affect the child?
- the way resources available to the family are used
- who is working in the household, their pattern of work and any changes. What impact does this have on the child? How is work or absence of work viewed by family members? How does it affect their relationship with the child? Includes children's experience of work and its impact on them.

(From the *Framework for the Assessment of Children in Need and their Families*)

The links between inequalities in income and health are well known and are clearly demonstrated by a large body of empirical evidence from around the world. People living in poverty (usually defined nowadays as those living on less than half the average earnings for their country) are more likely to suffer ill health, disability and premature death than their more affluent counterparts. Poor health and disability also contribute towards the risk of experiencing poverty (Blackburn 1991; Blaxter 1990; Bywaters and

McLeod 1996; Phillimore *et al.* 1994). This link provides a clear illustration of the ecological model, with mutual interactions between individuals and their environments demonstrated in study after study.

The association between inequalities of income and personal health and development is a particularly serious issue for children and families living in Britain. Since the late 1970s, income inequalities have risen more sharply in Britain than in any other developed country except New Zealand (Joseph Rowntree Foundation 1995; Steinhauer 1998). Although there have been signs that the pace of change has begun to slow, inequalities of this magnitude, like a super-tanker, take a long time to bring to a halt and turn around (Goodman, Johnson and Webb 1997). At the end of the twentieth century, Britain finds itself in the unenviable position of being 'top' of the European Union child poverty league. More than one in three British children are currently living below the poverty line, compared with an EU average of one in five, and only one in twenty in Denmark (Department of Social Security 1998; *The Guardian* 1997).

The Labour government, elected in 1997, has recognised the importance of tackling child poverty and has set itself the ambitious target of eliminating it altogether by the year 2019. Economic policies have been introduced: the national minimum wage, New Deals to improve employment opportunities, tax credits for working families, children and child care and increases to universal child benefit, which are designed to lift 700,000 children out of poverty within three years. Other programmes include 'Sure Start' for early child care and Action Zones to pilot ways of improving education, health and communities. These programmes should also have beneficial effects for the life chances and development of poor children in the future (*The Guardian* 1999 a and b).

The present levels of income inequality in the UK are particularly worrying when we realise that it is this very inequality, rather than a country's overall level of prosperity, which has the most direct effects on health. It is not the richest countries in the world which have the healthiest populations but the countries with the most equal distributions of income (Wilkinson 1996). This is where the emphasis on people's subjective experience of their circumstances in the ecological model comes to the fore. Comparisons that reveal particularly large or unfair differences in income among different members of the same society have particularly damaging effects on the health and wellbeing of those who are disadvantaged. The dramatic rise in income inequality seen in New Zealand in recent years has been matched by an equally steep rise in youth suicides and crime, to the point where both of these measures became the highest in the industrialised world (Steinhauer 1998). Health inequalities have also risen in Britain, whilst the more egalitarian societies such as Sweden and Japan show no comparable rises in health inequalities or health gradients according to socio-economic status (Wilkinson 1996).

Families with children are particularly vulnerable to these trends. While not all children living in poverty in one year will be in poverty in the following and subsequent years, many will experience recurrent or persistent poverty. As many as 25 per cent of children in Britain are now estimated to experience a state of permanent poverty (Goodman *et al.* 1997; HM Treasury 1999). The groups most at risk are those living in lone-parent families, families of minority ethnic origin and two-parent families with neither adult in employment (Platt and Noble 1999; Smaje 1995).

The negative effects of poverty on children can be widespread and potentially long-lasting. As indicated earlier in this chapter, earnings in later life tend to be largely determined by parental earnings during childhood and there are clear associations between poverty and rates of recorded child abuse and neglect and juvenile crime (Garbarino and Sherman 1980; Rutter and Giller 1983). Children growing up in poverty are also at much greater risk of developing conduct and emotional disorders and chronic illnesses, and of not reaching their full cognitive and educational potential (Duncan, Broots-Gunn and Klebanov 1994; Kumar 1993; Ross, Shillington and Lochhead 1994; Steinhauer 1998; Woodroffe *et al.* 1993). In addition there is a clear social class gradient with respect to both road traffic accidents and fatal accidents in the home for children (Spencer 1996).

It is also worth noting that unemployment poses specific risks to family functioning and parenting capacity in addition to the threats which may be posed by reduced income. For example, the risk of suffering psychiatric problems for both men and women has been found to rise threefold on becoming unemployed (Bebbington *et al.* 1981).

Key messages for assessment

- the effects of poverty and inequality on children mean that children who experience these conditions for any substantial period of their lives should be considered as possible 'children in need', requiring the provision of statutory services (under section 17 of the Children Act 1989), in the same way as children who suffer 'significant harm' or are 'disabled' (Aldgate and Tunstill 1995)

- poverty is not an isolated phenomenon – it interacts with a whole range of other factors, including education, health and housing. Assessments and the planning and delivery of services to meet the needs of children living in poverty therefore need to be undertaken on an inter-agency basis, planned at the local level through Children's Services Plans, which are based on detailed knowledge of the social demographics of the areas being served (Department of Health and Department for Education and Employment 1996)

- there is a growing research literature which can assist all agencies involved in drawing up Children's Services Plans to develop effective responses to the complex set of problems faced by children and families living in impoverished circumstances (Audit Commission 1994; Blackburn 1991; Bywaters and McLeod 1996; Cochran 1993; Coulton 1996; Donnison 1998; Weil 1996).

Summary

'We have to confront the constant tendency to regress to the individualisation of social problems.' (Smale *et al.* 1994, p.2)

A number of lessons, for both practitioners and managers, emerge from an ecological approach to assessing children and families. For practitioners and their immediate supervisors, an awareness of the cumulative effect of adverse family circumstances, and the potential for their negative impact on children's development to begin early and last through to adulthood, is obviously important. It is for this reason that the third domain, family and environment, is included in the *Framework for the Assessment of Children in Need and their Families*. Because of the positive potential of social support for families with children, assessments should take into account the informal support already available, particularly from close relatives and friends. Where deficits or problems are identified, the first priority should be to strengthen existing support or activate other potential sources of informal support in the community. Where formal support systems are required, these are most likely to be effective if they involve opportunities to give as well as to receive help, and when as much control as practicable is left in the hands of the family concerned. Assessments should also be informed by an awareness of the effects of demographic and structural aspects of the wider environment on children and families, including the characteristics of particular neighbourhoods and the ways in which social capital and integration can be increased and social isolation minimised. Finally, the corrosive effect of poverty and inequality on children and families requires that children living in impoverished circumstances are recognised as possible 'children in need' who may require responses from across the agencies to help families to meet their developmental needs successfully.

This last point leads on to the main implications of the ecological approach for senior managers. Without the collection and analysis of comprehensive social demographic data about the populations being served, planning and the allocation of agency resources are likely to be fatally flawed. The various existing indices of deprivation, including the 'Local Deprivation', 'Jarman', 'Townsend' and 'Breadline' indices (Lee and Murie 1997) are all useful for identifying national or large-scale patterns. However, more fine-grained analyses are required at local levels to develop meaningful and reliable profiles, which can identify the needs of different communities and different groups within those communities and which will provide the basis for planning appropriate inter-agency responses to 'children in need'.

Recommended reading

Bersford, B., Sloper, P., Baldwin, S. and Newman, T. (1996) *What Works in Services for Families with a Disabled Child?* Barkinside: Barnardo's.

McLeod, E. and Bywaters, P. (1999) *Social Work, Health and Equality.* London: Routledge.

Thompson, R. A. (1995) *Preventing Child Maltreatment Through Social Support.* Thousand Oaks: Sage.

References

Aldgate, J. and Tunstill, J. (1995) *Making Sense of Section 17. Implementing Services for Children in Need within the 1989 Children Act.* London: HMSO.

Audit Commission (1994) *Seen but not Heard: Coordinating Community Child Health and Social Services for Children in Need.* London: HMSO.

Baldwin, A. L., Baldwin, C. and Cole, R. E. (1990) 'Stress-resistant Families and Stress-resistant Children.' In J. Rolf, A. Masten, D. Cicchetti, K. Newchterlein and S. Wintraub (eds.) *Risk and Protective Factors in the Development of Psychopathology.* Cambridge: Cambridge University Press.

Barker, P. (1999) 'Moving with the times.' In *The Guardian (Society),* 4 August, pp.2–3.

Barker, R. (1978) *Habitats, Environments and Human Behaviour.* San Francisco: Josey-Bass.

Bebbington, P., Hurry, J., Tennant, C., Stuart, E. and Wing, J. (1981) 'Epidemiology of mental disorders in Camberwell.' In *Psychological Medicine, 11,* pp.561–79.

Beckman, P. J. (1991) 'Comparison of mothers' and fathers' perceptions of the effect of young children with and without disabilities.' In *American Journal on Mental Retardation, 95,* pp.585–95.

Bell, L. and Ribbens, J. (1994) 'Isolated Housewives and Complex Maternal Worlds – The Significance of Social Contacts between Women with Young Children in Industrial Societies.' In *The Sociological Review, 42*, 2, pp.227–62.

Belle, D. (ed.) (1989) *Children's Social Networks and Social Supports.* New York: John Wiley.

Belsky, J. (1984) 'The Determinants of Parenting: A Process Model.' In *Child Development, 55*, pp.83–96.

Beresford, B., Sloper, P., Baldwin, S. and Newman, T. (1996) *What Works in Services for Families with a Disabled Child?* Barkingside: Barnardo's.

Blackburn, C. (1991) *Poverty and Health: Working with Families.* Buckingham: Open University Press.

Blaxter, M. (1990) *Health and Lifestyles.* London: Routledge.

Bottoms, A. E. and Wiles, P. (1997) 'Environmental Criminology.' In M. Maguire, R. Morgan and R. Reiner (eds.) *The Oxford Handbook of Criminology* (2nd edn.), pp.305–59. Oxford: Clarendon Press.

Bradley, R. H., Whiteside, L., Mundfrom, D. J., Casey, P. H., Kelleher, K. J. and Pope, S. K. (1994) 'Early Indications of Resilience and their Relation to Experiences in the Home Environments of Low Birthweight, Premature Children Living in Poverty.' In *Child Development, 65*, pp.346–60.

Brassard, J. (1982) 'Beyond family structure: mother–child interaction and personal social networks.' Unpublished doctoral dissertation. Ithaca: Cornell University.

Bronfenbrenner, U. (1979) *The Ecology of Human Development.* Cambridge: Harvard University Press.

Bronfenbrenner, U. (1986) 'Ecology of the Family as a Context for Human Development: Research Perspectives.' In *Developmental Psychology, 22*, 6, pp.723–42.

Brooks-Gunn, J., Duncan, G. J., Kelbanov, P. K. and Sealand, N. (1993) 'Do Neighborhoods Influence Child and Adolescent Development?' In *American Journal of Sociology, 99*, 2, pp.353–95.

Brown, G. W. and Harris, T. (1978) *Social Origins of Depression.* London: Tavistock.

Brown, G. W., Andrews, B., Harris, T. O., Adler, Z. and Bridge, I. (1986) 'Social support, Self-esteem and Depression.' In *Psychological Medicine, 16*, pp.813–31.

Brownell, A. and Shumaker, S. A. (1984) 'Social Support: An Introduction to a Complex Phenomena.' In *Journal of Social Issues, 40*, pp.1–9.

Bywaters, P. and McLeod, E. (eds.) (1996) *Working for Equality in Health.* London: Routledge.

Cochran, M. (1993) 'Parenting and Personal Social Networks.' In T. Luster and L. Okagaki (eds.) *Parenting: An Ecological Perspective*, pp.149–78, Hillsdale, NJ: Lawrence Erlbaum Associates.

Cochran, M. M. and Brassard, J. A. (1979) 'Child Development and Personal Social Networks.' *Child Development, 50*, pp.601–15.

Cohen, S. and Wills, T. A. (1985) 'Stress, social support and the buffering hypothesis.' In *Psychological Review, 98*, 2, pp.310–57.

Coohey, C. (1996) 'Child Maltreatment: Testing the Social Isolation Hypothesis.' In *Child Abuse and Neglect, 20*, 3, pp.241–54.

Coulton, C. J. (1996) 'Poverty, Work and Community: A Research Agenda for an Era of Diminishing Federal Responsibility.' In *Social Work, 41*, 5, pp.509–20.

Coulton, C. J. Korbin, J. E., Su, M. and Chow, J. (1995) 'Community-Level Factors and Child Maltreatment Rates.' In *Child Development, 66*, pp.1262–76.

Crittenden, P. M. (1985) 'Social Networks, Quality of Child Rearing and Child Development.' In *Child Development, 56*, pp.1299–313.

Crnic, K. A. and Stormshak, E. (1997) 'The Effectiveness of Providing Social Support for Families of Children at Risk.' In M.J. Guralnick (ed.) *The Effectiveness of Early Intervention*, pp.209–25. Baltimore: Paul H. Brookes.

Crockenberg, S. (1988) 'Social Support and Parenting.' In H. Fitzgerald, B. Lester and M. Yogman (eds.) *Theory and Research in Behavioural Paediatrics (Vol.4)*, pp.67–92. New York: Plenum.

Cross, W. (1990) 'Race and Ethnicity: Effects on Social Networks.' In M. Cochran, M. Larner, D. Riley, L. Gunnarson and C. Henderson, Jr., (eds.) *Extending Families: The Social Networks of Parents and Their Children*, pp.67–85. London: Cambridge University Press.

Department of Health, Home Office and Department for Education and Employment (1995) *Child Protection: Messages from Research*. London: HMSO.

Department of Health, Department for Education and Employment and The Home Office (2000) *Framework for the Assessment of Children in Need and their Families*. London: The Stationery Office.

Department of Health and Department for Education and Employment (1996) *Children's Services Planning: Guidance*. London: HMSO.

Department of Social Security (1998) *A New Contract for Welfare*. London: The Stationery Office.

Donnison, D. (1998) *Policies for a Just Society*. Basingstoke: Macmillan.

Duncan, G. J., Brooks-Gunn, J. and Klebanov, P. K. (1994) 'Economic Deprivation and Early Childhood Development.' In *Child Development, 65*, pp.296–318.

Dunn, J. (1993) *Young Children's Close Relationships: Beyond Attachment*. London: Sage.

Dunst, C. J., Snyder, S. and Mankinen, M. (1988) 'Efficacy of early intervention.' In M. Wang, M. Reynolds and H. Walberg (eds.) *Handbook of Special Education: Research and Practice: Vol. 3 Low Incidence Conditions*, pp.259–94. Oxford: Pergamon Press.

Dunst, C. J. and Trivette, C. M. (1990) 'Assessment of Social Support in Early Intervention Programs.' In S. J. Meisels and J. P. Shonkoff (eds.) *Handbook of Early Childhood Education*. New York: Cambridge University Press.

Dunst, C. J., Trivette, C. M. and Jodry, W. (1997) 'Influences of Social Support on Children with Disabilities and Their Families.' In M.J. Guralnick (ed.) *The Effectiveness of Early Intervention*, pp.499–522. Baltimore: Paul H. Brookes.

Fischer, C. (1982) *To Dwell Among Friends: Personal Networks in Town and City*. Chicago: University of Chicago Press.

Furstenberg, F. F., Jr. (1993) 'How Families Manage Risk and Opportunity in Dangerous Neighbourhoods.' In W. Wilson (ed.) *Sociology and the Public Agenda*, pp.231–58, Newbury Park: Sage.

Garbarino, J. and Kostelny, K. (1992) 'Child Maltreatment as a Community Problem.' In *Child Abuse and Neglect, 16*, pp.455–64.

Garbarino, J. and Sherman, D. (1980) 'High-risk Neighbourhoods and High-risk Families: The Human Ecology of Child Maltreatment.' In *Child Development, 51*, pp.188–98.

Garmezy, N. (1994) 'Reflections and Commentary on Risk, Resilience and Development.' In R. J. Haggerty, L. R. Sherrod, N. Garmezy and M. Rutter (eds.) *Stress, Risk and Resilience in Children and Adolescents*. Cambridge: Cambridge University Press.

Gibbons, J. (1990) *Family Support and Prevention: Studies in Local Areas*. London: HMSO.

Goodman, A., Johnson, P. and Webb, S. (1997) *Inequality in the UK*. Oxford: Oxford University Press.

Gregg, P., Harkness, S. and Machin, S. (1999) *Child Development and Family Income*. York: York Publishing Services.

Grimshaw, R. and McGuire, C. (1998) *Evaluating Parenting Programmes: A Study of Stakeholders' Views*. London: National Children's Bureau.

Guardian, The (1997) 'Children in poverty: Britain tops the European league,' 28 April, p.1.

Guardian, The (1999a) 'Kind Uncle Gordon,' 10 March, p.18.

Guardian, The (1999b) 'Means to an end,' Society, 31 March, pp.6–7.

Gunnarsson, L. and Cochran, M. (1990) 'The Social Networks of Single Parents: Sweden and the United States.' In M. Cochran, M. Larner, D. Riley, L. Gunnarsson and C. Henderson, Jr. (eds.) *Extending Families: The Social Networks of Parents and Their Children*, pp.105–18, Cambridge: Cambridge University Press.

Hashima, P. Y. and Amato, P. R. (1994) 'Poverty, Social Support and Parental Behaviour.' In *Child Development, 65*, pp.394–403.

Hawtin, M., Hughes, G. and Percy-Smith, J. (1994) *Community profiling: Auditing Social Needs.* Buckingham: Open University Press.

Her Majesty's Treasury. (1999) *Tackling Poverty and Extending Opportunity.* London: The Stationery Office.

Howarth, C., Kennedy, P., Palmer, G. and Street, C. (1998) *Monitoring Poverty and Social Exclusion: Labour's Inheritance.* York: Joseph Rowntree Foundation (Findings, Dec. 1998).

Jack, G. (1997) 'Discourses of Child Protection and Child Welfare.' In *British Journal of Social Work, 27*, pp.659–78.

Jack, G. (1998) 'The Social Ecology of Parents and Children: Implications for the Development of Child Welfare Services in the UK.' In *International Journal of Child and Family Social Work, 2*, pp.109–20.

Jack, G. and Jordan, B. (1999) 'Social Capital and Child Welfare.' In *Children and Society, 13*, pp.242–256.

Jenkins, J. M. and Smith, M. A. (1990) 'Factors Protecting Children Living in Disharmonious Homes: Maternal Reports.' In *Journal of the American Academy of Child and Adolescent Psychiatry, 29*, pp.60–9.

Johnson, Z., Howell, F. and Molloy, B. (1993) 'Community Mothers' Programme: Randomised Controlled Trial of Non-professional Intervention in Parenting.' In *British Medical Journal, 306*, pp.1449–52.

Joseph Rowntree Foundation (1995) *The Joseph Rowntree Inquiry into Income and Wealth.* York: Joseph Rowntree Trust.

Kotch, J. B., Browne, D. C., Ringwalt, C. L., Dufart, V., Ruina, E., Stewart, P. W. and Jung, J. W. (1997) 'Stress, Social Support and Substantiated Maltreatment in the Second and Third Years of Life.' In *Child Abuse and Neglect, 21*, 11, pp.1025–37.

Kretzman, J. and McKnight, J. (1993) *Building Community from the Inside Out.* Evanston, Il: North-Western University, Center for Urban Affairs and Policy Research.

Kumar, V. (1993) *Poverty and Inequality in the UK: The Effects on Children.* London: National Children's Bureau.

Lacharit, C., Ethier, L. and Couture, G. (1996) 'The Influence of Partners on Parental Stress of Neglectful Mothers.' In *Child Abuse Review, 5*, pp.18–33.

Leavy, R. L. (1983) 'Social Support and Psychological Disorder. A Review.' In *Journal of Community Psychology, 11*, pp.3–21.

Lee, P. and Murie, A. (1997) *Poverty, Housing Tenure and Social Exclusion.* Bristol: The Policy Press.

Macdonald, G. and Roberts, H. (1995) *What Works in the Early Years.* Barkingside: Barnardo's.

MacMillan, H. L., MacMillan, J. H., Offord, D. R., Griffith, L. and MacMillan, A. (1994) 'Primary Prevention of Child Physical Abuse: A Critical Review, Part I.' In *Journal of Child Psychology and Psychiatry, 35*, 5, pp.835–56.

McKnight, J. (1987) 'Regenerating Community.' In *Social Policy*, Winter, 54–8.

McLaughlin, M. W., Irby, M. A. and Langman, J. (1994) *Urban Sanctuaries: Neighbourhood Organisations in the Lives and Futures of Inner-city Youth.* San Francisco: Jossey-Bass.

Maughan, B. (1994) 'School Influences.' In M. Rutter and D. Hay (eds.) *Development Through Life: A Handbook for Clinicians.* Oxford: Blackwell Scientific.

Mitchell, R. E., Billings, A. G. and Moos, R. H. (1982) 'Social Support and Well-being: Implications for Prevention Programs.' In *Journal of Primary Prevention, 3*, 77–98.

Monk, D. R. (1996) 'The Use of Geneograms to Identify Intergenerational Child Abuse.' Unpublished MPhil Thesis, University of Exeter.

Nelson, D. (1997) *The Building Blocks of Neighborhoods that Support Families.* Baltimore: Casey Foundation.

Olds, D. L., Henderson, C. R. and Kitzman, H. (1994) 'Does Parental and Infancy Nurse Home Visitation have Enduring Effects on Qualities of Parental Caregiving and Child Health at 25 to 50 months of life?' In *Pediatrics, 93*, 1, pp.89–98.

Oliver, J. E. (1993) 'Intergenerational Transmission of Child Abuse.' In *American Journal of Psychiatry, 150*, 9, pp.1315–24.

Perkins, D. D., Wandersman, A., Rich, R. C. and Taylor, R. B. (1993) 'The Physical Environment of Street Crime: Defensible Space, Territoriality and Incivilities.' In *Journal of Environmental Psychology, 13*, pp.29–49.

Phillimore, P., Beattie, A. and Townsend, P. (1994) 'The Widening Gap. Inequality in Health in Northern England 1981–1991.' In *British Medical Journal, 308*, pp.1125–28.

Pilling, D. (1990) *Escape from Disadvantage.* London: The Falmer Press.

Platt, L. and Noble, M. (1999) *Race, Place and Poverty: Ethnic Groups and Low Income Distributions.* York, Joseph Rowntree Foundation (Findings, Feb.).

Polansky, N. A., Gaudin, J. M., Ammons, P. W. and David, K. B. (1985) 'The Psychological Ecology of the Neglectful Mother.' In *Child Abuse and Neglect, 9*, pp.265–75.

Putnam, R. D., Leonardi, R. and Nanetti, R. Y. (1993) *Making Democracy Work: Civic Traditions in Modern Italy.* Princeton: Princeton University Press.

Ross, D. P., Shillington, E. R. and Lochhead, C. (1994) *The Canadian Fact Book on Poverty – 1994.* Ottowa, ON: Canadian Council on Social Development.

Rutter, M. (1984) 'Continuities and Discontinuities in Socioemotional Development: Empirical and Conceptual Perspectives.' In R. N. Emde and R. J. Harman (eds.) *Continuities and Discontinuities in Development.* New York: Plenum.

Rutter, M., Cox, A., Tupling, C., Berger, M. and Youle, W. (1975) 'Attainment and Adjustment in Two Geographical Areas. I. The Prevalence of Psychiatric Disorder.' In *British Journal of Psychiatry, 126*, pp.493–509.

Rutter, M. and Giller, H. J. (1983) *Juvenile Delinquency: Trends and Perspectives.* New York: Penguin Books.

Rutter, M. and Madge, N. (1976) *Cycles of Disadvantage.* London, Heinemann.

Rutter, M. and Quinton, D. (1977) 'Psychiatric Disorder – Ecological Factors and Concepts of Causation.' In H. McGurk (ed.) *Ecological Factors in Human Development*, pp.173–87. Amsterdam: North Holland.

Rutter, M., Quinton, D. and Hill, J., (1990) 'Adult Outcome of Institution-reared Children: Males and Females Compared.' In L. Robins and M. Rutter (eds.) *Straight and Devious Pathways from Childhood to Adulthood*, pp.135–57. Cambridge: Cambridge University Press.

Sampson, R. J., Raudenbush, S. W. and Earls, F. (1997) 'Neighbourhoods and Violent Crime: A Multi-level Study of Collective Efficacy.' In *Science, 277*, pp.1–7.

Sarason, B. R., Sarason, I. G. and Pierce, G. R., (eds.) (1990) *Social Support: An Interactional View.* New York: Wiley.

Shaw, C. R. and McKay, H. D. (1942) *Juvenile Delinquency and Urban Areas.* Chicago: Univ. of Chicago Press.

Sheppard, M. (1994) 'Childcare, Social Support and Maternal Depression: A Review and Application of Findings.' In *British Journal of Social Work, 24*, pp.287–310.

Smaje, C. (1995) *Health, 'Race' and Ethnicity: Making Sense of the Evidence.* London: King's Fund Institute.

Smale, G., Tuson, G., Ahmed, B., Darvill, G., Domoney, L. and Sainsbury, E. (1994) *Negotiating Care in the Community.* London: HMSO.

Spencer, N. (1996) 'Reducing Child Health Inequalities.' In P. Bywaters and E. McLeod (eds.) *Working for Equality in Health*, pp.143–60. London: Routledge.

Steinhauer, P. D. (1998) 'Developing Resiliency in Children from Disadvantaged Populations.' In *Canada Health Action, Building on the Legacy (Vol.1), Children and Youth.* Sainte-Foy, Quebec: Editions Multi-Mondes.

Sylva, K. (1994) 'School Influences on Children's Development.' In *Journal of Child Psychology and Psychiatry, 35*, pp.135–70.

Thompson, R. A. (1995) *Preventing Child Maltreatment Through Social Support.* Thousand Oaks: Sage.

Trivette, C. M., Dunst, C. J. and Deal, A. G. (1997) 'Resource-based Approach to Early Intervention.' In S. K. Thurman, J. R. Cornwell and S. R. Gottwald (eds.) *Contexts of Early Intervention: Systems and Settings*, pp.73–92. Baltimore: Paul H. Brookes.

Vinson, T., Baldry, W. and Hargreaves, J. (1996) 'Neighbourhoods, Networks and Child Abuse.' In *British Journal of Social Work, 26*, pp.523–43.

Warren, R. and Warren, D. (eds.) (1977) *The Neighborhood Organizer's Handbook.* South Bend: University of Notre Dame Press.

Weil, M. O. (1996) 'Community Building: Building Community Practice.' In *Social Work, 41*, 5, pp.481–500.

Werner, E., (1995) 'Resilience in Development. Current Directions in Psychological Science.' In *American Psychological Society 4*, 5, pp.81–5.

Werner, E. and Smith, R. (1992) *Overcoming the Odds: High-risk Children from Birth to Adulthood.* Ithaca: Cornell University Press.

Wilkinson, R. G. (1996) *Unhealthy Societies: The Afflictions of Inequality.* London: Routledge.

Wills, T. A. (1985) 'Supportive Functions of Interpersonal Relationships.' In S. Cohen and S. L. Syme (eds.) *Social Support and Health*, pp.61–82. Orlando: Academic Press.

Woodroffe, C., Glickman, M., Barker, B. and Power, C. (eds.) (1993) *Children, Teenagers and Health.* Milton Keynes: Open University Press.

Yoshikawa, H. (1994) 'Prevention as Cumulative Protection: Effects of Early Family Support and Education on Chronic Delinquency and its Risks.' In *Psychological Bulletin, 115*, 1, pp.28–54.

CHAPTER 4

The Core Assessment Process
How to Synthesise Information and Make Judgements
Margaret Adcock

Understanding what is happening to a vulnerable child within the context of his or her family and the local community cannot be achieved as a single event. It must necessarily be a process of gathering information from a variety of sources and making sense of it within the family and, very often, with several professionals concerned with the child's welfare.

(From the *Framework for the Assessment of Children in Need and their Families*, p.14, 1.51)

In this chapter we consider:

- planning a core assessment

- the process

- gathering information

- making sense of the information obtained

- analysing information using the domains of the Assessment Framework

- decision-making and planning interventions to meet the developmental needs of children.

Introduction

An assessment is the collection and evaluation of information relevant to an identified purpose. Assessment has several phases which overlap and lead into planning, action and review:

- the acquisition of information

- exploring facts and feelings

- putting meaning to the situation

- reaching an understanding with the family wherever possible, of what is happening, to include problems, strengths and difficulties, and their impact on the child

- drawing up an analysis of the child's needs and the parenting capacity as a basis for formulating a plan.

In this chapter the focus will be the core assessment in situations where there is concern about the parents' capacity to respond appropriately to their child's needs. The *Framework for the Assessment of Children in Need and their Families* (Department of Health *et al.* 2000) defines a core assessment as:

> an in-depth assessment which addresses the central or most important aspects of the needs of a child and the capacity of his or her parents or caregivers to respond appropriately to these needs within the wider family and community context. While this assessment is led by social services, it will invariably involve other agencies or independent professionals, who will either provide information they hold about the child or parents, contribute specialist knowledge or advice to social services or undertake specialist assessments... The findings from these should inform this assessment. At the conclusion of this phase of assessment there should be an analysis of the findings which will provide an understanding of the child's circumstances and inform planning, case objectives and the nature of service provision. (Department of Health *et al.* 2000, p.32, 3.11)

The core assessment is a means of acquiring and synthesising information. This information will assist practitioners and managers making decisions and planning for children and families in terms of the following questions, centred on the three domains of the Assessment Framework:

1. the developmental needs of the child

    What are the developmental needs of the child?
    How are these needs being met by the parent/carer?

Are other people meeting any of these child's needs?

Which needs are not being met?

What is the likely outcome for the child if these needs remain unmet?

2. parenting capacity

What are the parenting strengths and weaknesses in term of the dimensions of parenting capacity?

What parenting issues impact on parenting capacity?

What is the parents' attitude to the concerns expressed by the referrer and/or other professionals?

3. family and environmental factors

Are there members of the extended family or other people who could meet the child's needs?

Are there members of the community network who can meet the unmet needs of the child?

Within this chapter consideration is given to ways in which information regarding the above is acquired and synthesised through each phase of the core assessment process.

Planning the assessment

Preparation, process and outcome are inextricably interlinked. Assessments require careful planning. The purpose of assessing the particular child and family should always be kept in mind and the impact of the process on the child and family considered. The Assessment Framework is based on the following assessment principles:

- the aim of the assessment is to be helpful to the child and family

- the process should cause the least possible intrusion to the child and family

- families do not want to be subjected to repeated assessments (by social services departments alone, or in combination with other agencies)

- if, during the assessment, the child's safety is or becomes a concern, it must be secured before proceeding with the assessment.

Factors to consider when planning a core assessment

Effective planning should include a consideration of the following by practitioners and their managers.

SELECTING AN APPROPRIATE SOCIAL WORKER

The team manager should consider who would be the most suitable worker/s to undertake a core assessment with this particular family. Wynne (1993) suggests the following questions should be asked of the potential worker:

- Is the worker the right person to complete the assessment in terms of race and gender? Is he/she able to work in an anti-oppressive manner while recognising child welfare concerns (as discussed in Chapter 8)?

- Does the worker have the appropriate knowledge and understanding for making a core assessment of the child and family?

- What has been the family's previous involvement and experience of social services? How will it affect their ability to participate in an assessment?

- Can the worker be open and honest and work with this family, sharing concerns, goals and expectations?

USING AVAILABLE INFORMATION

No matter when workers become involved in an assessment, reference should always be made to the information that has been gathered in the preceding stages and any analysis and decisions made as part of those assessments. This information should form the basis for planning the core assessment and identifying any further information that may be required.

WORKING TOGETHER

The *Framework for the Assessment of Children in Need and their Families* states that the developmental needs of children can only be met by effective inter-agency cooperation and joint work between professionals. It is essential that the family and all those engaged in the assessment are clear about:

- the purpose and anticipated outputs from the assessment

- the respective roles of each professional involved

- which agency or professional has lead responsibility for the assessment

- which professional will take lead responsibility for gathering information, analysing the findings, constructing and implementing any plans for intervention

- ways in which the child and family will be involved in the assessment process

- the way in which information will be shared across professional boundaries and within agencies and be recorded.

(Department of Health *et al.* 2000, 1.23)

Specialist assessments involving a diverse range of professionals such as adult psychiatrists and drug workers may need to be considered in a range of situations which will include serious concerns about a child's physical development or mental health, and about parental capacity where poor mental health, learning disabilities, drug or alcohol abuse, violence or a history of childhood abuse appear to be impacting or are likely to impact adversely on the care of the child.

Methods of engaging a family

Assessment should not be seen just as a means of the worker gaining information. Family members should also be able to feel that they derive a benefit from the process. The assessment must be a dynamic interactive process between the worker and family members where each influences the other's understanding and within which opportunities for changes are created.

Appropriate ways must be found of gaining and maintaining the commitment and participation of the family members, as described in Chapter 6. Special care should be taken in working with parents and children with learning disabilities and families from a different race or culture from that of the worker.

Acquisition of information

As stated earlier, information from the family is required to enable practitioners to make decisions and plans for children. This information can be obtained in a variety of ways, for example through observation and the taking of a family history.

Factors to consider when acquiring information

It is important to establish at the beginning of the assessment process why the family thinks an assessment is being undertaken, what their attitude is to this, and what has been their previous experience of assessment. Information of this kind can help the social worker to understand the family's point of view and their own present situation and how the family members may receive further assessment. This can result in a discussion of what purpose a core assessment could serve and what advantages the family may gain from it.

If the child is living at home, the worker should try to ensure that their initial meeting includes the whole family. Parents and/ or partners also need to be seen individually and together. This is useful to explore both their own history and relationships and the impact this may have on their ability to respond to the needs of their child. The worker should also try to meet with the child to ascertain their perception of their needs, their relationship with their parents and their links with broader family and community networks. Bannister in Chapter 7 considers ways in which children can be engaged in the assessment process.

Taking a family history

In order to locate the sources of difficulties and to identify the unmet developmental needs of the child it is important to take a history from the child, as appropriate, the parents and other involved professionals. The history needs to include details about:

THE CHILD

- concerns about the child

- protective factors in the child's life

- a careful chronology of occasions when the child's needs have not been responded to

- a history of the child's successes and achievements

- a history of recorded difficulties for the child, for example non-attendance at school, eating problems.

THE PARENTS/CARERS

- a history of any traumatic events: for example, unemployment, bereavement, eviction or a move from a familiar neighbourhood

- a history of the family's coping mechanisms in response to previous stressful situations

- a history of any parental difficulties: for example, drug abuse, violent relationships

- history of the parents' own early life, relationships, abuse, etc.

THE FAMILY AND ENVIRONMENT

- identification of support networks used in the past by the child and the family

- support systems currently being used

- strengths and weaknesses of family and support networks

- identification of environmental factors that have affected family functioning in the past, for example poverty or social exclusion.

Family history and functioning

It will be important to establish whether the parent has had support from his or her own parent/s and whether this continues. The worker should also try to find out whether or not the parent would want their children to have a similar childhood to their own. If this is dismissed as irrelevant the practitioner should persist; a parent's or carer's view of their own childhood is likely to have a considerable effect on the quality of their relationship with their own child. The question concerns not so much what actually happened as how the parent now understands his or her own experience. *Protecting Children. A Guide for Social Workers Undertaking a Comprehensive Assessment* (Department of Health 1988) has a useful set of questions based on the work of Mary Main, a leading researcher in attachment theory, which elicits information in a way that more open-ended questions do not.

The worker needs to note how much the parent can remember about their childhood, whether the memories match the descriptive adjectives and how the parent feels now about what happened. Some parents will make it clear that they have come to terms with what happened. Others, however, will convey, either through denial, anger or continuing preoccupation with what happened, that their past is still very much influencing the present and how they relate with their own children.

Observation

It is very helpful to observe the adults and children together as soon as possible in order to assess the quality of their relationship and the child's attachment to each parent. The child's appearance and manner should be noted. Sometimes the worker may immediately note a developmental delay or be concerned about a child who seems very sad or very wary. The parent's or carer's ability to anticipate and respond to the child's needs and to show care and affection, the tone of voice when speaking to or about the child and the way in which the child is described are very relevant pieces of information. Observation of adult–child and sibling interactions and behaviours, particularly at mealtimes and bedtimes, may provide crucial information. In some cases a parent may be negative about a child who is trying very hard to please, whereas in other cases a child may seem to be quite unresponsive to adult requests and to be restless, rebellious and over-active. Observations of a child in the company of other adults may confirm the accuracy or otherwise of the parent's picture. The other parent, a child-minder, a teacher or other family members may, however, experience the child quite differently.

Collating the information acquired

Good recording of the information acquired is vitally important. Case records, together with reports from others, will provide the basis for analysis, decision-making and plans about a child and family. Records should contain information that reflects both the assessment process as well as the information gathered.

Process information should include:

- dates and details of meetings with family members, who was invited and who attended
- content of meetings, including observations, statements and any assessment instruments used
- contact and reports from other people
- succinct minutes of all meetings, including decisions made
- consultation with supervisor/manager
- initial analysis
- decisions made with both family and other professionals and rationale.

Information about the child and family should include:

- reasons for the referral and details obtained from the person who made it and other agencies involved

- family structure, names and ages

- an assessment of the developmental needs of the child

- chronology of any concerns about impairment of health and development and any ill treatment or neglect

- information regarding parenting capacity

- history of family events and of individual members

- community networks and resources used by the family

- environmental factors impacting on the needs of the child, for example unemployment.

In most cases the most accurate records of interviews and meetings with service users will be made at the time, so workers should therefore seek to negotiate with children and families to take notes during sessions. It will not be possible to record the total content but interactions and behaviours should be noted as well as important statements from family members and professionals. Recording will be much easier if time has been spent beforehand in planning the purpose and focus of each meeting.

Recording meetings and family sessions must be sufficiently accurate and detailed so as to provide the evidence for making judgements but must also be well organised and succinct. (Paragraphs with headings to denote a new topic or stage in the meeting are helpful). The first part of the record should be factual and descriptive; opinions should follow. An opinion, (for example 'the mother seemed cross') should not precede or substitute for a description of what actually happened or what was definitely said to provide the evidence which led the observer to decide that the mother was cross. The second part of the record might contain the worker's reflections after a session about the significance of what was done and how this may contribute to an understanding of concerns about the child and the family situation.

Putting meaning to the situation: reflection and explanations

Throughout the assessment the worker and the family should be engaged together in trying to understand why the present concerns have arisen (or why they might arise in future). The capacity for reflection and trying to understand and make sense of one's situation is an important indicator of parental capacity and strength (Kennedy 1997). An assessment provides an opportunity for families to engage in reflection with the aid of a helpful worker and to begin to develop explanations for concerns. Any insights may provide a way to find alternative coping strategies and possible solutions.

Factors to consider when putting meaning to the situation

STAGES OF FAMILY DEVELOPMENT

When searching for explanations of the family's current issues it is useful to think of the family as going through a number of stages as the children grow and develop. Adjusting to a new stage may create difficulties for a family which has previously functioned well enough. The family's ability to adjust to the new stage will be determined by the personality and temperament of both adults and children, by historical events and by current stresses, for example unemployment, illness or financial difficulties. Carter and McGoldrick (1980) state that the family with young children has to accept new members into the system and, in order to proceed developmentally, the marital or partnership system has to adjust to make space for children, parenting roles have to be taken on, and there has to be a re-alignment of relationships with extended family members.

DEVELOPMENTAL CHANGES IN CHILDREN

It needs to be remembered that children are likely to 're-work' previous problems at different stages in their lives as their cognitive abilities increase and as identity issues become more important. This is to be expected and is usual. It may, however, be very alarming and disappointing for parents who had thought that the child had at last dealt with issues arising from earlier difficulties, for example abuse, or a painful separation, a death in the family or the arrival of a new step-parent, only to find that old behaviours and feelings resurface in adolescence. (Fahlberg 1991 provides a very helpful discussion of all aspects of adolescence).

THE MEANING OF THE CHILD TO THE PARENT

Some parents may only have difficulties in respect of one particular child. Often this may be to do with a cluster of factors which did not arise with the other children. For example, Peter, aged 9, frequently had unexplained bruises, seemed to be scapegoated within the family, and his behaviour was often uncontrollable at school and at home. In talking with his parents and looking at the history, it became clear that the pregnancy had been unplanned, that he had been born at a time when his mother was looking after her own mother who was dying, and that a baby sister with a very placid temperament had been born 10 months later.

It is necessary to discover what parents like or dislike about the child; if they seem to focus only on his or her negative aspects, they can be asked how they think it may affect the child to hear her/himself described in that way. This may help to clarify the extent of any parental rejection.

STRESSFUL EVENTS

Sometimes difficulties may arise following a series of stressful events or a single trauma for a child in a family that previously had managed well enough. For instance, problems often arise after a parental relationship breaks up. A child may react to the events with difficult behaviour, which the already stressed parents cannot cope with. The child's behaviour may become worse and often he or she is then sent to stay perhaps with the other parent and/or with relatives. The school complains about the child's lack of concentration and poor achievement and the situation continues to deteriorate until by adolescence both parents say that the young person is unmanageable and must live elsewhere.

FAMILY RELATIONSHIPS

Attention should also be paid to family communication, particularly between the adults. In some cases a parent's difficulty in telling a partner, or anyone else, that he or she is under considerable stress may be an important part of the explanation for severe and unexpected injuries to a child in a family where no one had previously suspected that there was any cause for concern. In other situations the parents may be able to communicate with each other only through physical or verbal aggression because they have never learnt any strategies for resolving problems.

Social workers must also always be alert to the possibility of emotional abuse. Glaser (1995) lists five dimensions of emotional abuse. She suggests that the definition relies on qualitative as well as quantitative considerations, since aspects of emotionally abusive interactions probably occur sporadically in many parent–child interactions. Glaser says that emotional abuse may well have as its core the targeting of the child's emotional and psychological wellbeing and development through acts of omission and commission. The parent's intent may not be consciously malevolent and the harm is often caused by failure to attend to the child's needs and rights.

In families where an adult partnership has broken down, a history should be taken of the way the original separation occurred, what and how the children were told, how they reacted and how often the breakdown is talked about. The adults concerned may have been too preoccupied with their relationship to focus on how to help the children.

FAMILY PERCEPTIONS OF PROFESSIONALS

Current research (Farmer and Owen 1995) suggests that a therapeutic relationship with a helping professional may be a key factor in enabling change to occur in some situations. Jones (1998) warns, however, that the quality of professional intervention can also have an effect on the trajectory of a case, tending to turn initially optimistic cases into ones with poor outcomes and vice versa. In his study Jones found that unrealised expectations of professional help led to increasing disillusion for parents.

Situations are more likely to improve where parents are willing to work with professionals and to take responsibility by making an attempt to improve the situation. Workers, however, need to be realistic about both what they can offer and for how long they can offer it. They should also take a history of previous professional involvement to establish the family's perception of professionals, as this will influence the way the family relates to current professionals.

TIME-SCALES FOR CHILDREN

It is useful to think about the stages of child development and to recognise that the way in which age and stage-related tasks are achieved has the potential to affect the future outcome in good or less good directions.

Successful resolution of early-stage salient issues increases the possibility of subsequent successful resolution, and vice versa. Widom (1999) describes the compound effects of a negative process in the following way:

Deficits or dysfunctional behaviours at one developmental period will lay the groundwork for subsequent dysfunctional behaviours. Deficits manifest at one age continue to exercise an influence at the next stage unless an intervention occurs. For example, malnutrition in infancy in the neurological or medical domain may lead to an impaired intellectual or cognitive functioning in toddlers, which in turn may affect IQ, and in turn affect school performance in a negative way, and in turn lead to impaired performance as an adult.

Reaching an understanding of what is happening

By this stage of the core assessment the social worker and other professionals should have obtained the following:

- a history of any concerns noted by the parents or significant others

- observations of the child's appearance, growth, speech, behaviour, interactions with carers

- perceptions of the child by significant others, including parents, siblings, other relatives, school, etc.

- assessment of parental capacity and environmental factors

- any specialist assessments, for example by a paediatrician, school, etc.

To make sense of the information it is important to remember, however, that no one professional can expect to be able to identify or understand every aspect of a complex assessment on their own. The Assessment Framework suggests that specialist assessments may need to be part of the core assessment but also that specialist advice may be sought to help practitioners evaluate and analyse information at the end of the assessment.

Factors to consider when attempting to reach an understanding of what is happening

In order to reach an understanding of the child it is necessary to understand the causes and explanations for any delays regarding the child's development; to consider the risk factors that can increase the likelihood of future impairment of the child's health and development, and those protective factors which may mitigate impairment.

UNDERSTANDING THE DEVELOPMENTAL NEEDS OF CHILDREN

Although there is a great deal of agreement regarding the developmental needs of children, irrespective of culture, as Banks notes in Chapter 8, most child developmental models used in the United Kingdom are based on Eurocentric concepts and may not always be seen as entirely appropriate to people from other cultural groups. However, with this in mind, when considering age-appropriate development the Mary Sheridan Scales provide useful guidelines for physical growth and development for the under fives. Fahlberg (1991) and Bentovim (1998) provide guidance on the ages and stages of emotional development. Bentovim states that the key tasks the child should accomplish are:

- regulation of feelings. An adequately parented infant will demonstrate a resilient control of intense feelings in a variety of contexts.

- development of attachments. Children form models and a map of themselves and significant others based on their relationship history.

- development of a sense of self. As children become more aware of themselves during their second year they are able to use their capacity to play and communicate to convey their needs and feelings. But the relationship offered in response has a significant impact on how children's sense of themselves develops.

- forming peer relationships. The two main effects for children who have been harmed are those of showing physical and verbal aggression or a high degree of withdrawal or avoidance.

- adaptation to school. This includes integration into the peer group, acceptable class performance and orientation for achievement.

When considering how the child is achieving the developmental stages, the following questions should be considered:

- How is the baby or young child developing attachments? This is particularly important because forming attachments is such a key task of early development (see Chapter 12). Fahlberg (1991) says attachment influences a child's physical and intellectual development as well as forming the foundation for psychological development. The child's earliest attachments become the prototype for subsequent interpersonal development. If there are concerns it is important either to discuss this with a health visitor who is knowledgeable about attachment, or to ask the GP to refer the child to a community paediatrician designated to undertake such assessments.

- What is happening to a baby or young child's growth, motor development and speech? If a child's development seems much delayed it may be very harmful to do nothing except wait and see whether things change over time. A second opinion or a referral to a paediatrician may be essential to discover whether a child needs services to overcome any present impairment or prevent future harm.

- Are there concerns about a school-age child? Bentovim (1998) says that all aspects of school environment may prove difficult for the child who has already experienced harm, and failure occurs very readily, although there are some children who appear to think themselves into learning in order to avoid having to think about home stresses.

Teachers should be asked about the results of any base-line assessment (for children who have just started school) or SATS testing. It may be helpful for the social worker to ask both the school and the parents to complete the Strengths and Difficulties Questionnaire (Goodman in Department of Health *et al.* 2000) to get a clear picture of the child at home and at school.

If there are concerns about a child who is known to have physical or learning disabilities it is essential to talk, with the parents' permission, to any doctors or other professionals who have made previous assessments or who are involved with the child and family.

UNDERSTANDING THE CAUSES AND EXPLANATIONS FOR DELAYS AND CONCERNS

It is important to remember that development depends on a combination of different factors. Bentovim (1998) says that 'constitutional, genetic and environmental factors, for example the effects of physical illness, injury and handicapping considerations, and the family context in which the child grows, all play a part'. Culture, class factors, and inter-generational effects which derive from the parents' own experience of parenting may also be influential. Current views on development emphasise that what matters for development is that the various systems – biological and psychological – should be well integrated. In normal development there will be consolidation and growth at each stage; where development has been impaired there will be new forms of maladaptation and vulnerability. Disruptions in achieving developmental steps in earlier areas also have an implication for a child across his or her life span. Developmental liabilities may become enduring vulnerability factors that increase the risk of physical and mental health problems.

Therefore all other information about family relationships, parental capacity and the history of any concerns now need to be explored alongside the family history and information about the child's development in order to develop ideas about causation and explanations. Kaplan (1999) suggests that the effects of the child's 'temperament' need to be considered in the equation. She says the easy child will provoke positive responses and approaches, but it is also possible that the tendency to protest and cry less may result in the child receiving less stimulation and being ignored. On the other hand, the child with a strident cry will not escape attention, but this attention may be of a harsh and punitive nature. Vulnerability may be conferred on a child as a result of other intrinsic factors, such as low birth-weight and/or prematurity. These factors may reduce the range of arousal within which the infant operates, and so the child may be perceived as more difficult to care for because it is less responsive. Kaplan concludes that some children may be perceived as coping in the midst of striking adversity, but to depend on children's resilience is liable to lead to false optimism.

It is important to consider whether the professionals' concerns have always existed, in which case this may be an example of the 'pile up' effect described by Widom and Bentovim above, or whether they are of recent origin. Also it should be noted whether there were any important events that occurred about the time the concerns arose, for example, the parents separated, a new baby was born, the child had a long illness, the mother had a depression.

Fahlberg (1999) suggests that consideration needs to be given to the implications of developmental concerns. For example, if there are concerns about the child's educational needs, will the child need to attend a special school? What is the child likely to be able to achieve academically? Are the findings likely to raise or lower parental acceptance and/or concern for the child?

UNDERSTANDING RISK FACTORS THAT CAN INCREASE THE LIKELIHOOD OF IMPAIRMENT TO THE CHILD'S HEALTH AND DEVELOPMENT

A risk factor does not mean that a consequence will automatically follow. It means that protective actions are needed to try to reduce the child's vulnerability to such consequences occurring. A number of researchers have identified risk factors that are likely to increase the child's vulnerability to impairment of his or her development. For example, Wallace et al. (1997) noted that:

- poor parenting, marital discord and family dysfunction have all been associated with an increased rate of disorder in children. For example, harsh and/or inconsistent parenting, coercive interchanges between parent and child, and marital discord are all associated with antisocial behaviour in children

- large family size has been associated with increased rates of conduct disorder and delinquency in boys, independently of socio-demographic and parental factors

- specific parental psychiatric disorders are associated with increased rates of particular childhood disorders. For instance, parental alcoholism and antisocial behaviour are associated with increased rates of conduct disorder and depressive symptoms and disorder (especially in the adolescent age group)

- parental criminality is particularly associated with disorders of conduct and delinquency in children

- when social class is measured in terms of economic disadvantage, there is a strong and consistent relationship between the latter and childhood disorder

- children whose mothers suffer from a psychiatric disorder have a 2–4 times increased risk of mental health problems

- young children who have been exposed to physical abuse and those exposed to neglect are respectively at a twice and three times increased risk of mental health problems

- single traumatic life events can play a significant part in precipitating a wide range of childhood disorders.

Kaplan (1999) adds the following risk factors:

- level of stress, life events

- maternal anxiety, mood, attitude

- reduced family/social support

- low social/educational status of parents.

Crittenden and Claussen (1993) suggest that critical factors that will determine the outcome of any harm that has been done to the child and her or his development are:

- the chronicity of any maltreatment

- the degree of distortion of the child's self-perception

- limited access to developmentally normative and growth-producing experiences.

Kaplan (1999) points out that the literature stresses that one risk factor alone is probably not of great importance to a child if there are compensating factors, but that risk is cumulative. If there are two or more risk factors in a family where a child's care is a cause for concern, the risk to the child is multiply increased compared to that of a child in the normal population. The developmental risk factors for the child and other risks arising from environmental factors and parental capacity therefore need to be looked at carefully.

Reaching an understanding of what is happening: parental capacity

At the end of the assessment the various elements need to be weighed relative to one another and consideration given to the possibility of change. This is described in detail in Chapter 5. Jones (1998) suggests that it is probable that parental factors generally carry greater weight than other domains.

Parental capacity will depend in part on temperament and physical and mental health, but also on family relationships and other environmental factors. Both the possibility of making necessary changes and the possibility of future harm to the child's development need to be considered. Support of various kinds may or may not be a crucial factor in improving parental capacity sufficiently for the child's needs to be met within an appropriate time-scale. Part of the final assessment of parental capacity and the possibility of change may depend on discussions with parents about the results of the assessment and their reactions to it.

In the process of the assessment the parental capacity to meet the child's needs should have been considered together with any characteristics of the parent which may be relevant to their capacity to care for the child. Attention should also have been paid to the possibility and likelihood of change. In the analysis of the information the positive factors in both parents, the wider family and support networks, as well as vulnerabilities and difficulties should be examined first in order to decide whether and how well the child's needs are being met at present. After this there should be an assessment of all the factors which pose a risk to the child and then, finally, the possibility/likelihood of change should be considered.

Specialist assessments

If there are concerns about parenting issues a specialist assessment may have been obtained. It should be noted that the experts who provide these assessments will not necessarily be experts on parenting. For example, an adult psychiatrist would be able to provide an assessment of the parent's psychiatric condition and treatability and also prognosis. A forensic psychiatrist would comment similarly about dangerousness, and a substance addiction specialist about the nature and treatability of a drug or alcohol problem. Childcare social workers will then need to consider the reports in the light of their own observations and assessment of parenting interactions and child development. In some complex situations, particularly if the courts are involved, it may be necessary to ask a child psychiatrist to comment on parenting capacity.

Following the specialist assessment a discussion should be held with the family and professionals to consider all the information and to try to reach conclusions and form an agreement about future plans. It should be remembered that adult specialists may wish to advocate for the parents and their needs, and that in some cases this may conflict with the child's needs. It is most important that social workers present the child's needs clearly in any discussion. The adult specialist will then be able to tell the parent, 'Children and family social services say this is what the child needs,' and help the parent to accept this statement and the consequences without feeling that the specialist's own treatment role with the parent has been compromised.

Drawing up an analysis of the needs of the child and parenting capacity as a basis for formulating a plan

At this stage those undertaking the assessment should be answering the following questions:

- are there dimensions of the Assessment Framework where further information or assessment is required?
- what are the needs of the child?
- are there ways in which parenting capacity can be enhanced in order for the parents/carers to meet the needs of the child?
- what services, intervention and treatment would best assist the child and family?
- what needs to change and what will the process of change involve for the child and family?
- what will the criteria for success be?
- what is the time-scale for the child within which changes must occur?
- who will monitor and review the situation?

Factors to consider

CHANGE

The degree to which one or both parents assume some responsibility for the concerns about the children and want to work with the professionals to try to change the situation is exceedingly important and is considered in detail in Chapter 5. Bentovim, Elton and Tranter (1987) say that some potential for change, even in rigidly held beliefs and attitudes, should have been observed. In situations where parents have not been able to respond to the child's needs because of their own vulnerabilities or difficulties, they should have become able to take some responsibility for the state of the child, their difficulties in caring and, where this has occurred, their rejection of the child. They should accept the need for help within a specific context.

In some cases the parents may reach this position early on in the assessment. If this has not happened, the worker must arrange to meet them in order to provide honest feedback about the child and his or her needs and the parents' role in responding to them. There should be a discussion about what has to change and what the parents, aided by the relevant professionals, might achieve.

Workers need to think very carefully in advance about framing the information they give in order initially to establish a context of respect for the parents and acceptance of their difficulties, and then to try to assist parents to consider ways of changing and, if necessary, challenge them quite hard to think about the child's need for the situation to change. The outcome is hopeful if the child's needs are acknowledged and the parents' behaviour confirms the acknowledgement.

Professionals should consider very carefully what decisions to make in cases where more negative outcomes seem likely. Thought should be given to using the legal framework to protect the child, attempting a rapid 'trial for change' using specialist resources, or transferring care of the child to the other parent, extended family members or alternative carers.

A final assessment of parental capacity sometimes cannot be made until the results of the whole assessment have been discussed with the parents and, where appropriate, some or all of the changes suggested above have been implemented. Even at this late stage some parents may welcome assistance and make very great efforts to change the situation, whereas others are quite unable to do so.

Thought needs to be given to the question of appropriate services and interventions before meeting with the parents to give them the conclusions about the assessment. The parents will need advice at this meeting about what needs to change, how this can be done, and what services and supports could be provided.

MAKING JUDGEMENTS

Dalgleish (2000) draws a helpful distinction between judgements and decisions. Judgements are inferences drawn from data. A decision is a choice between alternative courses of action. It is very important to ensure that judgements are made and considered before decisions are taken. The Assessment Framework states that interventions should be considered first, on the basis of identified need and what is known to best address this need. The second stage is to make decisions regarding interventions in the light of the availability of resources.

Judgements about interventions will depend on consideration of the following factors:

- analysis of information about the child and any developmental needs which are not being responded to appropriately

- analysis of the information about parental capacity

- analysis of information about environmental factors and whether their effect on the child's needs is being responded to

- evidence, identified at this stage, of parental capacity to change.

Consideration then has to be given to what will be the effect on the child if nothing changes. Consultation with other professionals and reference to research findings will assist this process. The need for early identification and intervention where there is developmental delay has already been emphasised in this chapter.

The results of the above will facilitate consideration of what services and interventions might be helpful and why. Some problems may be relatively easy to address if, for example, they relate to child health or development issues; others may be more difficult. It is important that someone in the group making decisions has some knowledge of the success of different types of interventions and assessments.

Some families will need continuing services and support for long periods to supplement their parental care, for example, families with children who have severe impairments. In other cases parents need help to make changes to some aspects of their functioning, and will need support for a period of time in order to sustain these changes. However, parental care should be competent enough, with the assistance of supports and services, to respond to the child's needs within a space of three to six months. If this does not happen consideration will need to be given to whether the child should remain in the home. We have to accept, in a small number of cases (Adcock 1998), that it is not clear how some adult problems are best dealt with, or whether others can, in the present state of our knowledge or resources available, be resolved within a time-scale that also makes it possible to meet children's needs.

Summary

Undertaking a core assessment is a demanding task. It needs a high level of both knowledge and skill. It may need a team approach to make all the requisite skills and knowledge available for families. To achieve this may require changes from both managers and practitioners. It is, however, an exciting challenge because, as the government guidance states, 'The combination of evidence-based practice grounded in knowledge with finely balanced professional judgement is the foundation for effective practice with children and families' (Department of Health *et al.* 2000, p.16, 1.59).

Recommended reading

Adcock, M. and White, R. (eds.) (1998) *Significant Harm.* Croydon: Significant Publications.

Hill, M. (ed.) (1999) *Effective Ways of Working with Children and their Families.* London: Jessica Kingsley.

Reder, P. and Lucey, C. (eds.) (1995) *Assessment of Parenting.* London: Routledge.

Stevenson, O. (1998) *Neglected Children: Issues and Dilemmas.* Oxford: Blackwell.

References

Adcock, M. (1998) 'Significant Harm: Implications for Local Authorities.' In M. Adcock and R. White (eds.) *Significant Harm.* Croydon: Significant Publications.

Bentovim, A., Elton, A. and Tranter, M. (1987) 'Prognosis for Rehabilitation after Abuse.' In *Adoption and Fostering*, Vol.11, No 1.

Bentovim, A. (1998) 'Significant Harm in Context.' In M. Adcock and R. White (eds.) *Significant Harm.* Croydon: Significant Publications.

Carter, E. and McGoldrick, M. (1980) *The Family Life Cycle. A Framework for Family Therapy.* New York: Gardener Press.

Crittenden, P. and Claussen, H. (1993) 'Severity of Maltreatment; Assessment and Policy Implications.' In C. Hobbs and J. Wynne (eds.) *Clinical Paediatrics: Child Abuse*, Vol. 1, No. 1. Basilliere Tyndall.

Dalgliesh, L. (2000) 'Risk Assessment and Decision Making.' In *Risk and Decision in Child Protection.* London: Wiley.

Department of Health (1988) *Protecting Children. A Guide for Social Workers Undertaking a Comprehensive Assessment.* London: HMSO.

Department of Health, Department for Education and Employment and Home Office (2000) *Framework for the Assessment of Children in Need and their Families*. London: The Stationery Office.

Department of Health, Cox, A. and Bentovim, A. (2000) *The Family Assessment Pack of Questionnaires and Scales*. London: The Stationery Office.

Fahlberg, V. (1993) *A Child's Journey Through Placement*. London: BAAF.

Fahlberg, V. (1999) Personal communication to the author.

Farmer, E. and Owen, M. (1995) *Child Protection Practice: Private Risks and Public Remedies*. London: HMSO.

Glaser, D., (1995) 'Emotionally Abusive Experiences of Parenting.' In P. Reder and C. Lucey (eds.) *Assessment of Parenting*. London: Routledge.

Jones, D. (1998) 'The Effectiveness of Intervention.' In M. Adcock and R. White (eds.) *Significant Harm*. Croydon: Significant Publications.

Kaplan, C. (1999) 'The Real Risks Children Face: The Role and Perspective of the Child Psychiatrist.' In A. Weir and A. Douglas (eds.) *Child Protection and Adult Mental Health; Conflict of Interest?* London: Butterworth.

Kennedy, R. (1997) *Child Abuse, Psychotherapy and the Law*. Free Association Books.

Wallace, S., Crown, J., Berger, M. and Cox, A. (1997) 'Child and Adolescent Mental Health.' In A. Stevens and J. Raferty (eds.) *Health Care Needs Assessment*. Free Association Books.

Widom, C. (1999) 'Behavioural Consequences of Child Maltreatment.' In C. M. Reece, *The Treatment of Child Abuse*. Baltimore: John Hopkins University Press.

Wynne, M. (1993) Personal Communication to the author.

CHAPTER 5

Assessment of Parental Motivation to Change

Jan Horwath and Tony Morrison

It has to be recognised that in families where a child has been maltreated there are some parents who will not be able to change sufficiently within the child's time-scales in order to ensure their children do not continue to suffer significant harm... However, most parents are capable of change and following appropriate interventions, able to provide a safe family context for their child.

(From the *Framework for the Assessment of Children in Need and their Families*, p.58, 4.25)

In this chapter we look at:

- reasons for assessing parental motivation to change as part of an assessment of the developmental needs of children

- a model for the assessment of motivation and capacity to change

- engaging parents in the change process.

Introduction

The *Framework for the Assessment of Children in Need and their Families* (Department of Health *et al.* 2000) seeks to enable social workers to identify the developmental needs of the child and the parent's capacity to respond appropriately to those needs. If the assessment indicates that the health and development of the child is impaired or is likely to be impaired then part of the assessment should be to identify the changes that need to be made, which in turn should inform planning and appropriate interventions to bring about optimum outcomes for children. Some initial assessments may indicate that the required changes relate to the provision of services, such as day care. In other cases, the assessment may indicate that the health and development of the child is impaired as a result of the parent(s) not being able to respond to the child's needs, and consequently the parent(s) need to change their attitudes or behaviour. In these situations, while there still may be a requirement for services, there is also an expectation of more permanent change from family members. The assessment role of the social worker, working with other professionals, is thus to assess the ability of the parent(s) and their willingness to engage in therapeutic work to achieve and sustain the changes required of them. Each parent is an individual with different motivation and capacity to change. It is, therefore, important that this is taken into account during the assessment.

In addition, it is important that professionals recognise the ever-changing context in which assessment takes place, both for the family and practitioners. It is only by assessing the family over time that it is possible to discover the parental and familial capacity to change. Here we refer to cases which are beyond initial assessment – where social services departments are involved because there are significant concerns regarding the welfare of the child and/or risks of significant harm. In this chapter we explore the concept of change as the frame of reference in which assessment should be located. Consideration is given to a model of change, focusing in detail on the early stages of the change process, the process that is most relevant to assessment. We consider emotional reactions to change and explore ways in which the model can assist in the identification of the sources and strength of parental motivation to change.

Motivation and capacity for change: a model

The Assessment Framework uses the concept of parenting capacity to respond appropriately to the needs of children. Capacity has two elements: ability and motivation; if either one or other of these is missing then the parent will be unable to respond appropriately to the child's needs. For example, a parent with an alcohol problem may be able to describe exactly what he or she needs to do to improve the situation for the child or children, and indeed may have the ability to bring about the required changes. However, the ability to change is meaningless unless it is accompanied by the motivation to try to change the situation. Jones in Chapter 16, writing about parenting capacity, considers issues related to assessing parents' ability to change. In this chapter we consider issues related to the assessment of potential motivation. In order to assess motivation, professionals need to have some understanding of ways in which levels of motivation and change are linked.

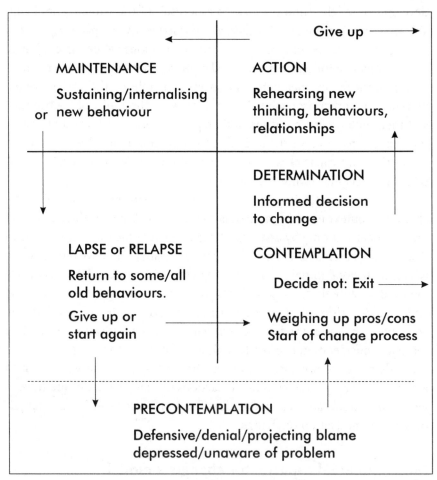

Figure 5.1 Comprehensive model of change (DiClimenti 1991).

Prochaska and DiClimenti's Comprehensive Model of Change (1982) is a useful tool for child and family assessment (see Figure 5.1). It can be applied to any family where change is required at personal and relationship levels, especially where there may be a need for external sanctions via court orders and where the parent's engagement in the system is involuntary at the outset at least. Equally it applies to situations in which the parent has sought advice and support about problems within the family.

The model's basic premises are:

- that change is a matter of balance, and that people change their behaviour when there are more motivational forces in favour of change than in favour of the status quo

- for the process of change to be effective, professionals must assess and work with the parent or carer at the stage which the parent has reached in terms of their readiness to accept or deny the need to change.

The model contains five stages of change which are explained below:

- contemplation

- determination

- action

- maintenance

- lapse.

There are also two blocks to change:

- pre-contemplation

- relapse.

Pre-contemplation

The vast majority of families are at this point when they come to the attention of social services departments. This is most likely to be the case when the family has been referred because the child is a cause for concern to professionals or neighbours. The parents who are in pre-contemplation are unaware of, or have a vague recognition of concerns, but at this stage they have not considered that their behaviour needs to change. Parents consequently respond in a variety of ways to the initial social work contact, as highlighted in the study by Cleaver and Freeman (1995). They may be scared and anxious when faced with the concerns of professionals and may be defensive, angry, and deny difficulties. Alternatively, there may be a helpless, passive response in which parents seemingly do not react to the professionals' concerns. The situation is likely to be exacerbated for black families who may already have negative experiences of 'authority figures' or where there are language/communication difficulties between workers and carers.

At this stage the agencies' concern to protect the child may involve practitioners in planning interventions to safeguard the wellbeing of the child. However, workers need to be aware that parents at the pre-contemplation stage are unable to make a full psychological commitment to plans for change as they have not yet come to terms with the need to change. Thus parents' commitment and/or motivation to change at this stage may simply be tokenism, or they may make commitments that are unrealistic, such as, 'We'll do anything you say'.

Contemplation

At this stage parents begin to consider the possibility that there is a problem and explore whether or not they are able to tackle it. The assessment process is an essential tool to facilitate the contemplation stage, but this can take time and may also be incompatible with the needs of the child or the time-scale given for assessment. Parents may be ambivalent and feel anxious about what change will mean. Part of parents' very early motivation may come from being subject to external intervention, perhaps by the name of their child being placed on the child protection register, or the possibility of child care proceedings, both of which give a potent message that things must change. The effectiveness of intervention will depend on whether this external motivation can be transformed into the internal motivation of the parent. The ability of workers to combine the use of external sanctions with the engagement of families is crucial if the intervention is to lead to change.

It is here that paying close attention to parents' engagement in careful assessment and enhancement of motivation becomes pivotal. Parents may need assistance to look at themselves and to come to terms with what they see. They may need time to appreciate their child's needs and to count the real costs of what change will mean, as well as to identify benefits and goals that have real meaning for them. The task for professionals is to assess sources of motivation, to recognise parents' ambivalence, their compliance, and genuine commitment and capacity to change. Workers must also recognise that individual parents may each be at different stages of the change process. In addition each parent may need to make a different type of change. For example, a perpetrator of domestic violence may need to change his violent behaviour, but be stuck in pre-contemplation by denial. His partner, however, may need to consider the consequences for the children of a relationship with a violent partner, and consider too whether she will remain in this relationship if the partner does not change. She may therefore be in the contemplation stage and struggling with ambivalent feelings aroused by this difficult issue. Some children have suffered from our failure to assess motivation; in contrast, other families who might have been engaged have been unintentionally denied the possibility of working towards change in our haste to protect children. Consideration should also be given to the part that can be played by the extended family in terms of positive and negative influences for encouraging and supporting change.

Later in this chapter the contemplation stage is analysed in more detail, as this is a critical stage in terms of assessment.

Determination

Determination is found when parents make a more formal expression of:

- the real nature of the problems they face and how these affect their children
- the changes they wish/should make
- what specific goals are to be achieved
- how parents and workers will cooperate in moving towards these goals
- what rewards and changes will arise once these goals are met – for instance, de-registration from the child protection register or the removal of court orders
- what the consequences might be if such changes are not achieved.

At this stage, clear agreements for work towards change may be negotiated among parents, children and professionals. These agreements should include specific detail about who does what, when and how. A study of post-registration practice by Calder and Horwath (2000) demonstrated that lack of clarity with regard to details of what was expected of both parents and professionals resulted in confusion about the purpose of interventions and gave parents little indication as to what they were expected to do to meet the needs of the child. For parents the agreements can reinforce the fact that progress will be incremental and achieved in small stages. Case planning and core group meetings are two fora where agreements can be developed. Parents are more likely to be motivated to change if they receive early support services as part of the assessment process (Farmer and Owen 1995). It is therefore important that agreements make explicit exactly what the parents can expect from professionals.

Action

At this point a parent has made a decision to change and is attempting to use the services and interventions provided by the agencies to put the change into practice. If parents are not properly prepared they may find it difficult to engage in the process of change. Targeting specific interventions for specific problems may be useful as the interventions enable parents to work in an ordered sequence, rather than finding themselves overwhelmed by all that is required and dropping out; for example, parents may stop attending a parents' group if they are not clear as to why they are attending. Dropping out or disengaging can often be labelled as failure or non-compliance, when in many cases it can be the result either of confusion with regard to aims and objectives, or because early agreements for change that were made with the parents precede discussion of issues related to contemplation.

Maintenance

At this stage the emphasis moves to consolidating changes already made. This may be achieved through rehearsal and testing of newly acquired skills and coping strategies, over time and under different conditions. More specific attention needs to be paid to relapse-prevention work that is aimed at anticipating stresses, and triggers that may undermine newly acquired coping skills. Relapse-prevention work involves parents and professionals in recognising and planning strategies to manage the impact of unforeseen stresses that are likely to occur and which can result in maintenance of change becoming very difficult. For example, a parent who has an alcohol problem may decide to abstain from its use. He or she may manage this effectively until a crisis occurs, when the temptation to drink becomes overwhelming. A situation such as the one illustrated needs to be anticipated, and strategies that build on known strengths and effective support systems – for example, extended family, community, and other agencies – should be identified. It is particularly important to recognise the impact of stresses on the parents when one parent changes while the other is left out of that process. The abandonment of one parent can occur if professional involvement centres on the other parent, frequently the mother, who is prepared to work with the professionals.

Maintenance is sometimes given little or no space in practice because the pressure on resources in turn creates pressure for the rapid turnover of cases. Typically, a family may make significant progress in a family centre, as a result of which the child is de-registered and services are terminated. However, if changes have not been sufficiently integrated into the family's daily life as well as internalised by the parents, the latter remain dependent on the supportive presence of family centre staff, with new stresses quickly overwhelming the fledgling confidence and skills of parents and children, leading to relapse.

Further complications arise if parents are unable to internalise the changes required of them. Change can only be maintained through the use of external resources, for example, family and community networks. Some parents with learning disabilities, for instance, are able to meet the developmental needs of the child with support from family and the community. Therefore, part of the assessment process needs to include an evaluation of both the effectiveness and viability of maintaining a support network as a long-term arrangement, in the event of the parents' present inability to internalise the required changes.

Lapse and relapse

One of the strengths of this cyclical model is that it allows for the reality that few people succeed the first time round. Change comes from repeated efforts, re-evaluation, renewal of commitment and incremental successes. However, the model distinguishes between lapse and relapse.

Lapses occur when individuals or families get themselves into high-risk situations – for instance, couples begin to argue once again over which of them should discipline the child. At this point it is vital that the couple recognise what is happening, and put into action their relapse prevention plan – for instance, to call a neighbour round to look after the child while each parent has a cooling-off period.

In contrast, a relapse occurs with a return to the unwanted behaviour – in this case abuse of a child – which may have serious consequences for the family's future. Lapse is thus a part of, and not simply an enemy of, change. In some cases of relapse, where the risk of the child's suffering harm is high, court orders may be required to monitor the process and to ensure that contingency plans will protect children from further harm, should the need arise.

Engaging with the change process

Engaging with the change process involves positively weighting, increasing or establishing motivators for change, while actively removing, decreasing or reframing barriers to change, whether these are material, psychological, individual or environmental. This can be understood only by recognising that motivation is an interactional phenomenon in which professionals are highly significant figures, especially where the future security of the family is in question. However, others also have influence; family, friends and community all form part of the wider motivational network. Part of the assessment process should therefore include an identification of the influences and attitudes of the wider network: supports, strengths, stressors, weaknesses or anti-therapeutic elements. Positive members of the network should be engaged in the change process; this can be achieved through such fora as family group conferences. Parents also influence each other in terms of their engagement with, and commitment to, change.

Earlier in this chapter we referred to the crucial stage of contemplation, which is probably the area most commonly overlooked in assessment work in many family situations. One of the major tasks for social workers utilising the *Framework for the Assessment of Children in Need and their Families* is to assess the parents' recognition of a problem and their capacity to change. Therefore we return to look in more detail at the contemplation stage by using the following framework, called the Seven Steps of Contemplation, which was developed by Morrison (1998).

The seven steps of contemplation

1. I accept that there is a problem: 'I accept my child is underweight.'

At this stage there may be only minimal agreement that there is a problem, but this needs to be capitalised on and not rejected as insufficient. Clearly, if further progress is not made this will not be a sufficient level of motivation for change to occur, and may indicate the need for external protective controls in the form of court orders or finding a placement for the child where his or her needs will be better met.

2. I accept that I have some responsibility for the problem: 'I never have enough time to feed her as she's such a slow eater.'

At this stage the parent may deny total responsibility, but there has to be some recognition of personal influence in the identified problems. It is important that professionals acknowledge with parents how hard it must be to be open about problems.

Note: it is essential that the parent acknowledges the part he or she has played in failing to respond to the needs of the child and begins to develop a real understanding of his or her responsibility to meet the child's unmet developmental needs. A person can acknowledge his or her behaviour without accepting responsibility. Acknowledging may not necessarily indicate reduced risk of harm to the child unless it is accompanied by other elements, such as remorse and empathy. For example, parents may acknowledge that they hit their child but justify this in terms such as, 'I was hit as a child and it never did me any harm.' 'Children need to know who is boss.' This is unlikely to lead to change unless the parent is able to understand the consequences for the child of being hit, and recognises that his or her behaviour is inappropriate.

3. I have some discomfort about the problem: 'I feel bad when I see how thin she is.'

Internal discomfort reveals that the parent's behaviour is at some level at odds with their values and beliefs about what is appropriate. Without some degree of internal dissonance, motivation will remain external, and may be no more than disguised compliance. Parents who have distorted beliefs about children may lack this dissonance, and believe, for instance, that a two-year-old's reluctance to eat is wilful defiance towards the parents. Whilst discomfort is an important stage to reach, it does not yet create sufficient conditions for change. The parent may feel helpless in the face of the problem and unable to do anything to change the situation; for example, 'But I just don't know how I can get her to eat. I've tried everything and nothing works.'

4. I believe that things must change: 'She really needs to put on weight.'

Here there is the realisation that something must change, but this does not mean that the parent knows what this is, or that all internal resistance and ambivalence has gone, although it does represent a public declaration of the need to change. It is also at this stage that the parent may say, in desperation: 'I'll do whatever you say.'

5. I can see that I can be part of the solution: 'I managed to feed the other one, so I am capable.'

Eliciting parents' sense of self-efficacy and helping them to make their own arguments for change, and confront their ambivalence about it, is crucial. Too often workers unintentionally take this process out of clients' hands by suggesting, persuading and imposing their ideas without trying to elicit parents' own problem-solving skills.

6. I can make a choice: 'If I don't do something about this she could be taken away.'

The recognition of a choice is important in clarifying in parents' minds that they have some power to choose, even if the choices are small or limited in scope. This is particularly important in working with involuntary situations (Ivanoff, Blythe and Tripodi 1994). However, the more the parents are aware of their strengths and capabilities the more they will recognise the choices available, hence the importance of following the sequence in which the steps are addressed. This means avoiding premature demands on parents to make difficult choices, for example, to leave an abusive partner.

7. I can see the next steps toward change: 'I think I will go to that family centre.'

At this point delay in provision of services or allocation of new workers can sabotage all the previous good work and leave children very vulnerable. The parents are ready, but delay can result in retreat into pre-contemplation, as parents may rationalise that their problems cannot be so serious if services are not made available.

Managing ambivalence as part of the change process

One of the crucial assessment tasks for the social worker is to assess the parents' real commitment to engaging and implementing change. Effective change occurs when individuals are in agreement with the change and are prepared to put in effort to effect it. As indicated, some parents may have difficulty in engaging with the change process and their responses may indicate whether the issue lies in acknowledging the need to change, or the effort they are prepared to put into either the change or their capacity to change. Horwath has developed a model to provide a framework for assessing parents' responses to change, which identifies four possible types of response (see Figure 5.2).

- dissent and/or avoidance
- tokenism
- genuine commitment
- compliance.

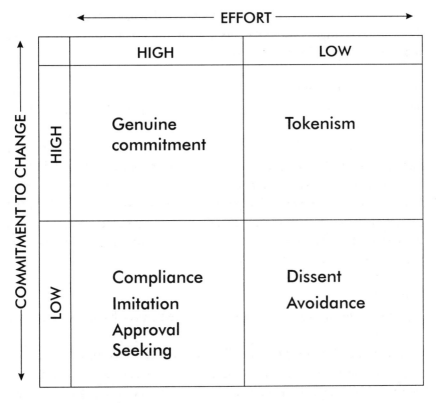

Figure 5.2 Response to change

Effort to implement change

Each of these responses is described in detail, with consideration given to assessment issues.

TOKENISM

'I am quite happy for Jane to go to nursery as long as you fetch her and bring her back in a taxi.'

In this situation the parent will agree with the professionals regarding the required changes but will put little effort into making change work. In other words, the parent engages superficially in the change process. It may well be that some change results, but no change that requires effort from the parent.

GENUINE COMMITMENT

'I know it's important for Jane to go to nursery, so I get everything ready in the evening so we don't have to rush in the morning.'

The parent recognises the need to change and makes real efforts to bring about these changes. These parents are the ones who are most likely to maximise the use of resources provided to support change.

DISSENT AND/OR AVOIDANCE

'The nursery seems to be doing more harm than good: she comes back really tired so why bother?'

Dissent can range from proactively sabotaging efforts to bring about change to passively disengaging from the process. One of the most difficult forms of dissent to assess and manage is that of parents who do not admit their lack of commitment to change but work subversively to undermine the process. This is especially likely in cases involving perpetrators of sexual abuse and fabricated or induced illness by proxy (also known as Munchausen Syndrome by Proxy).

COMPLIANCE

'I get her to the nursery at nine-thirty because that is what is written in the care plan.'

In this situation the parents will do what is expected of them because they have been 'told' to do it. Change may occur but has not been internalised because the parents are acting without having gone through the process of thinking and responding emotionally to the need to change.

The practitioner needs to work with parents to identify both facilitating and inhibiting factors in terms of both agreement to the change and effort to implement it. It is at this stage that the parents' own strengths and family and community supports can be identified to assist them in bringing about the change required to promote the welfare of the child.

AMBIVALENCE

'I know that Jane benefits from nursery but I cannot see that it will harm her to miss sessions when I cannot get my act together in the mornings.'

Very few people can both agree to change and implement it by changing their attitudes and behaviour without any lapses. It is most likely that commitment and effort will vary not only from individual to individual but at different stages of the change process. For example, parents may make a genuine commitment to change at the start of the process because they are frightened of losing their children. However, as a care plan is created and implemented, this fear may subside and levels of commitment may waver as ambivalence returns.

As Millar and Rollnick (1991) note, change will occur only if the perceived benefits of change outweigh the perceived fears and costs. At times within the change process, it is inevitable that parents are going to feel ambivalent and may demonstrate behaviours that the social worker perceives as disengagement from the change process. The assessment task for the social worker is to be watchful for signs of ambivalence throughout the process of working with the family, and to assess ways in which the parents manage ambivalence, and how professionals can help them move through ambivalence to achieve change. Professionals need to work with parents by using the parents' personal strengths and support networks to enable them to maintain change, rather than relapsing and exiting from the change process.

Who needs to change what?

Research by Farmer and Owen (1995) highlights the problem of assessment which focuses solely on the mother, particularly if the father is aggressive. It is crucial that assessment involves both parents instead of focusing only on one of them. Each parent is likely to have a different level of commitment to change and may well be ambivalent towards it in response to different motivational factors. Unless the practitioner assesses both parents' responses to the required changes, one parent could be negatively influencing and undermining the change that is being implemented by the other.

The method of the parents' entry into the social services system also has considerable impact on the prognosis for constructive engagement with change (as noted by Ivanoff et al. 1994). Being forced to engage in change is likely to increase the parents' sense of failure, uncertainty and low self-efficacy. In turn, this means that they are likely to respond negatively to agencies' requirements, either through superficial compliance or subversive dissent. So it is of critical importance to involve the parents as much as possible in decision-making. Whilst this is important for all families, it is particularly important for parents who may have a low sense of self-worth from their experiences of discrimination. Two examples might be of parents from minority ethnic groups or parents with learning disabilities. In the above-mentioned situations an assessment contract is required to ensure that parents are clear about:

- the role and powers of workers
- the expectations of each parent
- how the worker will respond to non-compliance

- options and choices for the parents

- specific goals

- opportunities for early success and incentives for progress.

(Ivanoff *et al.* 1994)

Summary

Parents are too easily labelled as 'failures' and 'non-compliant' because we expect them to change at our pace rather than at their own. Less commonly, but just as importantly, workers may overestimate parental motivation and readiness to change. If we are to assess parents' commitment, motivation and capacity to bring about meaningful change that is designed to promote the welfare of their children, workers must draw on models of motivation and change. Furthermore, professionals need to be aware not only of models of motivation and change but also of their own influence on the change process. Professionals should have the knowledge and skills to use appropriate interviewing techniques. An overview of these techniques is beyond the remit of this chapter, but readers are strongly recommended to read the texts listed below. The crucial assessment task for the social worker is to consider ways in which parents can positively engage in the change process at a pace that will ensure that the needs of the child are met. The models of change and the seven steps in particular can provide a framework in which parenting capacity and commitment can be brought together at a time when professionals have to make major decisions about the child's welfare and safety. Too often assessments focus on information-gathering, but fail either to consider and understand motivation and change, or to engage parents in that process.

Recommended reading

Jenkins, D. (1990) *Invitation to Responsibility*. London: Dulwich Press.

Miller, W. and Rollnick, S. (1991) *Motivational Interviewing*. London: Guilford Press.

Morrison, T. (1998) 'Partnership, Collaboration and Change under the Children Act.' In M. Adcock and M. White (eds.) *Significant Harm: Its Management and Outcome* (2nd edition). Croydon: Significant Publications.

References

Alexander, L. (1991) 'Strategy Implementation: The Nature of the Problem.' In D. E. Hussey (ed.) *International Review of Strategic Management.* Chichester: John Wiley and Sons.

Calder, M. and Horwath, J. (2000) 'Challenging Passive Partnerships with Parents and Children in the Core Group Forum: A Framework for a Proactive Approach.' In *Children and Family Social Work* Vol. 5, 2.

Cleaver, H. and Freeman, P. (1995) *Parental Perspectives in Cases of Suspected Child Abuse.* London: HMSO.

DiClimenti, C. (1991) 'Motivational Interviewing and the Stages of Change.' In W. Miller and S. Rollnick *Motivational Interviewing.* London: Guilford Press.

Department of Health (1988) *Protecting Children. A Guide for Social Workers Undertaking a Comprehensive Assessment.* London: HMSO.

Department of Health, Department for Education and Employment and Home Office (2000) *Framework for the Assessment of Children in Need and their Families.* London: The Stationery Office.

Farmer, E. and Owen, M. (1995) *Child Protection Practice: Private Risks and Public Remedies.* London: HMSO.

Ivanoff, A., Blythe, B. and Tripodi, T. (1994) *Involuntary Clients in Social Work Practice.* New York: Aldine de Gruyter.

Millar, W. and Rollnick, S. (1991) *Motivational Interviewing.* London: Guilford Press.

Morrison, T. (1998) 'Partnership, Collaboration and Change under the Children Act.' In M. Adcock and R. White (eds.) *Significant Harm: Its Management and Outcome* (2nd edition). Croydon: Significant Publications.

Prochaska, J. and Di Clementi, C. (1982) 'Transtheoretical Therapy: Towards a More Integrative Model of Change'. In *Psychotherapy Theory, Research and Practice 19*, 3.

CHAPTER 6

Empowering Children and Family Members to Participate in the Assessment Process

Yvonne Shemmings and David Shemmings

Gathering information and making sense of a family's situation are key phases in the process of assessment. It is not possible to do this without the knowledge and involvement of the family. It requires direct work with children and families, explaining what is happening, why an assessment is being undertaken and what is likely to be the outcome. Gaining the family's cooperation and commitment to the work is crucially important.

(From the *Framework for the Assessment of Children in Need and their Families,* p.38, 3.32)

In this chapter we consider the following:

- empowerment in assessment processes
- the benefits of empowerment
- factors that promote empowerment
- working with resistant family members
- engaging men in the assessment process
- empowering children and young people
- tips for participative practice.

Introduction

Apparently, one of the mathematicians involved in breaking the Enigma codes during World War II asked some of his colleagues, 'Which way round do the hands of a clock turn?' No doubt wondering if he had been working a little too hard, but nonetheless intrigued by the question, one of the group said, 'Surely, that's obvious; everyone would see it the same way, wouldn't they?' 'Yes, everyone probably would … everyone except the clock, that is,' was the reply.

In this chapter we explore involving parents, carers and children in assessment processes by changing the perspective from that of the outsider to that of the child or parent, by moving away from the clock-watcher's or outsider's viewpoint and getting closer to the vantage-point of the clock itself; considering what it is like to be involved in an assessment from the service user's perspective. The following three quotes each give a flavour of the user's perspective. The first excerpt is from an interview with a young person (taken from Walker 1999) and the second two are parents talking about social workers (taken from Thoburn, Lewis and Shemmings 1995):

> It is important for young people to be involved in deciding whether there needs to be a meeting, who needs to be at that meeting, who needs to be involved in what discussions, what discussions need to be had, whether the young person needs somebody to represent them, whether there is some way that somebody can talk to the young person, whether there needs to be a split meeting between the young person and an unbiased representative and then that representative [brought] into the meeting, whether the young person needs additional support to be in the meeting, whether … if somebody was physically disabled in some way there are a lot of systems set up to give them what they need. For example, any important document will automatically be translated into Braille for the blind if they request it… Now if at the end of the day they lose out because their point is not getting across they are being discriminated against (Walker 1999, p.46).

> She was very friendly, a likeable person, constructive and not accusative and it came through genuinely. She made us talk about things that made us think and that we should have talked about before (Thoburn et al. 1995, p.58).

> She was compassionate, she listened to us, she was very supportive and understanding, especially over the allegations. She was terrific. We trusted her because when she said she would do something, she did.

She always phoned and left a message for us and told us she would be unable to see us because of working part-time or holidays (Thoburn *et al.* 1995, p.58).

The research on the subject of participation and empowerment in child welfare is now vast. Rather than try to cover everything, instead we summarise the key literature on what empowerment might mean in the context of an assessment of children in need and their families and then we suggest ways of working with resistant family members. We conclude by outlining ten 'Tips for Participative Practice'.

Empowerment in assessment process

Jack distinguishes between two different meanings of empowerment. The first is *enablement* 'which, being about the development of another's capabilities, is a professional skill ...', whereas *empowerment*, 'being about the struggle for power and control, is essentially a political activity' (Jack 1995, p.11). Perhaps not surprisingly, professionals tend to see empowerment as 'enablement'. Additionally, the literature on users' views about family participation reveals that, early on, the preoccupations of professionals often differ from those of parents, carers and young people (Shemmings and Shemmings 1995; Shemmings and Shemmings 1996). Professionals tend to stress the procedural aspects of empowerment – for example, sharing records, attending meetings, knowing about complaints procedures – whereas family members usually stress both the procedural and the relational aspects – typically, developing trust, being transparent, genuine and even-handed, and being direct, yet sensitive.

The benefits of empowerment

As a result of their research into 220 families involved in the child protection process, Thoburn *et al.* (1995) identified three reasons why empowerment is important, both to professionals and to family members:

1. It leads to better safeguarding of the child's welfare.

2. It recognises that family members possess unique knowledge about their own and each other's strengths and weaknesses.

3. It acknowledges explicitly the rights of family members, which helps develop trust.

Promoting empowerment

Given the potentially conflictual nature of a visit by a social worker regarding the safety of a child, the finding that only 2 per cent of families could be considered as true 'partners' in the assessment process is not surprising. However, it was also found that in the early stages of an initial assessment, most families could at the very least be 'informed, involved and consulted' (Thoburn *et al.* 1995).

The *Framework for the Assessment of Children in Need and their Families* (Department of Health *et al.* 2000) encourages an approach which builds on strengths as well as identifying difficulties, as described in Chapter 2. This should encourage greater participation during the early stages of assessment, as carers should feel they are not being labelled as parents who can do nothing right. Research studies highlight a number of factors that help participation in assessment to happen, particularly in terms of the kind of relationship that has to be developed and then nurtured between professionals and family.

ENGAGING FAMILIES

Cleaver and Freeman (1995) found that families wanted to be kept fully informed, treated with courtesy and involved at all stages of the social work process. From our own reviews of the literature on users' perspectives we found that honesty, answerability and even-handedness were three conditions of participative practice with families; but there is a fourth condition – sensitivity – which, from the family member's viewpoint, has to act as an envelope to contain the other three (Shemmings and Shemmings 1995; Shemmings and Shemmings 1996). We also found that for trust to develop, family members wanted all four conditions to be demonstrated, typically by being invited to attend meetings, seeing records and being informed of their rights and options. But the responsibility for developing empowerment in practice does not rest solely with professionals.

AGENCY POLICIES

Agency policies can confirm or obstruct openness in assessment. For example, workers trying to empower family members whose first language is not English will find it virtually impossible if interpreting facilities are difficult to access. The following extract summarises the relationship between professional practice and agency policy: 'Whilst failure to work in partnership can sometimes be attributed to aspects of the case itself ... differences between cases where family members were informed, involved and consulted and those where they were not seemed almost always attributable to either the agency policy and procedures or the social work practices or both together' (Thoburn, Lewis and Shemmings 1996, p.140).

A GUIDED CONVERSATION

Empowerment and participation are difficult to achieve during the initial assessment because, for many families, it will be the first time they have met the worker; also, the time available for assessment may be limited. After the purpose of the assessment has been clarified the aim should be to conduct a 'guided conversation' rather than use a set formula. Assessment forms consisting of lists of questions can inhibit open participation. Referring to the current Looked-after Children Action and Assessment Records, one of the young people in Walker's research captures the problems of taking an over-bureaucratic approach to the use of recording materials: 'And they say stuff like "Have you ever made anyone pregnant?" or "Are you pregnant?" "Are you disabled?" ... "Do you do drugs?" ... I get so fed up with them ... some of it just does my head in.' (Walker 1999, p29)

Although the respondent was referring to the contents of the form itself she went on to talk about the way in which some social workers seemed to use the Action and Assessment Record Forms, just reading the questions out and then expecting her to answer them 'on the spot', as she put it, rather than discussing the issues and recording the outcomes of the discussion. (The latter method is how the Action and Assessment Records are designed to be used.) The new Assessment Framework provides the worker with a structure for the overall direction and focus to the assessment, not a question and answer format for interviewing each child.

AVOID ASSUMPTIONS

When undertaking assessments, one of the barriers to empowerment practice can be professionals' assumptions. By considering one dimension of the Family and Environment Factors domain – poverty – as used in the *Framework for the Assessment of Children in Need and their Families*, we now illustrate some of the effects this can have.

In one of the ice-breaking exercises in training which we have both used, participants are asked to rank a number of statements on two scales – 'This is not unusual in families', and 'I disagree with this'. One of the statements is 'Buying an 8-year-old a pair of trainers for £120'. The most typical response is, 'It depends whether they can afford it', but subsequent small group discussions uncover a set of assumptions about poverty which are often incongruent with research findings and which inevitably act as a barrier to participative practice. Some participants, however, make the point that a parent living in poverty might well buy their child a present if, for example, they had a small win on the lottery. They often argue that, far from being profligate, their behaviour could be seen as selfless – in that they are not spending it on themselves – and actually protective of a child who may have been ridiculed or even bullied as a result of wearing unfashionable trainers.

In a similar vein, Graham points out that mothers, when 'caring in poverty', tend initially to cut back on their own consumption; second, they look to outside sources of support (for example, family, child benefit, moneylenders); third, but in parallel, they may depend heavily on routines such as watching TV, listening to the radio, smoking, taking tranquillisers and buying sweets for their children – what Graham refers to as 'a way of coping with the constant and unremitting demands of caring, a way of temporarily escaping without leaving the room' (Graham 1993, p.73). Various studies have shown that such selfless behaviour is often part of living in poverty. Such knowledge is essential and, provided it does not lead to collusion, an ability to put oneself in the position of family members leads to practice which is more participative and empowering.

One of the most important points for professionals to remember when trying to empower users is to consider the significance of each domain of the *Framework for the Assessment of Children in Need and their Families* for this particular family. Hence, it is the interaction between, say, poverty and, for example, the strength of a specific parent/child relationship that a professional needs to assess, rather than to rely upon generalised links between poverty and the needs of children and families.

With regard to culture, as Kenney (1999) points out, nonverbal communication is particularly prone to assumptions and misinterpretation during assessment: the service user may consider silence an example of 'good manners' while the worker considers it 'surliness'. Maintaining eye contact might be understood as 'bold' or 'insolent' by the worker, but a sign of respect by the family member. An absence of eye-contact could be interpreted as 'evasive', 'withdrawn' or as indicative of 'low self-esteem'.

Thompson reminds us that anti-oppressive practice means that professionals must achieve three different objectives:

- recognise the impact of discrimination and oppression on people's lives

- avoid the pitfall of reinforcing or exacerbating such discrimination and oppression

- challenge and undermine the oppressive structures, attitudes and actions that disadvantage certain groups in society.

(Thompson 1996, p.153)

To increase the involvement of people from different cultural groups it is important to distinguish between two overlapping approaches. First, workers need actively to resist and challenge their own and others' oppressive practices (including those of both organisations and individuals) when undertaking assessments. So, for example, they should routinely and assertively question the use of language and practices which either implicitly or explicitly exclude family members. They also need to understand how eurocentric beliefs – for example, concerning the relative weight given to the individual versus the community – and stereotypical views of families from other cultures, all affect how and why assessments are produced. One obvious way to do this is by working closely with religious and self-help groups (for example Black Sisters). Second, workers must also work to promote greater understanding of cultural differences, for example by considering the diversity of child-rearing practices. Thus, it is not enough for workers to challenge oppressive practice; they must also take account of family members' cultural backgrounds and beliefs. The provision of ethnically diverse assessment practice based upon a greater participation with family members is also the responsibility of organisations. Hence not only must translation and interpretation services be funded adequately, partly to prevent the inappropriate use of children as interpreters, but also there needs to be a clear policy on anti-oppressive practice. Extensive consultation with people from local cultural groups should inform written policies and procedures.

Disabled children and their families

With respect to empowering disabled children and their families, professionals will need to consider that the child is likely to have experienced a multiplicity of different assessments. For families with a disabled child 'assessment' may be a very familiar process. Russell identifies eight types of assessment which disabled children and family members may have experienced, only one of which is a 'family assessment' (Russell 1996). It is possible that 'assessment fatigue' could set in for these children and their families and that the degree to which any of them will become engaged in a further assessment may be affected by their past experiences. To work in partnership with families, professionals should take account of these past experiences and their impact on the child's and the family's attitude to assessment and professionals. Research indicates that care is needed to explore possible assumptions and prejudices which may be held by professionals about disabled people. Advice could be sought from those working within the disability specialism, as well as considering whether an advocate should be identified for an individual child or family. It is likely that other agencies will have worked with the child and his or her parents and it will be helpful to ask those who know the family how best to involve them (having sought the parents' permission). Additionally, to develop empowerment practice in assessments it is important not to marginalise disabled children by favouring family members who are more vocal.

Working with resistant family members

A powerful measure of the success of empowerment practice is its effectiveness with family members who are reluctant or resistant. The research literature stresses the need for workers to begin by considering why the family member appears resistant (Cleaver and Freeman 1995; Trotter 1999). For example, they may be fearful or they may have had negative experiences of health and welfare agencies in the past; similarly, professionals themselves may be contributing inadvertently to the difficulties.

Egan (1994) is not alone in making the point that 'It is impossible to be in the business of helping people for long without encountering both reluctance and resistance' (p.147). This is particularly true during assessment processes, as they usually take place early on in the relationship at a time when trust may not have developed sufficiently for more challenging ideas to be expressed; yet, however sensitively done, child and family assessments are often perceived by family members to be anxiety-provoking and challenging.

Egan reminds us that 'involuntary clients' are more likely to be reluctant or resistant. He discusses some practical tips (1994, pp.147–53), which we have modified and summarised under four question-type headings.

How might resistance show itself?

- by only being prepared to consider 'safe' or low priority areas for discussion

- by not turning up for appointments or by being too cooperative with professionals

- by being verbally and/or physically aggressive
- by minimising the issues.

When might resistance show itself?

- when there is fear of intensity and high levels of empathy being expressed by the child or family
- in situations in which lack of trust or fear of betrayal are present
- when the family member feels that he or she has no choice but to take part
- when there is resentment of third-party referrers (e.g. teachers, other family members)
- when the goals of each party are different
- with people who have negative experiences or images of social services departments
- when people feel that to ask for help is an admission of failure
- when people feel that their rights are not respected
- when people feel they are not participants in the process
- if the worker is disliked.

What might we be doing, or have done already, to make matters worse?

- becoming impatient and hostile
- doing nothing, hoping the resistance will go away (this might work if it was based on a calculated assessment)
- lowering expectations or blaming the family member
- absorbing the family member's anger (again, sometimes this could work if used as a response to an identified need)
- inappropriately allowing the family member to control the assessment
- becoming unrealistic by, for example, arguing that all family members should be willing and self-referring
- believing that family members must like and trust us before assessment can proceed

- ignoring the enforcing role of some aspects of child protection work, and hence refusing to place any demands on family members.

Are there productive approaches to working with 'reluctant and resistant' people during assessment?

- give practical, emotional support – especially by being available, predictable and consistent, thus modelling a secure attachment style

- see some reluctance and resistance as normal

- explore our own resistance to change and examine the quality of our own interventions and communication style

- establish a strong and well-articulated relationship by clarifying all the rules of sharing records, by inviting people to meetings, sharing with them how and why you have to make decisions, and explaining the complaints procedure

- help family members to identify incentives for moving beyond resistance (e.g. by helping them see that they can be in charge of their own lives again, or that they and their child can benefit from support)

- tap the potential of other people who are respected as partners by the family member

- understand that reluctance and resistance may be 'avoidance' or, of course, it could be us not doing our job as well as we might. Either way, try never to 'blame the service user'.

Involving men in the assessment process

When thinking about the question of involving men in the assessment process, research clearly indicates that there are additional factors to consider (Ryan 2000), many of which concern the gendered nature of what constitutes 'parenting practice', still seen by many as 'mothering'. Even tasks within families are usually perceived and experienced differently between, and by, men and women. In some families, for example, the man tends to plan for and budget the family finances, leaving the woman to manage the money (Graham 1993). The effect of this delegation can be that it is the woman who daily confronts the ignominy of poverty.

When child welfare professionals wonder, like Milner, why they 'spend most of (their) time working with mothers and ignoring fathers' (Milner 1993), part of the answer is that there are historical and structural reasons why it has been in men's interests to remain invisible. This protection of the self can be marked: Bentovim, for example, found that men will often allow the family to be split up rather than admit abuse (Bentovim 1987). Sometimes men's part in child abuse and their role in therapeutic work is overlooked or even excused by professionals. Whilst there is a danger here of stereotyping all 'men', research consistently uncovers the same pattern: men disappear (or are ignored by professionals) when children's welfare is discussed, even though many studies draw attention to the part played by men in child maltreatment (Milner 1993; Ryan 2000).

The implications for empowering family members during assessment are more complicated when considering men's involvement because one of the problems is that (some) men have exercised an excess of power. Hence, to empower certain family members, professionals may imply a need to restrict the power of others. Indeed, as Humphries (1999) points out, when there is family violence, helping women to leave men may become the primary objective.

Empowering children and young people

Practitioners can find it difficult to engage children in the assessment processes. For some children, being involved in aspects of the adult world is familiar, but the degree to which they have been involved in decision-making will vary and will depend on a number of factors that include their family composition and wider culture, their place in the family and their age. Practitioners should therefore consider how to involve each child in the assessment process according to age and understanding and past experiences.

It has been shown that the ability of very young children, as well as of those with severe learning disabilities (Larson and Gerber 1992), to engage in metacognitive thinking – or 'thinking about thinking' – is quite marked; similar results have been found concerning the young age at which children become interested in how other people are thinking – 'mind-reading', or 'theory of mind' as it is referred to in child development research (Baron-Cohen 1995). Unfortunately, however, both metacognitive thought and 'mind-reading' may not be as well developed in children who have been abused. Hence, a role for child welfare professionals who are trying to involve children in assessments is to gauge a child's ability to describe what other family members' viewpoints are about important issues in her or his life. A child's answers to questions such as, 'What do you think mummy thinks about?' are not only powerful indicators of cognitive and emotional development, they also paint a picture of the extent to which the child has developed self-protective and resilient frames of reference: to appreciate that other people have 'minds' helps children not to feel responsible when they have suffered maltreatment from adults.

Summary: tips for participation

We conclude our chapter by outlining ten practice-based tips for developing a more participative approach to assessing families and children in need:

1. Be clear with families right from the start what your role is ... and what it is not. Don't wait to be asked for information; offer it freely in the form of leaflets, etc. Make sure you have considered family members who have specific communication needs (for example, by using interpreters or advocates).

2. Offer to show family members what you are recording about them, addressing third-party confidentiality. Invite them to meetings, etc., but prepare them well – not just for the practicalities but also for the more 'emotional' aspects of involvement in decision-making.

3. Use forms and checklists as part of a 'guided conversation', not bureaucratically. You are aiming to produce an improvised performance each time you do an assessment with family members, rather than learning lines for a scripted play.

4. Continue to acquire more knowledge about the impact of culture, gender, sexuality, disability and poverty in the lives of families, and to develop skills in relating this knowledge to decisions about how best to help children and their families.

5. Communicate in straightforward, jargon-free language appropriate to the specific family member(s) with whom you are working. Keep family members informed of developments and progress.

6. To work in a participative way with family members you need to share your thinking at appropriate points in the assessment. They will want to know how you plan to undertake your assessment and on what basis you are making judgements about the child's needs.

7. Finally, work from and with the strengths of family members. Treat all family members as you would want to be treated: with courtesy and respect, yet with honesty if you have concerns about the child's welfare.

The last three tips refer specifically to children and young people:

8. To help children of different ages to express their wishes and feelings, always take what Brandon, Schofield and Trinder (1998) refer to as a 'kit-bag', consisting of handy materials which can be used with children of different ages. Their recommended list includes: play people, animals, puppets, play-dough, drawing materials and coloured paper. Additionally, the resource pack 'Turning Points' (NSPCC 1997) contains activities and materials designed specifically to help children express thoughts and feelings which they find difficult to talk about. And, as expected with advances in technology, computer software is now being designed to involve children in decision-making in family support processes (see, for example, Brandon *et al.* 1998, p.82).

9. Involvement of children in decision-making meetings is sometimes more complex. Because young people tend to express their needs differently, a model of children's involvement was devised by Shemmings and Shemmings (1996) and more recently incorporated into a cartoon character for younger children called Identikid (see Shemmings, D. 1999, p.89–90). The model involves working out with a child how he or she links together the following four participation variables:

    (i) seeing what is happening

    (ii) being seen oneself

    (iii) hearing what others are saying

    (iv) being heard oneself (in other words, 'speaking').

    Provided they remember to take account of the unique needs of disabled children, the model reminds workers that 'being involved' in decision-making not only means attendance at the meeting but may incorporate participating in a telephone or video link, writing a letter or making a tape-recording.

10. Some young people cannot trust a 'professional' but will confide in an advocate or supporter who, as long as they are given

training and support, can provide an effective way for children to express their wishes and feelings. A combined approach, using advocates and 'paid' professionals, is often the optimal way of increasing children's confidence and feelings of self-efficacy, both of which are known resilience factors capable of providing a child with positive experiences to enhance and strengthen self-esteem.

Recommended reading

Butler, I. and Williamson, H. (1994) *Children Speak: Children, Trauma and Social Work*. London: NSPCC/Longman.

Ferguson, H., Gilligan, R. and Torode, R. (1993) *Surviving Childhood Adversity: Issues in Policy and Practice*. Dublin: Trinity College.

Platt, D. and Shemmings, D. (1996) *Managing Enquiries into Alleged Child Abuse and Neglect: Partnership with Families*. Chichester: John Wiley.

Shemmings D. (ed.) (1999) *Children's Involvement in Family Support and Child Protection*. London: The Stationery Office.

References

Baron-Cohen, S. (1995) *Mindblindness: An Essay on Autism and Theory of Mind*. London: MIT Press.

Bentovim, A. (1987) 'Clinical Work with Children and Families where Sexual Abuse has Occurred.' Paper presented to the Midlands Forensic Research Group, Leicester University, 16 September 1987.

Brandon, H., Schofield, G. and Trinder, I. (1998) *Social Work with Children*. Basingstoke: MacMillan.

Cleaver, H. and Freeman, P. (1995) *Parental Perspectives in Cases of Suspected Child Abuse*. London: HMSO.

Department of Health, Department for Education and Employment and Home Office (2000) *Framework for the Assessment of Children in Need and their Families*. London: The Stationery Office.

Egan, G. (1994) *The Skilled Helper* (5th Edition). Monterey: Brooks/Cole.

Ferguson, H., Gilligan, R. and Torode, R. (1993) *Surviving Childhood Adversity: Issues in Policy and Practice*. Dublin; Trinity College.

Graham, H. (1993) 'Caring for Children in Poverty.' In H. Ferguson, R. Gilligan and R. Torode. *Surviving Childhood Adversity: Issues in Policy and Practice*. Dublin: Trinity College.

Humphries, C. (1999) 'Avoidance and Confrontation: Social Work Practice in Relation to Domestic Violence and Child Abuse.' In *Child and Family Social Work, 4*, 1, pp.77–87.

Jack, R. (ed.) (1995) *Empowerment in Community Care*. London: Chapman and Hall.

Kenney, C. (1999) 'Using Professional Judgement.' In D. Shemmings (ed.) *Children's Involvement in Family Support and Child Protection*. London: The Stationery Office.

Larson, K. A. and Gerber, M. M. (1992) 'Metacognition.' In N. N. Singh and J. L. Beale (eds.) *Learning Disabilities: Nature, Theory and Treatment*. New York: Springer-Verlag.

Milner, J. (1993) 'Avoiding Violent Men: The Gendered Nature of Child Protection Policy and Practice.' In H. Ferguson, R. Gilligan and R. Torode (1993) *Surviving Childhood Adversity: Issues in Policy and Practice*. Dublin: Trinity College.

NSPCC (1997) *Turning Points: A Resource Pack for Communicating with Children.* London: NSPCC publications.

Russell, P. (1996) 'Children with Disabilities and Special Needs: Current Issues and Concerns for Child Protection Procedures.' In D. Platt and D. Shemmings (eds.) *Managing Enquiries into Alleged Child Abuse and Neglect: Partnership with Families.* Chichester: John Wiley.

Ryan, M. (2000) *Working with Fathers.* Oxford: Radcliffe Medical Press.

Shemmings, D. (ed.) (1999) *Children's Involvement in Family Support and Child Protection.* London: The Stationery Office.

Shemmings, D. and Shemmings, Y. (1995) 'Defining Participative Practice in Health and Welfare.' In R. Jack (ed.) *Empowerment in Community Care.* London: Chapman and Hall.

Shemmings, D. and Shemmings, Y. (1996) 'Building Trust when Making Enquiries.' In D. Platt and D. Shemmings (eds.) *Making Enquiries into Alleged Child Abuse and Neglect: Partnership with Families.* Chichester: John Wiley.

Thoburn, J., Lewis, A. and Shemmings, D. (1995) *Paternalism or Partnership? Family Involvement in the Child Protection Process.* London: HMSO.

Thoburn, J., Lewis, A. and Shemmings, D. (1996) 'Partnership-based Practice in Child Protection Work.' In M. Hill and J. Aldgate (eds.) *Child Welfare Services: Developments in Law, Policy, Practice and Research.* London: Jessica Kingsley.

Thompson, N. (1996) *People Skills.* London: Macmillan.

Trotter, C. (1999) *Working with Involuntary Clients: A Guide to Practice.* London: Sage.

Walker, S. (1999) *Children's Perceptions of their Participation in Looked After Children Reviews.* Unpublished MA dissertation, University of East Anglia: Norwich.

CHAPTER 7

Entering the Child's World

Communicating with Children to Assess their Needs

Anne Bannister

Fundamental to establishing whether a child is in need and how those needs should be best met is that the approach must be child centred. This means that the child is seen and kept in focus throughout the assessment and that account is always taken of the child's perspective.

(From the *Framework for the Assessment of Children in Need and their Families*, p.10, 1.34)

This chapter considers the following:

- the benefits of engaging children in an assessment of their needs
- establishing relationships with children whose needs are being assessed
- creating a safe climate for the exploration of views and feelings
- methods of communication
- therapeutic containment
- completing the assessment – the needs of young people.

Introduction

A practitioner who is assessing a child using the *Framework for the Assessment of Children in Need and their Families* (Department of Health *et al.* 2000) must ensure that the child's views and feelings are sought. They should ascertain the child's views on his or her place in the family and community and their perception of the carer's ability to respond to the child's needs. In addition, through communication with the child, a social worker will be able to assess the developmental stage of that child. For example, the verbal communication skills of the child will give some indication as to whether the child who is able to communicate verbally is communicating at a level appropriate to his or her age and ability. In situations where there are concerns that a child is suffering or has suffered significant harm, this chapter should be read in conjunction with *Working Together to Safeguard Children* (Department of Health, Home Office and Department for Education and Employment 1999) and the *Memorandum of Good Practice* (Home Office and Department of Health 1992).

Why enter the child's world?

Research studies have demonstrated that children and young people know what their needs are and can usually communicate these needs if practitioners take the time and develop the skills to listen to them. For example, Butler and Williamson (1995), in their study *Children Speak*, interviewed children to obtain their views about 'harm' and what supports they would like. They found that children often have strong opinions about their needs and ways in which these can be met, and are able to express their views and feelings if professionals create the right atmosphere. Despite the Children Act 1989, emphasising that practitioners should ascertain the wishes and feelings of children and ascertain what the child wants to see happen, parents and carers remain the main source of information on children's views. To understand how events affect children's lives, workers should empathise fully with the position of children and put aside their own anxieties and views regarding communicating with children about sensitive issues.

Ascertaining children's wishes and feelings in the assessment process: the child centred approach

There is no quick formula for engaging with children in order to understand their perspectives. The differences in age, developmental level, disability, gender and culture of the young person means that the worker will have to establish with each child the most appropriate method for communication; for example, some children may prefer to communicate through play, others through discussion.

Although it is vital for the practitioner to be empathic and trustworthy, as well as honest and accepting, it may not be enough when working with children. Young people, especially those whose needs may have been ignored or misinterpreted within their families, may believe that their voices will automatically be silenced or misunderstood. They may never have learned to express openly their feelings or emotions. It may be that workers making assessments are the first people to try to ascertain these. As a result of this children may test professionals to see if it is safe to discuss feelings.

In addition many children, depending on their age, culture and inclination, may use verbal communication only as an adjunct to more basic communication using body language. All babies communicate first of all with cries (to attract attention) and with body and facial expressions. Parents and carers may learn to interpret these, but other children (such as older siblings) are often much more adept at helping infants to communicate their needs. Brothers and sisters 'translate' what infants are showing rather than what they are saying. Practitioners should therefore consider what they see and feel, as well as what they hear.

The tasks of professionals who are trying to ascertain the views of children as part of the assessment process can be divided into three stages:

- to build a rapport in which the child gains trust, feels understood and accepted

- to create a safe space where the child's needs can be expressed

- to reassure the child that his or her voice has been heard and that their opinions will be taken into consideration.

These are considered in detail below.

Stage 1: Building rapport

Those who have carried out research with children, or who have evaluated programmes for children, report that 'asking too many questions' or 'too many hard questions' will not be appreciated and will not help to build rapport. Interviews with adults tend to be based on the question-and-answer format and those with children often follow the same format, relying, yet again, on spoken language. However, the importance of children's play, for a range of reasons, has been stressed throughout the last century by those who have studied childhood: children learn through play (see for instance Froebel 1912); child development, physical, emotional and social, depends on the quality of play (see Piaget 1954); children's play is also a means of communication (see Stern 1985). It is important therefore that in the first interaction with children there is recognition of the importance of play, particularly for younger children, and assurance that children are not over-burdened with talk.

In order to develop a relationship in which the child feels safe and able to trust the worker it is useful to give him or her some information about oneself and one's roles. For instance, giving them cards with contact telephone numbers might be useful for older children.

MAKING AN AGREEMENT

Making an agreement regarding the limits to confidentiality is vitally important. Practitioners should refer to guidance regarding confidentiality in *Working Together to Safeguard Children* and the *Framework for the Assessment of Children in Need and their Families* and take account of the child's circumstances before discussing confidentiality with the child. This agreement may be written by the child or the worker, depending on the child's developmental level.

METHODS OF COMMUNICATION

Inviting children to draw or play with small figures (people and animals, fantasy figures), helps most children to relax and build a rapport with the worker. If the figures include some which are relevant to the domain to be assessed — for example, for assessing under family and environmental factors, 'community people' such as doctors and policemen and women, as well as 'extended family figures' such as grandparents – they may be used to elicit views from a child who may not understand the written word. Adolescents can be offered felt-tip pens and paper, although many will be comfortable and intrigued with using small figures, especially if 'cult' figures from TV series are included. If a person is offered a method of communication which is familiar, it gives her or him some control over the situation, which helps to erode the obvious power imbalance in any meeting between adult and child. Normally, in a first meeting, the content of the communication with the child is relatively unimportant. It is the process which matters (the exception is when children are being interviewed because of concerns about their safety). So the child may be given an open brief to draw (anything they like) or to look at the small figures and choose which ones they like best, or to write something (a poem, a message to someone, etc.). The workers may then build rapport by sharing something of themselves (their own drawing or writing, or their own favourite small figures). Children who are withdrawn or aggressively silent may still respond if given an open brief. For examples of suitable techniques see the case studies in Oaklander (1978); Bannister (1997); Bannister (1998).

These methods of communication may be helpful with children of varying abilities and from different cultures. The aim, at this stage, is not to interpret the work which children produce but to establish communication. A child who is unable to hold a pen or who has a motor disability may use the small figures or may prefer soft toys or puppets. The practitioner needs to take time to establish the child's preferred mode of communication. Chapter 3 in *Assessing Children in Need and their Families: Practice Guidance* (Department of Health 2000) provides more information on communication with disabled children.

PARENTAL PARTICIPATION

Parental participation, where it is suspected a child is suffering or has suffered significant harm, should be considered in the context of the Government guidance *Working Together to Safeguard Children*. However, when assessing children it is important to engage whenever possible with the parents or carers at a very early stage, and so the first meeting with the child, if appropriate, should be conducted in part or in whole in the presence of a parent or carer. For some children this will help to create safety so that they feel more confident about being alone with the worker in subsequent meetings. In some situations, for example in cases of suspected child sexual abuse by the parent or carer, it may not be appropriate to involve parents at this early stage. Parental presence can create problems, however, if parents are anxious to express their points of view or if they seem to be controlling the child in words or actions. Professionals should give parents the opportunity to express their own feelings separately, for example, through an initial interview with the parents in the absence of the child. An assessment can then be made as to whether the parent/s should be present for the whole or part of the first interview with the child. Of course, when assessing the attachment of the child to parents or carers it will be important to spend some time looking at the adult–child interaction, but a balance should be drawn between the necessity for this and the importance of gaining the child's trust. In any event a parent should be asked to prepare the child for the meeting with the worker, but if the parent is unwilling to do this then a person whom the child trusts should be asked to assist.

Stage 2: Creating a safe space

Careful consideration should always be given to the place where interviews with the child are carried out. In recognition of the fact that many workers may not have access to ideal facilities for working with children, the following questions should be asked:

- is the child's home neutral territory?

- can privacy be guaranteed?

- what is the child's preference for a suitable location?

- does the chosen venue have undesirable associations for the child?

Ideally the child should have sufficient space within the room to withdraw temporarily from direct engagement with the worker, although a very large room may feel unsafe and a very small room may be too oppressive.

UNCONDITIONAL REGARD

Creating safety also relies on the worker's ability to enable the child to express feelings, needs and opinions without the fear of being judged, denied or punished. Most people, especially those who feel vulnerable or powerless, as many children do, need to feel accepted before they can express feelings. This is especially so if the feelings are of fear or anger (which may be deemed unacceptable for children in some families). In addition, expressing negative feelings regarding parents or carers may feel unacceptable to children who are not securely attached or have a dys-functional attachment to a carer, as described in Chapter 12.

To create an accepting relationship with a child the practitioner must also be honest and unafraid to set boundaries, especially concerning unacceptable behaviour. Setting limits also helps to create safety and trust, especially when it is made clear that it is the behaviour, not the child, that is unacceptable.

BODY LANGUAGE

It is important to be aware of the body language of the young person and his or her overall affect or emotional tone. It may be helpful to convey to the child that the latter has been noticed: for example, 'It looks to me as if you are feeling pretty sad today.' If this is then denied, the worker might apologise and share the way in which his or her own body sometimes shows others that they are sad (hunched shoulders, downcast eyes, etc.). This may be an opportunity for a child to explain how in their family, or their culture, downcast eyes may simply be a sign of respect when in the presence of an adult. Copying or mirroring of body postures between the worker and the child during this kind of exchange facilitates communication and trust. Indeed, it imitates the behaviour which caring parents use unconsciously to facilitate the development of their children.

Mirroring the body posture of the other person is also common, unconscious behaviour when two friends are having a private conversation during which both are paying close attention. In other words, it is behaviour which signals equality and respect, and is also listening behaviour. This message is important to children. In a study by Bannister and Gallagher (1997), one boy evaluated his workers positively and noted, 'They asked me what I wanted and they really listened.'

THERAPEUTIC ROLE

Sometimes 'listening' can mean 'witnessing'. Allowing a child to talk about difficult experiences may mean that the worker almost inadvertently moves from an assessment role to a therapeutic role as the child expresses feelings about current or past events which may not have been communicated to anyone else. Assessing the needs of the child includes the child's perception of, and feelings concerning, past and present events within the family, and it is usually necessary to listen carefully to the child's view of these events before asking her or him to look at how things might be different. The worker should therefore have an understanding of therapeutic boundaries and containment, so that any areas which are 'opened up' in sessions are carefully 'closed down' before the session is over.

It is also important that no areas are barred from discussion within the assessment, unless there are legal reasons so to do. Children may complain about their teachers, about their health care workers, social workers and other professionals, and these complaints should be taken seriously and discussed further, if necessary, just as they would be if an adult had made a complaint. The effect of 'the system' (upon children who engage in an assessment of their needs) can be extremely powerful and should not be underestimated. If workers are consistent in showing their respect for the opinions of children then it is more likely that the child will feel safe to express more intimate feelings and needs.

FAMILY RELATIONSHIPS AND SOCIAL NETWORKS

Once a relationship has developed and the assessment of the child's views is under way it may be necessary to obtain factual information and to ask the child more direct questions. With younger children this can be done through the medium of drawing or use of figures. For instance, it will be important to ascertain who in the child's family is most important, or to whom he or she is closest. This kind of sociometric testing (Moreno 1993) is a long-established method enabling the child to describe his or her closest relationships, whether positive or negative. This can include extended family, friends and community. A child is asked to draw or to place figures in some kind of relationship to him or herself (represented by another figure or drawing) and then talk about the reasons for these choices. The children may then move the figures around, or change the drawings, to try out any changes they think they would like. This can lead to discussion of past configurations. It is important to emphasise with children that they may include people who are no longer part of the family because of bereavement, distance or estrangement.

At this stage of the work it can be helpful to assist the young person in looking at his or her situation with some objectivity. For very young children this will probably not be possible, but school-age children may be able to sit back and look at a drawing or a collection of small figures which they have been using. They can be helped to disengage from their own role and asked to play a 'judge' or 'wise person' who is trying to 'sort out any muddles'. This sometimes enables a child to express needs and feelings more clearly. This 'role reversal' is a natural developmental response in most children from the ages of 4 or 5. Children realise their own potential to incorporate into their personalities roles which have previously felt unattainable and possessed only by adults. It is particularly helpful for children who are otherwise feeling disempowered to be encouraged to take this role.

Stage 3: Reassuring, clarifying and moving on

Although an agreement about confidentiality should have been made at an early stage, it is important that the agreement is reiterated in the final part of the assessment. Both worker and child need to be clear about what material can be shared with parents and other professionals. It may be that during the course of the assessment the child has managed to clarify his or her own needs and to disentangle those needs from those of the parent(s). The child may need reassurance that his or her own viewpoint is perfectly valid and that it is important for this to be heard.

Stage 4: Therapeutic containment

For busy practitioners there may be a temptation to shorten, or even to omit, this final stage of the assessment. The worker may have carefully set the scene and engaged the child and explored the feelings, opinions and possibilities for the future. This process, however, is akin to the therapeutic process and unconscious fears and desires will have been brought to consciousness. Most adults in this situation will have carefully filtered their unconscious feelings and shared with the worker only those emotions which are containable. In any case, most adults will have a wide repertoire of containing and coping mechanisms to enable them to function. Children, however, are still trying out different ways of coping and are generally much closer to their unconscious material. Children in assessment situations may also be discussing events which are very damaging to them as well as very recent. Whereas adults who discuss the same events will have tried and tested ways of coping with similar situations, some children may find the events unique and will be struggling to cope at all. It is important, therefore, that children are reminded of what they have said and that they are allowed to change their minds, or to add to what they have said, if necessary. They may need reassurance about not being punished for their opinions and about not being blamed for family problems.

Children need to know if their opinions have been truly heard, and so clarification is important. Children of primary-school age and younger may benefit again from the use of drawings and figures. This time the worker can portray 'an action scene' where an explanation of the child's needs is given to 'the wise person'. Most adolescents will prefer verbal feedback or a sum of the report which the worker is to write, but young people with learning disabilities may also prefer an 'action scene'.

This clarifying scene or discussion helps the child to 'close down' and return to his or her usual ways of coping. Most children will then be able to understand the limits to the powers of the worker who is undertaking the assessment, and the long time-scales which may be involved before difficult situations are fully resolved. Younger children may not understand these abstract concepts and may simply need reassurance about their current situation, if that is realistic.

Some children, especially those with insecure attachments to current carers, may have become over-attached to the worker completing the assessment. This will need careful handling and a more gradual detachment may be necessary for these children. On the other hand, some young people may have experienced, in the past or currently, multiple caring relationships with adults and may cope with the short relationship with the assessment worker in a particularly easy fashion. Workers should bear in mind that family history and functioning can contribute to the response of the child. Workers should not make assumptions as to how a child will respond to termination of the assessment without looking at the child's history very carefully.

Summary

For many children, having their needs assessed by a skilful practitioner can be an empowering, rather than a stressful event. However, those who work with children often feel that the powerlessness and vulnerability of the young service users impact on their own lives. Good supervision for workers is essential, therefore. The supervision should be provided by someone who is able to assist the worker to separate her or his own feelings from those of the child. This is considered in detail in Chapter 9. We should not underestimate the strength which is gained from having our own needs heard and from expressing our feelings.

Recommended reading

Bannister, A. (ed.) (1998) *From Hearing to Healing: Working with the Aftermath of Child Sexual Abuse.* Chichester: Wiley.

Brandon, M., Schofield, G. and Trinder, L. (1998) *Social Work with Children.* Basingstoke: Macmillan.

Cattanach, A. (1992) *Play Therapy with Abused Children.* London: Jessica Kingsley.

Gaibannio, J., and Stott, F. M. (1992) *What Children Can Tell us: Eliciting, Interpreting and Evaluating Critical Information from Children.* San Francisco: Jossey-Bass.

References

Bannister, A. (1997) *The Healing Drama: Psychodrama and Dramatherapy with Abused Children.* London: Free Association Books.

Bannister, A. and Gallagher, E. (1997) 'Children Who Sexually Abuse Other Children.' In J. Bates, R. Pugh and N. Thompson. *Protecting Children: Challenges and Change.* Aldershot: Arena.

Bannister, A. (1998) *From Hearing to Healing: Working with the Aftermath of Child Sexual Abuse* (2nd edition). Chichester: Wiley.

Butler, I. and Williamson, H. (1995) *Children Speak.* London: NSPCC/Longman.

Department of Health, Home Office and Department for Education and Employment (1999) *Working Together to Safeguard Children.* London: The Stationery Office.

Department of Health, Department for Education and Employment and Home Office (2000) *Framework for the Assessment of Children in Need and their Families.* London: The Stationery Office.

Department of Health (2000) *Assessing Children in Need and their Families: Practice Guidance.* London: The Stationery Office.

Froebel, F. (1912) *Chief Writings on Education* (trans. S. S. F. Fletcher and J. Welton). London: Arnold.

Home Office and Department of Health (1992) *Memorandum of Good Practice: On Video Recorded Interviews with Child Witnesses for Criminal Proceedings.* London: HMSO.

Moreno, J. L. (1993) *Who Shall Survive?* (student edition). Roanoke, Virginia: Royal Publishing.

Oaklander, V. (1978) *Windows to our Children.* Utah: Real People Press.

Piaget, J. (1954) *The Construction of Reality of the Child.* New York: Ballone.

Stern, D. (1985) *The Interpersonal World of the Infant.* New York: Basic Books.

CHAPTER 8

Assessing Children and Families Who Belong to Minority Ethnic Groups

Nick Banks

Since discrimination of all kinds is an everyday reality in many children's lives, every effort must be made to ensure that agencies' responses do not reflect or reinforce that experience and indeed, should counteract it.

(From the *Framework for the Assessment of Children in Need and their Families,* p.12, 1.42)

In this chapter the following issues are considered:

- an exploration of the term 'minority ethnic'

- the *Framework for the Assessment of Children in Need and their Families* and its application to minority ethnic groups

- assessment of minority ethnic children and families, the implications for practice.

Introduction

The primary focus of this chapter is to identify ways in which assessments using the *Framework for the Assessment of Children in Need and their Families* (Department of Health *et al.* 2000) can be completed effectively with children and families from minority ethnic groups. The effectiveness will depend on the ability of the practitioner to work in a way that is both anti-oppressive and which recognises cultural difference. The aim must be to identify and meet the developmental needs of minority ethnic children. This chapter seeks to consider the task for social workers undertaking assessments of the needs of children and families from minority ethnic groups.

What is meant by 'minority ethnic'?

In considering the application of the *Framework for the Assessment of Children in Need and their Families* in the context of families from minority ethnic groups, it is useful to discuss what is meant by the term 'minority ethnic'. Banton (1988) has noted that in using the term 'ethnic' for naming groups, two tendencies have become apparent. First, there is a tendency to regard ethnicity as an attribute of minorities. Secondly, there has been an assumption that racial groups are distinguished by physical appearance and that ethnic groups are distinguished by cultural characteristics such as language, history, and shared perspectives. The term 'minority' relates not only to physical numbers in the population but also includes an implicit reference to the unequal power relations between groups. Thus the term 'minority ethnic families' means those families who do not share common physical, religious and cultural similarities to the dominant group in society – in the British context: white British people. It should be recognised from the outset that the basic psychological defining feature of being a 'minority ethnic' person is that of an interaction of the self-definition of distinctiveness and the perception of difference as seen by other groups.

The United Kingdom is culturally rich and diverse. Examples of the issues involved in assessment are drawn in this chapter from two of the largest minority ethnic groups: the African-Caribbean and South Asian communities. The 1991 census indicates that approximately 6 per cent of the population or some three million people fall into these two categories. It is recognised that there are many differences within and between these groups. There is also a growing population of 'mixed parentage' or 'dual heritage' people. The issue of mixed parentage has become increasingly important for social workers working with children and families because there is an over-representation of mixed parentage children in care statistics (Barn *et al.* 1997). Also, the research of Rowe *et al.* (1984) Thoburn, Norford and Rashid (1997) and Charles, Rashid and Thoburn (1992) indicates that children of mixed parentage are more likely to be permanently separated from their birth families and transracially placed with white carers, and their placements are more prone to disruption. This presents a picture of a growing group with considerable vulnerability.

The *Framework for the Assessment of Children in Need and their Families* and minority ethnic groups

The Assessment Framework has three domains: the developmental needs of the child, parenting capacity to respond to the child's needs, and family and environmental factors. It is important for professionals undertaking assessment of children in need from minority ethnic groups to consider how the domains and their dimensions are influenced by cultural difference.

The developmental needs of the child

While there is a great deal of agreement regarding the developmental needs of children, irrespective of culture, the worker should be aware that most child development models used in the United Kingdom are based on Eurocentric concepts and may not always be seen as entirely appropriate to people of other cultural groups. Attachment behaviours may need to be considered in an extended family caregiving context. Also, there may be distinct cross-cultural conflicts with the white majority culture to ensure that the developmental needs of children are met. For example, Masten and Coatsworth (1998) suggest that it is a key developmental task to form close friendships within and across gender. This is an ethnocentric view. Some cultural groups explicitly discourage cross-gender relations in adolescence. Encouragement to form such relationships by those from outside of the culture is likely to lead to family discord and may isolate the adolescent from his or her family and community network.

Children from minority ethnic groups have specific identity needs related to knowledge about origins of self, of culture and identity, which may require considered and systematic input if the child is to develop psychological completeness. To ignore this need is to ignore a fundamental developmental need of a child, with the effect of disadvantaging the child in later life in its understanding and degree of comfort with self. This point is explored in detail in the *Practice Guidance* to the *Framework for the Assessment of Children in Need and their Families* (Department of Health 2000).

Parenting capacity

When assessing the needs of minority ethnic children it is important that workers do not translate a 'culturally sensitive' assessment of parenting into one with less stringent criteria. The criteria should be culturally relevant and, most important, child centred. In considering the domain of parenting capacity in a relevant cultural context, there are additional issues which arise in terms of the specific dimensions. For example, in considering basic care needs it is likely that minority ethnic children will have additional needs to those of white children. There will be specialist hair and skin products that will require effort (and cost) to provide. There are dietary considerations such as the availability of halal food for Muslim children, the avoidance of pork for Muslim and some Caribbean groups, and vegetarian food for many cultural groups. Meeting these needs requires additional effort, expense and knowledge. To ensure safety one must take a wide view to include the likely experience of a black child experiencing racist taunts. Is the child prepared in advance for the possibility of taunts? Is the child helped to respond to these within the expectations of a school – that is, not to fight? What direct action does the carer take in dealing with the taunts? Is the child comforted? Is the school or club notified and expected to take protective action? The view that the taunts should just be ignored is not acceptable, as the child may develop a self-blaming attitude. This has implications for carers who are not part of the child's culture.

Assessing parenting capacity should also take into account different approaches to parenting tasks. For example, notions of the value and advantages of demand versus scheduled time feeding, and breast versus bottle-feeding are essentially culturally driven, as is the appropriate time to discontinue breast-feeding. The mechanisms of stimulation may also be culturally embedded. For example, an infant being carried on his or her mother's back or front for long periods during the day may be contrasted to the infant that is left in a pram or cot to sleep, and issues are thus raised about maternal closeness and availability.

Environmental factors

Of considerable importance in this domain is the perception that the worker may hold of the family and how this may or may not coincide with the view of the family itself. A way of avoiding stereotypes and erroneous assumptions about family structure and support systems may be to map the family's self-perceptions of important people and their roles in offering support and guidance in the parent-and-child network. This requires the worker to work directly with the family (in whatever form it presents) in order to discover who is available in its kinship and social support network. The network may include extended family members who, although not living in the family home, may offer a source of psychological support and influence in family functioning. Membership of church, temple or mosque may also be a source of family support. Specific stereotypes to avoid are the 'strong, black, African-Caribbean mother' who is perceived as faultless and able to cope without additional support or resources, and the 'quiet but able Asian mother' who is (mis)perceived as following good cultural expectations about child care when she is not. Stereotypes among workers about avoidant, domineering, absent fathers also exist. These should be questioned and challenged by the supervisor if they are unsubstantiated by evidence.

The assessment of minority ethnic children: practice implications

The literature indicates that it is not so much the nature of difference between cultural groups that is an issue when assessing children and families from minority ethnic groups, but rather the response to the perception of difference by the assessing agencies and social workers, which may lead the assessment process astray (Cheetham 1982; Ahmed, Cheetham and Small 1987; Coombe and Little 1986; Dominelli 1988; Maitra 1995; Banks 1999). In order to avoid the assessment process going astray workers and their supervisors should consider the following.

A need for cultural familiarity

There is a danger of culture and ethnicity being silent or ignored factors in the assessment process. The social worker should always be aware of the need for cultural familiarity in undertaking an assessment. Familiarity is not, in this case, necessarily synonymous with awareness or knowledge. Familiarity suggests a higher level of understanding born of engagement in the cultural experience of others, outside a problem-centred assessment process. An understanding of the positive guiding influences of culture on a family's way of living, rather than a restrictingly narrow view of cultural behaviour as exotic, mysterious, or bizarre, is required.

CULTURAL CONTEXT

Cultural demands and expectations may be part of the presenting problem. Perceived non-cooperation with, or resistance to, working with an agency may be related to a conflict between minority cultural beliefs and majority cultural expectations. For example, a parent may resist meetings or appointments on certain days if these conflict with religious requirements. As another example, an African-Caribbean member of the Seventh Day Adventist religious persuasion may resist meetings on Fridays when the time approaches dusk, due to the religious prohibition on doing, thinking or talking about work after this period on Friday until Saturday at dusk. Some members of the Jewish faith may share similar religious prohibitions. It is not uncommon to hear in child protection case conferences, when there is anxiety about a lack of cultural knowledge, the comment 'we must focus on the child, not the parent's culture'. You cannot assess a child out of his or her cultural context.

USE OF LANGUAGE

Possible difficulties in interpretation or meaning of language subtleties may exist and lead the worker to draw the wrong conclusion. Use of the terms 'beating', 'smacking', 'whipping', 'thrashing', 'licks' and 'hitting' to describe physical punishment may be used and interpreted differently in severity of action by different groups. A worker should explore the actual behaviour involved in the physical punishment rather than subjectively interpret the phrase used.

CULTURAL MISATTRIBUTION

The term cultural misattribution involves the emotional reactions of the worker of one ethnic group projected on to the client of another ethnic group. The mere presence of a client from another ethnic group may spark intense emotions in the worker and influence the total process and outcome of the risk assessment. For example, a worker may find the appearance of a father intimidating because the father wears his hair in dreadlocks and this evokes a response of fear in the worker, who then avoids the father. The reactions are caused by the worker's personal bias and anxiety and often have nothing to do with the service user's presenting behaviour. The failure of the worker to resolve or at least to recognise his or her feelings results in a misperception of the service user, which is likely to affect both the assessment process and outcome. Any service user may provoke these feelings but it is likely that black users may provoke more frequent and complicated reactions than white service users (Banks 1999). The worker may be defensive about his or her feelings and this makes them less likely to acknowledge their effect in and on the assessment process. The danger is that, while locked into this state of distortion, workers are unlikely effectively to test the reality of a family's functioning.

Adapting Ridley's (1995) work to the assessment process suggests that the existence of misattribution factors can place black service users in a double-bind situation where they can neither win nor lose, as the outcome of the assessment is not dependent on their efforts, but on the personal bias of the worker and on the power dynamics and tensions in the worker-client relationship. This misattribution dynamic does not always present itself in a hostile or dominating behaviour pattern on the part of the worker. Ridley notes that some white workers may expend considerable effort trying to gain service users' acceptance or approval. Beneath the approval-seeking is likely to be 'the worker's desire to be absolved of guilt, whether real or imagined, for being racist'. Here again white workers are working on their own issues and not on those of the client. In attempting to gain the black client's approval, workers may resort to subtle manipulation of the client. Their goal is to appear 'right on' and non-racist. By using subtle behaviours workers attempt to prove they are different from white racists. This process may be recognised by service users, who tune in to the emotional dependency of the worker, with the result that this starts a counter-manipulation reaction in the client. The assessment becomes worker-focused rather than user-focused. The worker may feel paralysed by a wish to help the black service user fight the injustice in society, rather than concentrating on the needs of the child and family members. The assessment becomes sidetracked to meet feelings of approval-seeking and guilt. The supervisor should be aware of cultural misattribution and ensure that this is considered and addressed in the supervision of workers undertaking assessments.

AN OVER-RELIANCE ON CULTURAL EXPLANATIONS

Although there is a need for cultural familiarity in the assessment process, there is also the possibility of an over-reliance on cultural explanations. A preoccupation with culture conflict among family members may lead to denial of the importance of other factors operating within the family's background; in turn, this may lead to an over-simplification and distortion of the child's needs. Here there is a danger of ignoring facts and information that may affect the worker's perception and analysis of the presenting difficulty. As with any family, regardless of culture, there may be tensions related to dysfunctional family relationships which need to be addressed. Any tendency to see dysfunction or pathology in family and child relationships as stemming only from cultural origins suggests that the professional has pathologised the culture, as he or she has come to see the difficulty as arising from the culture, not from individual behaviour. This view pathologises the culture and normalises any unacceptable behaviour of adults and carers, and has the potential to allow professional inaction or ineffective intervention.

Just as there are difficulties with a colour-blind assessment where no consideration is given to the culture of the family, there can be colour-conscious errors (Ridley 1995), where the view is taken that all difficulties arise from being a minority group member living in a white society. This view rests on a foundation of truth, but may still be a distortion of reality. The colour-conscious professional may place too much emphasis on the family's ethnic background while overlooking the person's contribution to the difficulties. One would need to consider whether the parents' difficulties stem from ignorance, cultural difference in belief from the worker, or outright resistance or inability to consider parenting change (independent of culture). The outcome of colour-consciousness is that the worker may fail to identify the difficulties in family functioning by attributing these difficulties to cultural differences between the worker and the family. The role of the supervisor is crucial. Supervisors should challenge white workers' views if they consider the latter are distorting the assessment.

One way forward may be to engage a black worker to deal with black families. This does something to help the agency meet its professional responsibility to black families, but it is not sufficient in itself as it may also reflect organisational avoidance of a significant difficulty in agency functioning. Black workers, in isolation, cannot work independently of the organisational culture. They may become frustrated and stressed by the additional responsibility and workload placed on them.

Summary

Sensitive and effective assessment of family functioning within a specific cultural context is likely to occur if:

- practitioners and managers acknowledge right from the onset that the worker may not know what the family's cultural norms are, and that if these are to be taken into account in assessment they must be obtained from the family. The culturally implicit should be made explicit

- workers are clear they are assessing within a legal context, and are explicit about the criteria they are using for assessing children's needs

- workers have adequate skills, knowledge and understanding of issues of 'difference' in the sense of acknowledging cultural, and in some instances value-based, distinctiveness. Racist or ethnocentric attitudes may well rule out workers for direct work with children and families

- assessment approaches support the minority ethnic child's social, psychological and physical connectedness with their respective communities, with no attempt to pathologise the family's cultural beliefs or behaviour

- concrete learning of facts about cultural difference is recognised as insufficient in itself to prepare an assessment. Culture is not static; it is an evolving dynamic within and between groups. Although cultural understanding is an important part of the assessment process, one should not be preoccupied with cultural explanations as this may mean that the effect/influence of structural inequalities and issues of power are denied or minimised

- awareness that an over-focus on culture, to the degree that it promotes a preoccupation with the exotic and unusual while other salient factors are ignored, may lead the worker to stereotyping which can result in inaccuracies when determining decisions in child-care planning

- clear policy and procedural guidelines are necessary. It is essential that these should be informed by anti-oppressive and anti-racist training that considers organisational practices and relates these to desirable, measurable outcomes

- supervisors ensure that the primary focus of the assessment is to promote and safeguard the welfare of the child. This should be undertaken in a way that recognises cultural differences without making the assessment subjective.

Recommended reading

Banks, N. (1999) 'Assessing Risk in Black Families: The Influence of Psychological Dynamics.' In *Representing Children, 12*, No. 1.

Jackson, V. (1996) *Racism and Child Protection: The Black Experience of Child Sexual Abuse.* London: Cassell.

Shams, M. (1995) 'Differences in Perceived Parental Care and Protection and Related Psychological Distress between Asian and non-Asian Adolescents.' In *Journal of Adolescence, 18*, 3, pp.329–348.

Thanki, V. (1994) 'Ethnic Diversity and Child Protection.' In *Children and Society 8*, 3, pp.232–244.

References

Ahmed, S., Cheetham, J. and Small, J. (1987) *Social Work with Black Children and their Families.* London: Batsford.

Banks, N. (1999) 'Assessing Risk in Black Families: the Influence of Psychological Dynamics.' In *Representing Children 12*, No. 1.

Banton, M., (1988) *Racial Consciousness.* London: Longman.

Barn, R. (1993) *Black Children in the Public Care System.* London: Batsford/BAAF.

Charles, M., Rashid, S. and Thoburn J. (1992) 'The Placement of Black Children with Permanent New Families.' In *Adoption and Fostering, 16*, 3, pp.13–18.

Cheetham J. (1982) *Social Work and Ethnicity.* London: George Allen and Unwin.

Coombe, V. and Little, A. (1986) *Race and Social Work: A Guide to Training.* London: Tavistock Publications.

Department of Health (1988) *Protecting Children: A Guide to Social Workers Undertaking a Comprehensive Assessment.* London: HMSO.

Department of Health (2000) *Assessing Children in Need and their Families, Practice Guidance.* London: The Stationery Office.

Department of Health, Department for Education and Employment and Home Office (2000) *Framework for the Assessment of Children in Need and their Families.* London: The Stationery Office.

Dominelli, L. (1988) *Anti-Racist Social Work.* London: BASW/Macmillan.

Maitra, B. (1995) 'Giving due consideration to the family's racial and cultural background.' In P. Reder and C. Lucey (eds.) *Assessment of Parenting: Psychiatric and Psychological Contributions.* London: Routledge, pp.151–168.

Masten, A. and Coatsworth, D. (1998) 'Development of Competence in Favourable and Unfavourable Environments.' In *American Psychologist*, February 1998.

Phillips, M. and Dutt, R. (1990) *Towards a Black Perspective in Child Protection.* London: Race Equality Unit.

Ridley, C. (1995) *Overcoming Unintentional Racism in Counselling and Therapy.* Thousand Oaks CA: Sage.

Rowe, J., Cain, H., Hundleby, M. and Keane, A. (1984) *Long-term Foster Care.* London: Batsford Academic/BAAF.

Thoburn, J., Norford, L. and Rashid, S. (1997) *Ten Years On: The Placement of Black Children with Permanent New Families.* School of Social Work, University of East Anglia.

CHAPTER 9

Supervising Assessments of Children and Families

The Role of the Front Line Manager

Rosemary Gordon and Enid Hendry

Staff who are in the front line of practice must be well supported by effective supervision. 'Supervision of workers carrying out family assessment is essential, as the assessment can have far reaching effects on the planning of care and whether families can meet children's needs within their time frames.' (Bentovim and Bingley Miller, forthcoming).

(From the *Framework for the Assessment of Children in Need and their Families,* p.85, 6.26)

Here we consider the following points:

- the core principles of supervisory practice

- a critique of current practice in the supervision of assessment work

- the function of supervision in the context of the assessment of children in need

- supervising the assessment process – the supervisory tasks

- factors that impact on the assessment process.

Introduction

Just as the assessment process is pivotal to the planning and delivery of effective outcomes for children, so supervision is a key factor in ensuring the quality of assessment work. Using the *Framework for the Assessment of Children in Need and their Families* (Department of Health *et al.* 2000) requires relevant information to be critically analysed by the practitioner, and professional judgement to be exercised in order to decide, based on an understanding of the child's developmental needs, how best to safeguard and promote the wellbeing of the child.

This chapter focuses on the crucial role and tasks of the front-line manager, to plan the assessment, to supervise the process of using the framework, to make professional judgements and decisions based on the evidence and understanding gained through the assessment, and to review progress. The focus is on the role of the front-line manager as a professional supervisor of practice, as distinct from the more managerial aspects of the role.

Professional supervision is defined as:

> a process in which one worker is given responsibility to work with another worker(s) in order to meet certain organisational, professional and personal objectives. These objectives are competent, accountable performance, continuing professional development and personal support. (adapted from Harries 1987, quoted in Morrison 1993, p.13)

To provide effective supervision of assessment practice supervisors need to ensure that:

- the ethos and principles of the Assessment Framework are understood and used by practitioners

- there is a planned process for introducing changes to existing assessment practice

- training and development opportunities are provided to workers, both to facilitate the change from current assessment practice and also to address individual learning needs

- they themselves have the relevant professional expertise to inform decision-making and planning and 'have a sound knowledge of child development, family dynamics and recent child care research findings' (Noakes and Hearn 1998, p.6).

Core principles of supervisory practice

The supervision of assessment work can be carried out by a range of front-line managers in a number of different settings, for example: area office teams, disability teams, family centres and family placement teams. While each of these areas of assessment practice has some distinctive characteristics which have implications for supervision, there are core principles of effective supervision which are held in common. These core principles are examined in more detail in the texts recommended at the end of this chapter, but can be summarised as follows.

Supervision should be:

- regular

- uninterrupted

- well structured and purposeful

- recorded

- based on an agreement which includes how issues of power and difference will be addressed

- periodically reviewed

- within the context of an agency policy on supervision.

Local supervision policies should outline agencies' interpretation of these principles for supervision practice. Whatever the context or purpose of assessments in child care settings, supervisors must ensure that they remain child-centred and give consideration to both safeguarding and promoting children's welfare, regardless of how the initial requirement for an assessment arose. Supervision should encourage reflective practice amongst professionals who are seeking to ensure children's safety while promoting their welfare.

Current practice in supervison of the assessment of children and families

A study of a wide range of child care inspections undertaken by the Social Services Inspectorate between 1992 and 1997 was carried out by Pont on behalf of the Department of Health (2000b) in order to identify key messages in relation to various aspects of assessment. This included a consideration of supervision of assessment practice, and what inhibits or enhances practice. While it proved difficult to find specific references to supervision of assessment work in the inspection reports, key areas of concern were identified that have significant implications for the quality of assessments. In summary, characteristic areas of weakness found by inspectors were:

- inadequate recording of supervision
- lack of expertise and specialist knowledge in supervisors
- lack of rigour in ensuring compliance with policies and procedures
- infrequent and unstructured supervision, with interruptions
- failure to challenge decisions, and lack of rigour in examining the basis of decisions
- failure to record decisions on case files or routinely to monitor case files
- failure to address the professional development needs of workers.

Pont concluded that 'social workers require specialist supervision and consultation in carrying out complex assessments', and that 'the quality of supervision is related to the skills, competence and experience of individual supervisors'. She highlighted the importance of guidance for decision-making for managers on how cases should be prioritised, monitored and allocated.

The *Framework for the Assessment of Children in Need and their Families* helps to address many of the deficiencies identified by Pont. It provides a structured and systematic basis for determining a child's developmental needs with the child and his or her carers, whether a child's health and development is being, or is likely to be, impaired by his or her current circumstances, and what services are required in terms of support or intervention. The Government has set time-scales within which assessments must be completed (Department of Health 1999). The three domains and the dimensions within them require systematic and comprehensive gathering and recording of information. The Assessment Framework assists supervisors to identify the evidence base which informs judgements and decisions. There is an expectation that assessments result in a recorded statement which summarises both needs, objectives and plans. This provides a basis for supervisors to monitor and review progress against the objectives.

The functions of supervision in the context of the assessment of children in need

Richards and Payne (1990) describe four principal functions for supervision: management, education, support and mediation. What follows summarises briefly how these different aspects apply to the supervision of assessments using the new framework.

Management function

- to clarify the purpose of assessment
- to ensure principles of assessment are addressed
- to ensure rigour
- to ensure information gathered is analysed, drawing on the most up-to-date research
- to ensure professional judgement informs decisions on plans, interventions and methods.

Managers are responsible for ensuring that assessments lead to optimal outcomes for children. They must ensure the quality of assessments and their compliance with national and agency policy, procedures and any agreed standards. This means checking that time-scales for assessments are met, that salient information is recorded and that case files are regularly reviewed.

Educational function

- to encourage reflective practice
- to encourage the application of theory, research and practice developments.

It is particularly important at a time when a new approach to assessment is being introduced, when new areas of skills and knowledge, and attitudinal issues or blocks are highlighted, that the developmental aspect of supervision for front-line staff receives adequate attention. Social workers should be encouraged to reflect critically on their performance when using the framework with children and families, and be helped by the supervisor to identify how their professional development needs can be addressed. A number of studies – Gadsby Waters (1992), Marsh and Triseliotis (1996), and Noakes et al. (1998) – have identified that this aspect of supervision is often neglected in favour of a managerial focus.

Support function

- to consider the use of self in assessment
- to address subjectivity.

Assessment work can be a source of anxiety and uncertainty, particularly where there are concerns about a child's safety, or about how long to continue providing help for needy parents when, despite this supplement to their parenting capacity, a child's developmental and emotional needs still are not being appropriately addressed. These situations call for the supervisor to provide 'a safe context within which to explore the impact of the work on the worker, particularly where this may be blocking their ability to offer an effective service' (Noakes *et al.* 1998, p.14).

Mediation function

- to identify areas of conflict or difference between social workers and other professionals or family members
- to work with practitioners and others to develop strategies for managing conflict or difference.

Supervisors may be required to mediate between different agencies and disciplines in order to get the necessary professional contributions to an assessment or to secure the supportive services that are identified as necessary.

Supervising the assessment process: the supervisory tasks

The tasks associated with the assessment will be determined by its purpose, scale and breadth. The role of the supervisor is to consider the following when supervising assessment.

Stage 1: setting up and beginning

WHAT IS THE PURPOSE OF THE ASSESSMENT?

What questions require answering through the assessment, what are the issues and what are the likely consequences for the child's health and development of the present situation?

Is/are the child/ren safe, now? Has there been or is there risk of significant harm?

Who is most worried about this child or family – does any one else have concerns; are they the same? Who is requesting this assessment?

Who is involved – which children, family members, workers, agencies, court?

Has the family been assessed before and for what purpose(s)?

Are there any special considerations?

What is the family's first language, culture, religion or identity?

Are any family members disabled? What is their main communication method?

Is there a need for an interpreter?

Who can best help understand and work with this family?

ARE THERE ANY LIKELY OR POSSIBLE BARRIERS
TO CARRYING OUT THIS ASSESSMENT?

Is there agreement with the family and between family members about the need for and purpose of the assessment?

Is there agreement within the professional group about the need for and purpose of an assessment?

Is there agreement about respective professional roles and responsibilities, what information will be shared and who has lead responsibility?

Are other types of assessment concurrent?

Are there adequate resources to carry out the assessment?

Is the worker competent and does he or she possess the necessary knowledge and experience to carry out the assessment, working to the framework?

Stage 2: during the assessment
IS THE ASSESSMENT CHILD-FOCUSED?

Is the worker taking a developmental approach to assessing the child's needs?

Does the worker understand and draw on relevant theory and research findings?

Is the worker seeking the views of the child (according to his or her age, ability and understanding)?

Is the child's identity understood from the perspective of the child?

DOES THE ASSESSMENT INVOLVE WORKING WITH THE PARENTS AND CARERS?

Refer to *The Challenge of Partnership in Child Protection: Practice Guide* (Department of Health 1995a) for guidance on working with parents/carers in difficult situations.

Is there agreement about the concerns and reasons for assessment?

Are parents and/or carers clear as to the purpose and the possible outcomes?

Is there a written agreement? If not, why not?

Is the worker communicating effectively with the parents/carers?

Is the father, substitute father or absent father involved?

Is the family's identity understood and taken account of sensitively but appropriately?

Are there issues of safety for the worker in working with this family?

IS THE ASSESSMENT TAKING ACCOUNT OF FAMILY AND ENVIRONMENTAL FACTORS?

Is the family history known and its significance for the child fully understood?

Are there other significant family members who should be involved – for example, grandparents, aunts, uncles, and step-parents (past and present)?

What is the quality of housing and the local community environment?

What supports are there either within or outside of the family, including day care?

Is the family socially excluded – for example, through racism?

HOW IS THE WORK PROGRESSING IN RELATION TO TIME-SCALES?

Is the worker aware of the expected time-scales for progressing an assessment?

Is the worker planning the work appropriately and realistically?

Is there a recognisable beginning, middle and end (in sight)?

HOW IS THE WORKER MAKING USE OF SELF DURING THE PROCESS?

Is supervision addressing the possible impact of this piece of work?

How does the worker perceive this family? This will relate to his or her own value base, personal experiences, history and levels of anxiety.

How does the worker think the family perceives him or her? Are gender, age or identity playing a part? Are there fears about safety?

Stage 3: analysis and decision-making

This is possibly the most difficult part of supervising assessment work. It is easy to become mechanistic and to check that tasks are being carried out to time-scales, but it is less easy to bring the necessary objectivity, challenge and rigour to this part of the process in a way that is supportive and constructive to the worker.

IS THE ASSESSMENT PROVIDING ADEQUATE EVIDENCE TO ANALYSE BEFORE MAKING JUDGEMENTS LEADING TO DECISIONS ABOUT FUTURE ACTIONS?

Is the worker distinguishing between fact and opinion?

Is there reasonable cause to suspect that a child is suffering, or is likely to suffer, from significant harm?

Has the assessment revealed significant unmet needs for support and services?

If the decision is not to provide services, this is itself a decision. What is the next step?

Is the worker able to evaluate evidence drawing on his or her understanding of theory: for example, child development?

Is the worker drawing on knowledge of research?

Is the worker informing the family (including the children) of the outcome and recommendations arising from the assessment?

IS THE SUPERVISOR ENSURING THAT RIGOUR AND CHALLENGE FORM PART OF THE SUPERVISION?

Is the supervisor able to ask questions, to challenge and probe where necessary? This may mean asking obvious or unpopular questions.

Is the supervisor encouraging both factual analysis and reflective practice?

Is the supervisor able to address the areas of potential impact on the worker?

Is there a supervisory agreement in place that allows for constructive challenge and feedback?

Is the supervisor evaluating how the worker is currently making judgements?

What is given priority and why?

Which factors are marginalised and why?

Which factors are causing most discussion and debate in terms of determining priority and why?

What is this saying about their current practice?

Approaches to the assessment

The way in which the assessment is being carried out is important in terms of ensuring that the appropriate individuals are being seen in the most appropriate and useful settings.

ARE THE CHILDREN INTERVIEWED INDIVIDUALLY?

Is the child who is the focus of the assessment being seen on his or her own?

Are siblings being seen, separately?

What methods are being used to interview the children?

Does the worker have a good understanding of different communication methods?

Is the worker able to relate to children on their terms?

Might it be appropriate to set up infant observation sessions?

IS THE FAMILY BEING INTERVIEWED TOGETHER, WHEN APPROPRIATE?

Are the parents being seen together if appropriate – even if they are separated?

Are any other family members included? They may have crucial information.

Are the parent/s and children being seen together? Are they seen at the office or at home, or both?

Are there some family members who should not be seen together, because to do so would place the child at risk of suffering harm?

WHO ELSE IS INVOLVED AND HOW ARE THEY WORKING WITH THE FAMILY?

Is the health visitor involved? What methods is he or she using?

Is the school involved? How are they approaching the assessment? Is there a Special Educational Needs Statement in relation to the child/ren?

Is the youth offending team involved? Have they prepared an assessment profile (ASSET) or a risk of harm assessment?

If a child has a parent who is in prison, have the probation and prison service been contacted?

Are other 'specialists' involved who may be better placed to assist with issues of identity, communication, interpreting, etc.?

Is there a role for a specialist assessment, for example, by a child psychiatrist, child psychotherapist, child psychologist, educational psychologist, NSPCC or Family Service Unit?

Is there a place for using specific assessment questionnaires and scales? (See Department of Health, Bentovim and Cox 2000c). Who is best placed to use these?

IS THE ASSESSMENT BEING RECORDED?

Is the worker organised and methodical about recording?

Is there adequate administrative support?

Is the information being collated as part of the process?

Is the recording accurate and reflective of the actual work being undertaken?

Is the amount of recording compatible with the scale of the assessment?

If required, is a report for court under way?

Factors that impact on the assessment process: issues for supervisors

Subjectivity

The supervisor should be alert to reactive behaviour. This is behaviour that is a response by the worker to some of the hidden processes within the work, rather than to the actual facts generated. This can cause:

- distortion of judgement
- stereotyping of individuals (within the family or the professional network)
- a 'fixed idea' about the situation
- over-cynicism or
- over-optimism about the family.

All these are common reactive processes.

Staff stress and morale

Account should be taken of levels of staff stress, both personal, team or organisational. If the individual is preoccupied with personal difficulties these may be triggered by the present situation and block or distort professional perception, or may cause the worker to become disengaged and withdrawn from the process. If the team or the organisation is facing change or reorganisation, or has experienced a recent inspection or case review, then this is likely to have an impact on staff morale. The adoption of the Assessment Framework may raise anxieties for workers and supervisors alike. Stress and low morale can have a dangerous impact on the assessment process.

A checklist approach

The use of checklists of risks of significant harm indicators undeniably has its attractions as it gives the worker a sense of security and helps structure thinking about the complex life of families. However, dependence on checklists or tools to aid judgement can lead to an over-emphasis on risk and incidence at the expense of making a holistic assessment of need. On the other hand, a careful use of specific tools as part of the whole approach can be an advantage. As is stated in the guidance, good tools cannot substitute for good practice, but good practice and good tools together can achieve excellence.

Sliding into therapy

This is a common pitfall in assessment work. It often occurs in a context where the team or the worker has a therapeutic ethos. The danger signals of a slide into therapy prior to completing a core assessment are: lack of purpose, no shared agreement with the family, no boundaries and no clear time-scales. The difficulty in spotting the pitfalls is that the skills involved in assessment are very similar to those required in therapeutic work and, in addition, the process of assessment should have a therapeutic component, which is to the service user's advantage. The boundaries of assessment and therapy are permeable, but it is important to be clear which mode one is working in at any one point in time.

Assessment and no planned intervention

This can occur in a context where there is a specialist assessment team working to a commissioning authority – usually a local authority social services team. The specialist team usually has greater resources to invest in the assessment than the commissioning authority has to invest in the services. Gibbons, Conroy and Bell (1995) found that in these circumstances recommendations were often not carried out; despite the effort and cost of assessments, they are often seen to carry little weight with professionals. Katz (1997) commented that 'if things are going relatively well at the end of the assessment, there is a tendency to "leave well alone" until the next crisis occurs and intervention becomes necessary'.

Unfocused work

There is a danger of unfocused assessment work becoming an end in itself. It can be detrimental as it 'confuses parents and carers who may feel under endless critical observation' (Department of Health 1995b). Unless there is a very clear, written agreement, parents and carers may have no idea about time-scales and be powerless to challenge the assessment process. Equally, if there is no agreement with those completing the assessment that specifies roles, responsibilities and the explicit relationship between assessment, planning and services, there is a risk that the assessment will lose its focus and children and families may disengage.

Summary

The supervisor has a key part to play in ensuring quality assessment work. Needless to say, the quality of supervision will depend on senior managers recognising that supervisors should have the time available and the support, guidance and backing to meet the supervisory needs of practitioners. In addition, supervisors need training in their own right, enabling them to develop the knowledge, values, skills and professional confidence required to undertake this complex task; their development needs are just as important as those of practitioners who carry out assessments.

Recommended reading

Brown, A. and Bourne, I. (1996) *The Social Work Supervisor.* Buckingham: Open University.

Morrison, T. (1993) *Staff Supervision in Social Care.* London: Longman.

Noakes, S. and Hearn, B. with Burton, S. and Wonnacott, J. (1998) *Developing Good Child Protection Practice: A Guide for First Line Managers.* London: National Children's Bureau.

Pritchard, J. (1995) (ed.) *Good Practice in Supervision.* London: Jessica Kingsley.

References

Department of Health (1995a) *The Challenge of Partnership in Child Protection: Practice Guide.* London: HMSO.

Department of Health (1995b) *Child Protection: Messages from Research.* London: HMSO.

Department of Health (1999) *The Government's Objectives for Children's Social Services.* London: Department of Health.

Department of Health, Department for Education and Employment and Home Office (2000a) *Framework for the Assessment of Children in Need and their Families.* London: The Stationery Office.

Department of Health (2000b) *Studies Informing the Framework for the Assessment of Children in Need and their Families.* London: The Stationery Office.

Department of Health, Bentovim, A. and Cox, A. (2000c) *The Family Assessment Pack of Questionnaires and Scales.* London: The Stationery Office.

Gadsby Waters, J. (1992) *The Supervision of Child Protection Work.* Avebury.

Gibbons, J., Conroy, S. and Bell, C. (1995) *Operating the Child Protection System: A Study of Child Protection Practices in English Authorities.* London: HMSO.

Harries, M. (1987) 'Discussion Paper on Social Work Supervision,' Western Australia Branch of the Australian Association of Social Workers.

Katz, I. (1997) *Current Issues in Comprehensive Assessment.* London: NSPCC.

Marsh, P. and Triseliotis, J. (1996) *Readiness to Practise? The Training of Social Workers in Scotland and their First Year of Work.* Aldershot: Avebury.

Morrison, T. (1993) *Staff Supervision in Social Care.* London: Longman.

Noakes, S. and Hearn, B. with Burton, S. and Wonnacott, J. (1998) *Developing Good Child Protection Practice: A Guide for First Line Managers.* London: National Children's Bureau.

Pont, C. (2000) 'Assessment Summary of Findings from Child Care Inspections (1992–97).' In *Studies Informing the Framework for the Assessment of Children in Need and their Families.* London: The Stationery Office.

Richards, M. and Payne, C. (1990) *Staff Supervision in Child Protection Work.* London: National Institute for Social Work.

Part III

Assessing the Developmental Needs of Children

CHAPTER 10

The Developmental Needs of Children

Implications for Assessment

Harriet Ward

Children have a range of different and complex developmental needs, which must be met during different stages of childhood if optimal outcomes are to be achieved.

(From the *Framework for the Assessment of Children in Need and their Families*, p.101, 1.36)

In this chapter consideration is given to the following:

- who are children in need?

- the seven dimensions of children's developmental needs

- the relationship between the *Framework for the Assessment of Children in Need and their Families* and the *Looking After Children* Assessment and Action Records

- resources to assist effective assessment of children in need.

Introduction: towards a *Framework for the Assessment of Children in Need and their Families*

Under the Children Act 1989, local authorities are required to 'safeguard and promote the welfare of children within their area who are in need by providing a range and level of services appropriate to those children's needs' (section 17). But which children are 'in need'? Judged by commonly accepted indicators of deprivation, potentially vast numbers of children could fit this category. For instance, about 3.5 million children are being brought up in families dependent on income support; about 2.4 million are living in single-parent families; about 360,000 have impairments or other special needs.

As Rose points out in Chapter 2, it is clear from the Children Act 1989 (section 17(10)) that not all children who are disadvantaged are necessarily 'in need': the term applies only to those whose vulnerability is such that they are unlikely to reach a satisfactory standard of health and development, or their health and development will be significantly impaired without the provision of services. Many children living in extremely difficult family circumstances receive sufficient support from parents, friends, relatives and the wider community to compensate for potential disadvantage and are not thought to require additional services from a local authority.

It can be argued that the primary purpose of providing child welfare services is to support families in responding to children's needs as they grow towards adulthood, with the aim of promoting their satisfactory development. At a very basic level, all children have similar developmental needs, such as for food, clothing, shelter, intellectual stimulation and social interaction; we know that children are more likely to achieve a satisfactory standard of development if these needs are met, usually by parents, but with additional support from universally available services such as those provided by doctors, teachers, and so on. However, some children have extensive special needs which cannot be adequately met without their families receiving additional services. Other families require additional support from social services because the circumstances of the parents are such that they cannot meet their children's needs without extra assistance: it is these children who, according to the terms of the Children Act 1989, are 'children in need' (see Ward 1998).

The *Framework for the Assessment of Children in Need and their Families* (Department of Health *et al.* 2000) is designed to help professionals adopt a common approach to deciding whether a child is in need and how best to respond to the identified needs. The domain of 'child developmental needs' identifies the seven dimensions along which children must progress if they are to achieve long-term wellbeing in adulthood; within each of these dimensions, children's needs must be met either by themselves as they grow older, or by parents or parent figures, whose capacity can be separated out into six further dimensions. Learning disability, mental illness or alcoholism can inhibit parental capacity, as is demonstrated in Chapters 17 and 18. Other factors within the parents' and child's immediate social and physical environment can either enhance or inhibit both parental capacity and children's successful development: these form the third domain which an assessment should consider. The *Framework for the Assessment of Children in Need and their Families*, therefore, offers a structure which should make it easier for social workers to:

- distinguish between those families which do and those which do not require additional assistance

- identify those areas of need and parental capacity which can benefit from the provision of specific services to enhance children's health and development

- evaluate the outcomes of such services in terms of their potential or perceived impact on children's developmental progress.

A standardised approach to the assessment of developmental need

The *Framework for the Assessment of Children in Need and their Families* takes further some of the thinking that went into the development of the *Looking After Children* (LAC) Assessment and Action Records used for identifying and meeting the needs of children looked after by the local authority. The latter are based on a theoretical model whose relevant features are that:

- all children need to progress across a spectrum of development if they are to achieve satisfactory wellbeing in adulthood

- they will make satisfactory progress only if their developmental needs are met

- attempts to evaluate the outcomes of services should not only take account of children's developmental progress, but also the extent to which they have been offered experiences that are relevant to success (Parker *et al.* 1991).

The spectrum of development along which children progress can be broken down into seven interlocking dimensions.

- *Health*: includes growth and development as well as physical and mental wellbeing. Children's health needs are more likely to be met if, for instance, they are taken to the doctor when they are ill, and receive dental and optical care; if they are given an adequate, nutritious diet; if younger children receive immunisations and developmental checks, and if older children and teenagers are given appropriate advice about issues such as sexual behaviour, smoking, alcohol consumption and substance abuse.

- *Education*: covers all areas of cognitive development from birth onwards. Children's education needs are more likely to be met if, for instance, they have frequent opportunities to play and interact with other children; if they have access to books; if they are given opportunities to acquire a range of skills and interests; if those with special educational needs receive appropriate support at school; if an adult is interested in the child's educational activities.

- *Identity*: concerns the child's growing sense of self as a separate and valued being. Children make successful progress on this dimension if they become confident about themselves and their abilities, if they feel accepted by their family and by the wider society, and if they develop a strong sense of their own individuality and a positive view of their abilities. Children's needs on this dimension are more likely to be met if, for instance, they encounter positive role models of their own gender and culture; if they are frequently praised and encouraged; if parents and parent figures are open about relationships within the family, such as the presence of a step-parent or an adopted child.

- *Family and social relationships*: involve the child's ability to make friends and get on with other people. Although younger children's relationships with parents and parent figures may be central to their development along this dimension, the quality of friendships with peers will become increasingly important. Children's needs on this dimension are more likely to be met if they experience a stable family life, with changes of carer kept to the minimum; if they are given opportunities to socialise and are encouraged to bring friends home; if parents and parent figures show appropriate physical affection.

- *Social presentation*: concerns children's growing understanding of the way in which their appearance and behaviour are perceived by the outside world. This area of development is often undervalued, yet it is of central importance; the primary concern is that children should learn to pick up messages about the impression they are creating, not necessarily that they should feel forced to conform. Their needs on this dimension are more likely to be met if parents take an interest in children's appearance and make sure that they are reasonably clean, pay attention to personal hygiene and are appropriately dressed, bearing in mind their age, gender, culture and religion; if children have opportunities to learn that behaviour and appearance can be adjusted to different situations; if teenagers feel able to ask for (though not necessarily accept) advice about appropriate ways of presenting themselves on important occasions such as job interviews.

- *Emotional and behavioural development:* concerns the appropriateness of response in children's feelings and actions, initially to parents and parent figures and increasingly to others beyond the family. It includes children's growing ability to adapt to change, to respond appropriately to stress and to demonstrate self-control. It also covers children's ability to empathise with others and to 'pick up' social signals. Development will be affected by the nature and quality of children's early attachments and also by the temperament of the individual child. Children's needs on this dimension are more likely to be met if they are given the security of consistent boundaries within a context of emotional warmth and approval.

- *Self-care skills:* the competencies, both practical and emotional, that all children and young people need to acquire if they are to achieve independence in adulthood. Children's needs on this dimension are more likely to be met if they are encouraged to acquire appropriate self-care skills from a very early age: parents can, for instance, help toddlers to learn how to dress and feed themselves; older children need opportunities to learn how to cross roads safely and to use public transport; young people approaching independence need to learn how to cook and to manage a budget.

All children need to progress along all seven of these dimensions if they are to achieve long-term wellbeing in adulthood. Even though, for instance, one might be more concerned if a fifteen-year-old were having difficulty in establishing a strong sense of identity than if the same were true of a three-year-old, if children's needs in this and every dimension are not met from an early age, they will be increasingly likely to experience difficulties as they grow up.

Similarly, progress along all of these dimensions is important for all children, regardless of their race, culture or ability. Children who experience discrimination because, for instance, they come from a minority ethnic group or have an impairment may require additional support to develop a positive sense of self-esteem; those with learning disabilities may have different educational objectives from their peers; those with physical disabilities may require extra support in the acquisition of self-care skills. Nevertheless, evidence of progress across the complete range of dimensions is inherent to the successful development of all children.

Within each dimension it is possible to identify specific objectives and to match these with the parental tasks required to help children achieve them. Both objectives and tasks will change as children progress from birth to adulthood. Thus health objectives for a two-year-old might be that he or she is thriving and reasonably protected against common childhood accidents; for the same child at fifteen, the objectives might be that his or her weight is within normal limits for his or her height and that he or she does not put his or her health at risk by smoking, drug or alcohol abuse or unprotected sex. Parents can help to meet the health needs of a two-year-old by, for instance, making sure that he or she has an adequate, nutritious diet and by keeping medicines and household poisons out of reach. At fifteen, similar support might be provided by encouraging the young person to avoid unhealthy food and to take exercise, and by making sure that he or she is adequately informed about the potential consequences of behaviours that can jeopardise his or her health.

Although each child will progress at a different pace, it is nevertheless possible to group children into six age bands that mark different stages of psycho-social development: under one, 1–2; 3–4; 5–9; 10–14, and 15 and over. The unequal spans demonstrate the unevenness of children's development, which progresses particularly rapidly in all dimensions in the early years. Although the cut-off points mark progression from one stage of development to another, and cover issues such as those defined in Chapter 17, they also reflect socially determined requirements imposed externally on children by, for instance, the education system.

How the *Framework for the Assessment of Children in Need and their Families* relates to the *Looking After Children* (LAC) Assessment and Action Records

The LAC Assessment and Action Records were developed for use with children looked after away from home. At the time of their construction it was assumed that the various regulations would ensure that children cared for by the local authority would be living in a reasonably safe and hygienic environment and looked after by adults who were free from difficulties, such as mental illness or drug addiction, which might jeopardise their caring or parenting capacity. This is not the place to consider how far this assumption was justified; however, we do know that the presence of such factors is likely to have a significant effect on parents' capacity to respond to children's needs.

The *Framework for the Assessment of Children in Need and their Families* builds on the thinking behind the LAC Assessment and Action Records by linking the capacity of parents or parent-substitutes to perform those tasks necessary to promote children's successful development to those factors within their own or the child's circumstances, or the wider family and environment, that promote or inhibit their ability to do so. The key factors in the family and environment domain – income, employment, housing; the family's history, functioning and integration; the support or lack of it from the wider family and the resources available within the community – are all considered in depth in Chapter 3. The key factors in the parenting capacity domain – basic care; ensuring safety; emotional warmth; stimulation; guidance and boundaries and stability – are explored in Chapter 16. The effect that these factors have on the extent to which children's developmental needs are met is well documented (see for instance Cleaver, Unell and Aldgate 1999). It is evident, for instance, that parents who are living in acute poverty have difficulty in providing basic care in the form of nutritious food or adequate housing, and that this has a detrimental effect on children's long-term health chances; parents who feel themselves isolated may find it difficult to promote children's friendships, and so on. Factors within the environment may also exacerbate parents' difficulties, making them more prone to problems such as alcoholism, domestic violence or mental illness, which, as Cleaver points out in Chapter 17, further inhibit their capacity to promote children's wellbeing. The research by Moyers and Mason (1995), was able to demonstrate that the greater the combination of circumstances that served to weaken parenting capacity, the more likely were children to be 'in need'. It is the purpose of the Assessment Framework to provide a structure that will enable practitioners to identify systematically those factors which may obstruct children's successful development, assess whether there are sufficient strengths within the family or the wider community to mitigate the potential effects of adversity, and to decide which services might be required to safeguard and promote the welfare of the child.

Is the Assessment Framework applicable to all children?

We know that each child is unique. His or her experience will be determined by a vast diversity of cultural expectations, family situations and living conditions. How can we be sure that the Assessment Framework will be of use in helping professionals assess the needs of any child?

In 1993, in response to initial doubts that the LAC Assessment and Action Records set the expectations of parents too high, the *Looking After Children* research team tested them with a representative sample of 400 children living at home, in order to find out how far the contents represent the preoccupations and needs of ordinary families. They found that the seven dimensions of development are almost universally recognised as the key areas in which children need to progress if they are to achieve satisfactory wellbeing in adulthood. Within each dimension almost all parents, from all walks of life, hold similar, basic, age-related objectives for their children. Moreover, the vast majority of parents are aware of the type of experiences that children require if they are to meet these objectives. The difference lies in parents' ability to make use of this knowledge (Moyers and Mason 1995).

So far, therefore, we know that the dimensions of development covered by the Assessment Framework are relevant to all children. We also know that environmental factors can seriously affect children's long-term wellbeing (see Page, forthcoming). The relationship between areas of parenting and children's wellbeing is also well known, although the specific dimensions of parenting capacity identified in the framework have yet to be tested out; the various parenting tasks identified as necessary in the LAC Assessment and Action Records can, however, be categorised in this way as illustrated in the work of the Department of Health and Cleaver (2000).

One final question remains: are there some children who have needs that cannot be identified through the Assessment Framework? Will we find, for instance, that the framework fails to address issues that are relevant to the culture of children from minority ethnic groups because it is has been created to assess the needs of a different, mainstream society? Will we also find that the assumption that all children have similar developmental requirements is inappropriate when assessing the needs of those with multiple disabilities?

Children from minority ethnic groups

The framework addresses the very fundamental needs that all children hold in common. As outlined in the guidance, all children, whatever their racial background, have the same inherent developmental needs; however, the effects of racism may mean that black children growing up in a pre-dominantly white society may require different services to counteract additional disadvantage. Different cultural groups may also meet children's developmental needs in different ways: parents in pre-literate societies may help children develop their language skills by telling stories rather than by reading to them; patterns of attachment may be different from those of nuclear families in cultures with strong kinship networks. The Assessment Framework is, nevertheless, likely to address sufficiently fundamental issues to avoid the charge of cultural specificity: all children need to grow, to learn to communicate, and to develop attachments: at this very basic level it is the manner in which these needs are met rather than the needs themselves that may differ from one culture to another. The application of the LAC Assessment and Action Records appears to confirm this view, for they have been used successfully with such culturally diverse populations as the Aboriginal peoples of Western Australia and the Inuit of Labrador, as well as many other majority and minority ethnic groups in Britain, Canada, Australia, Sweden, Russia and Hungary.

Disabled children

There are also obvious issues to be addressed concerning the extent to which a methodology based on a concept of normative development can be applicable to children with extensive disabilities, whose progress may be very different from that of their peers. However, attempts to identify different stages of development or different objectives for some children do not necessarily solve the problem. It would be valuable to develop criteria that would help social workers identify those children whose disability is so severe that normative measures are inappropriate in every area of develop-ment; however, few children will be included in this category. Moreover, the range of disability is so extensive that alternative indicators would only be applicable to very small groups of children; numerous subsets would be necessary, causing further difficulties in determining how children might be grouped. Second, providing a separate methodology for disabled children undermines the now widely accepted principle that such children are 'children first'; to regard them as having different needs and objectives from their peers could be regarded as discriminatory in that it would encourage practitioners to collude with the assumption that, because disability prevents children from progressing in some areas of development, it will restrict them in every area. It is, for instance, inappropriate to assess the overall development of children with learning disabilities by using measures designed for children of a much younger age, for, although their cognitive development may be restricted, their physical development may not, and issues such as maturational changes at adolescence will need to be addressed at the appropriate chronological age. The seven dimensions of development are important for all children, regardless of ability. The challenge is to offer a methodology that allows assessors to set different objectives for those areas of development that will be unavoidably restricted by the disability of a child, to ensure that additional experiences are offered by parents or parent figures in those areas where disability might otherwise restrict progress, and to use normative measures in those areas which are unaffected.

Resources to assist effective assessment of children in need

As indicated in the *Framework for the Assessment of Children in Need and their Families*, practice materials are being developed at national and local level to assist practitioners systematically to collect and analyse information in order to make decisions regarding children in need. Some materials currently being developed are considered below.

Inter-agency materials

One of the primary aims of the Assessment Framework is to ensure that families are not subject to a barrage of overlapping assessments undertaken by a range of professionals, all of whom may reach different conclusions. To this purpose, in some authorities, multidisciplinary assessment materials are currently being developed by a consortium of agencies which are seeking to identify common standards to be used by a range of professionals in identifying children who are (or are not) 'in need'.

Tools such as the Children and Family Assessment Forms currently being developed and piloted in North Lincolnshire ask child welfare professionals to translate information about deficits in children's experiences and progress into indicators of different levels of concern. Concerns may arise from factors within the child's physical environment, or from parenting difficulties or children's special needs within any of the seven dimensions of development. Indicators of mild concern are unlikely to have a significant effect on the child's development, but might suggest that families could make greater use of universally available services. Indicators of moderate concern are those which could result in a child being 'unlikely to achieve or maintain or to have the opportunity of achieving or maintaining a reasonable standard of health or development without the provision of services. Indicators of serious concern are those which could result in a child's health or development being significantly impaired or further impaired, without the provision of services. For instance, in terms of the educational dimension, an assessment of a 9-year-old might reveal mild concerns if no one attends school parents' evenings, moderate concerns if there is no contact between the school and the child's family, and serious concerns if the child is not sent to school. Additional concerns might be raised if, for instance, a child with an identified learning disability is not receiving extra assistance, or if a child with no apparent disability is not learning to read, write and count.

The materials do not help agencies decide what will be an acceptable or reasonable standard of development. Thresholds change over time, and are to some extent determined by local eligibility criteria. However, they are intended to ensure that all professionals who are asked to identify families in need use a common language and the same criteria, and to prevent cases which might be more appropriately supported by health authorities, education departments, voluntary agencies and so on from being automatically referred to social services. (Ward, forthcoming).

Age-related assessment records for children in need

Where social services may be required to provide long-term or complex packages of support, a core assessment should be completed. As with the initial assessment, professionals will need to consider children's experience and progress in each of the seven dimensions of development; particular attention will need to be given to the interplay between those factors in both the children's and the parents' circumstances which can diminish life chances, and those compensatory elements such as the presence in the household of a concerned and capable adult who might protect the child from disadvantage.

Similar in concept to the LAC Assessment and Action Records, the Assessment Recording Forms (Department of Health and Cleaver 2000) are intended to help social workers make detailed assessments of parents' capacity to respond appropriately to children's needs within each of the areas of development. The attention of those completing the records is drawn to relevant research evidence, included in order to help social workers contextualise their observations and to make clear to children and parents some of the evidence on which professional judgements are made. The records require social workers to complete a methodical and detailed assessment procedure that is designed to ensure that identified needs are matched with appropriate provision from both adult and children's services.

Questionnaires and scales

These records can be complemented by more specialist instruments, such as those which were piloted by social workers in some local authorities. The Strengths and Difficulties Questionnaire, the Parenting Daily Hassles Scale, the Adult Wellbeing Scale and the Home Circumstances Scale (Department of Health *et al.* 2000) are designed to provide detailed, objective, structured information that will help practitioners approach with greater confidence complicated issues such as whether adults or children require referral to mental health services, whether family relationships are such as to require specialist intervention, or whether the housing or immediate environment pose a threat to children's wellbeing.

Summary

The guidance itself and the tools produced to assist social services departments and other child welfare agencies to assess children in need will inevitably necessitate revisions to the Assessment and Action Records and other Looked After Children materials. The long-term aim is to produce a unified system for assessing children's needs and the extent and nature of additional services required to support parents, parent figures, families, the community and their immediate environment in ensuring that they are met. The outcomes of such services will be assessed whether children are supported at home or placed in care or accommodation as a way of meeting their needs.

Recommended reading

Ward, H. (ed.) (1995) *Looking After Children: Research into Practice.* London: HMSO.

Rose, W. and Ward, H. (forthcoming) *Approaches to Needs Assessment in Children's Services.* London: Jessica Kingsley.

Jackson, S. and Kilroe, S. (1996) *Looking After Children: Good Parenting, Good Outcomes: A Reader.* London: HMSO.

References

Cleaver, H. (forthcoming) 'Assessing children's needs and parents' responses.' In W. Rose and H. Ward. *Approaches to Needs Assessment in Children's Services.* London: Jessica Kingsley.

Cleaver, H., Unell, I. and Aldgate, J. (1999) *Children's Needs – Parenting Capacity: The Impact of Parental Mental Illness, Problem Alcohol and Drug Use, and Domestic Violence on Children's Development.* London: The Stationery Office.

Department of Health, Department for Education and Employment and Home Office (2000) *Framework for the Assessment of Children in Need and their Families.* London: The Stationery Office.

Department of Health and Cleaver, H. (2000) *Assessment Recording Forms.* London: The Stationery Office.

Department of Health, Cox, A. and Bentovim, A. (2000) *The Family Assessment Pack of Questionnaires and Scales.* London: The Stationery Office.

Moyers, S. and Mason, A. (1995). 'Identifying standards of parenting.' In H. Ward (ed.) *Looking After Children: Research into Practice.* London: HMSO.

Page, R. (forthcoming) 'Towards Social Exclusion: Can Childhood Disadvantages be Overcome?' In W. Rose and H. Ward. *Approaches to Needs Assessment in Children's Services.* London: Jessica Kingsley.

Parker, R., Ward, H., Jackson, S., Aldgate, J. and Wedge, P. (eds.) (1991) *Looking After Children – Assessing Outcomes in Child Care.* London: HMSO.

Rose, W. and Ward, H. (forthcoming) *Approaches to Needs Assessment in Children's Services.* London: Jessica Kingsley.

Ward, H. (1998) 'Using a Child Development Model to Assess the Outcomes of Social Work Interventions with Families.' In *Children and Society, 12,* 3, pp.202–11.

Ward, H. (forthcoming) 'An Inter-agency Approach to Needs Assessment.' In W. Rose and H. Ward. *Approaches to Needs Assessment in Children's Services.* London: Jessica Kingsley.

CHAPTER 11

Promoting Positive Outcomes for Children in Need

The Assessment of Protective Factors

Robbie Gilligan

The self-esteem of children ... is critical to the outcome of longer term interventions. Good experiences are important when many other aspects of family life may be in chaos or problems feel insurmountable.

(From the *Framework for the Assessment of Children in Need and their Families,* p.57, 4.20)

The following issues are considered in this chapter:

- sources of vulnerability in children
- variables that influence outcomes for children
- children's development and the importance of turning points
- identifying protective and harmful factors in the child's life
- security, self-esteem and self-efficacy as qualities that enhance resilience
- community resources as protective factors
- messages for assessment practice.

Introduction

> Successful children [who do well despite adversity] remind us that children grow up in multiple contexts – in families, schools, peer groups, baseball teams, religious organisations, and many other groups – and each context is a potential source of protective as well as risk factors. These children demonstrate that children are protected not only by the self-righting nature of development, but also by the actions of adults, by their own actions, by the nurturing of their assets, by opportunities to succeed and by the experience of success.

> (Masten and Coatsworth 1998, p.216)

These observations on resilient development from two American researchers remind us of the different influences on children's development that are reflected in the *Framework for the Assessment of Children in Need and their Families* (Department of Health *et al.* 2000).

The quote also highlights the many protective forces that may be at work or waiting to be tapped, even in the most unpromising circumstances. Professionals working with children at risk of significant harm tend to be preoccupied with deficits and pathology in children, their social experience, their care-givers or their social environment. We are good at asking what is wrong, or who or what seems to be causing the wrong. We are less good at asking what is going well, and who is available who could help the child. Comparatively little attention is paid to assets and strengths which may be present within the child's own profile or their family or social context. Too often professionals are prone to think of help coming in the form of professional intervention and services. We may too easily underestimate the healing potential that may lie naturally within children, in their normal daily experience or their social networks. Instead we may be drawn excessively and prematurely to professional and clinical responses which may not engage the child, or may not resolve the problem (or may aggravate it) or, worst of all, may discourage interest by natural network members who may be left feeling irrelevant, marginalised or de-skilled.

This chapter considers some of the key concepts relevant to understanding what promotes resilience in children in need, and explores the implications for assessment.

Vulnerability and resilience

Children's day-to-day functioning and their development over time are shaped by the balance between harmful and protective factors in their lives.

In assessing vulnerability and resilience in a child, it is important to consider both qualities in terms of the three domains of the Assessment Framework: the child, the parental context, and the wider social world surrounding both child and family. As outlined in Table 11.1, a range of sources of vulnerability and resilience exists in each domain which may influence the outcome for children; a number of factors can have an important bearing on the impact of an adverse experience on a child, and these include:

CHILD	
Sources of Vulnerability	**Sources of Resilience**
young age	higher IQ
disability	good attachment
earlier history of abuse	good self-esteem
	good relationship with sibling
PARENT/CARER	
Sources of Vulnerability	**Sources of Resilience**
domestic violence	social support
serious substance misuse	positive parental childhood
chronic serious psychiatric illness	good parental health
	education
	workrole
FAMILY AND ENVIRONMENT	
Sources of Vulnerability	**Sources of Resilience**
run-down neighbourhood	committed adult
poor relationship with school	good school experience
weak fabric of social support	strong community
poverty	good services/supports
social isolation	

Table 11.1 Potential sources of vulnerability and resilience in terms of the three domains of the Assessment Framework.

Timing

The timing of an adverse experience may have an important bearing on its impact on a child's development. It is increasingly being suggested, for example, that traumatic early experiences through maltreatment may have a very disruptive and long-term impact on brain development, and on the child's processing of experiences and general functioning (Perry and Pollard 1998).

Isolation

Turning to particular negative factors which may have special significance in terms of resilience, it is important to be wary of circumstances where children seem to be isolated from both support and natural surveillance of their daily care and circumstances. Overt sources of vulnerability may come readily to mind: abuse in all its forms, neglect, domestic violence; parents' substance misuse or serious psychiatric illness; the absence of natural supports in the child's or the family's daily life. But there are more covert sources of vulnerability: for example, the family who by choice or default is socially isolated. Social isolation cuts off potential support and removes the child from easy view and unobtrusive surveillance. Social isolation can arise for various reasons which may include parental depression, defensiveness or distrust. Helpers may find themselves distanced by the family, a cause for concern where families have given cause for serious child protection concerns (Reder *et al.* 1993). It is also important to remember that a child may be isolated from help not only by the family's situation, but by young age or disability which could prevent the child from articulating his or her concern. In such circumstances, adverse characteristics of the child and the family and the wider social context may all contribute to a cumulative, and therefore worrying, vulnerability.

Gender and minority status

Other factors may complicate the ability of professionals or concerned adults to read the signs correctly: for example, a young person's gender or minority ethnic status. A boy may find it harder than a girl to discuss or have recognised his sexually abused status. Cultural differences may make it harder for a girl from a minority group to report her emotional abuse or to have it recognised as such by professionals insufficiently versed in the behavioural cues of a certain culture. It is important to acknowledge that children from minority groups are not necessarily more vulnerable than other children, and there may be features of their cultural background which tend to envelop the child within a protective framework (Boushel 1994; Bachay and Cingel 1999).

Variables that influence outcomes for children

Negative experiences such as sexual abuse do not have the same impact on every child in the short or long term (Kendall-Tackett, Williams and Finkelhor 1993; Jones and Ramchandani 1999). Many variables influence the actual outcome for a given child. To take the example of sexual abuse: its impact on the child may be related to factors such as the age of the child; the balance of other harmful and protective factors; the child's intelligence and the child's own appraisal of the nature of the abuse experience and of his or her own responsibility. Abuse factors such as the nature, frequency, duration of abuse and the child's relationship to the abuser(s) will also influence the impact, as will the context in which the abuse occurs: for example, the level of support the child receives following disclosure, the extent of social stress in the household, and so on. A child performing well at school and socially with peers, and who is intelligent, has good social skills and has support from mother, teachers and friends may recover more readily from the experience of abuse, whereas a child who is less able, who finds school a struggle academically and socially and has little in the way of social support may be more likely to suffer long-term negative effects from sexual abuse.

In assessing the significance of harmful experiences and a child's capacity to recover, it is therefore important to look for strengths in the child's make-up and social circumstances (Kirby and Fraser 1997). It is often difficult to eliminate negative factors in a child's life – for example, a father's alcoholism, or parenting behaviour which is in some ways neglect-ful. But it may be possible to play to strengths in the way an intervention is framed. While we may not be able to eliminate any or all of the negative factors in a child's life, it may be possible to counteract or cushion the negative effects by inserting or strengthening countervailing protective factors. What may tilt the balance in a favourable direction may be a relationship with a committed adult, inside or outside the home (Jenkins and Smith 1990). Where home life is difficult, a concerned adult outside the home (relative or not) may prove to be a vital role model and source of hope and encouragement (Barker 1998).

Research suggests that adversity seems most debilitating when it comes in multiple forms. As adversities mount up – abuse or neglect, plus domestic violence, plus educational failure, plus family poverty – the cumulative negative impact really begins to bite (Rutter 1990). A build-up of stressors may, for example, have the effect of reducing IQ over time (Sameroff *et al.* 1993). It seems that children may be able to cope with one or two fairly serious adversities in their lives without too much ill effect, but, as the number of adversities rises to three or beyond, the development of young people begins to show serious strain. Happily there is evidence that cumulative protective factors work in the opposite direction – they may have disproportionately positive effects (Runyan *et al.* 1998). Thus the aim of intervention should be to reduce the number of problems and build the number of strengths so as to lower the net total of negative factors in a child's life. Reducing the accumulation of problem areas as a child grows up seems to reduce the risk of later problems (Stattin and Magnusson 1996). This suggests that even a small overall improvement within a child's situation may lend momentum to a virtuous rather than vicious spiral of change and development.

We now consider some aspects of children's development which may be important in understanding resilience in the face of adverse experience.

Pathways and turning points in development

Children may be said to follow a pathway of development as they grow up (Bowlby 1988). This can be a smooth upward curve if things are going well for them, but they may veer off course in a zig-zag fashion if there are too many negative forces in play. Small incidents may have long-term effects for good or ill. One positive experience may be a turning-point in a child's or young person's trajectory of development. This concept of turning-points is influential in thinking about child development (Clausen 1995). Getting on with a particular foster carer, learning more about an absent father, successful treatment of a mother's alcoholism, are examples of what might be key turning-points in a child's life. The idea of turning-points would seem to be a useful concept for those assessing the needs of children. From this perspective of pathways and turning-points, relatively small incidents can make a big difference. A single experience, a positive relationship, even if short-lived, may prove to be a turning-point. Everyday living may be peppered with mundane yet vital opportunities for healing and development for the child in need. Possible examples of this 'therapy on the hoof' might include an aunt whose warm concern reassures a child of his or her essential lovability, an art teacher who encourages a latent talent, or a grandparent who helps a child to have a more positive sense of personal and family history.

For those who remain doubtful that change can come in such simple forms, it is worth remembering that it is neither necessary nor possible to try to change everything in one single step. Systems thinking emphasises that even a small change in one part of the system has a ripple effect on the whole system. This may sound excessively optimistic or simplistic to some who may think that change requires something deeper or more complex. But the ripple effect of one strength being unearthed or harnessed may ultimately set off a positive spiral of change in the whole system that is the child's life. For those who are sceptical that such an approach has any relevance in tackling seemingly intractable problems, it is worth remembering that most such problems have acquired their intractability gradually, and that effective earlier intervention on perhaps a quite modest scale might have had the desired pre-emptive effect.

Secure base and a sense of belonging

As indicated in the dimensions used within the Assessment Framework, children need to feel a sense of belonging to people who matter to them and to whom they matter. This sense of belonging gives rise to a feeling of security in the child which promotes growth and exploration, safe in the knowledge that his or her needs will be responded to by the committed adult. The child can explore the world and new experience, safe in knowing that he or she can retreat to a secure base, to be comforted and protected in times of distress, and prepared for further adventures when ready (Bowlby 1988). The consistent and reliable responsiveness of people who constitute the child's secure base teaches the child that the world is fundamentally a safe place, that people can be trusted and that new experiences are worth trying.

To promote their development children need people who have a partisan commitment to their wellbeing. While primary attachments are likely to be with parents or parent-type figures it is now recognised that most children have a hierarchy of attachments of greater and lesser emotional significance involving others (Trinke and Bartholomew 1997) such as siblings, grandparents, aunts, uncles, neighbours, teachers, friends, sports coaches and so on (Gilligan 1999a). For a child with difficult home circumstances, these relationships may assume a special importance (Werner and Smith 1992). For example, relationships with siblings are especially significant where there is adversity and disharmony at home (Jenkins and Smith 1990). Similarly, it has been suggested that children may seek comfort in other areas of their lives (school, leisure-time interests, part-time workplace) when home life is stressful (Thiede Call 1996). Positive friendships may, for example, help some young people transcend the effects of chronic mal-treatment (Bolger, Patterson and Kupersmidt 1998).

It is important, therefore, that professionals who assess children's needs are alert to the potential protective value of relationships and contexts which go beyond parents and home, when considering the third domain of the Assessment Framework (family and environmental factors). This is not to relegate or dismiss the importance of parents and home (Gilligan 1999b). It is merely to recognise that in circumstances where home life and parent–child relationships are stressful, it should not be assumed that there are no alternative sources of support and solidarity for the child within naturally occurring social networks. The Eco-Map (Hartman 1995) and the Social Network Map (Tracy 1990) are two useful tools social workers can use to assist the child and the family to identify possible support network members, and their possible significance in terms of providing positive emotional and practical support for the young person.

Identity: promoting self-esteem and self-efficacy

As indicated in the *Framework for the Assessment of Children in Need and their Families*, children need a sense of self as a valued being. Acceptance by people whose relationships children value and the accomplishment of tasks they value contribute to their positive self-esteem, their sense of self-worth (Rutter 1990). Self-esteem is also linked to the important quality of self-efficacy, a belief in one's own competence and capacity to develop and follow through on (big or small) plans in life. Self-efficacy can be nurtured by successful rehearsal, positive expectation by caring adults, and consistent encouragement and support (Sandler *et al.* 1989). People with positive self-esteem and self-efficacy seem to be cushioned from the worst effects of adversities which may befall them (Rutter 1990). Thus it would seem that children can be protected not only by attachment-type relationships of varying intensity, as discussed by Howe in Chapter 12, but also by success, by their own standards, in tasks they value. Two arenas which are important in this regard are school and spare-time activities.

Community resources as protective factors

The value of positive school experience and achievements

Next to the family, school is by far the most important institution in the lives of children between five and sixteen years. Yet its contribution to children's lives can easily be overlooked by professionals (Gilligan 1998). It is important not just in terms of the educational needs and possible achievements of the child, but also as a rich source of social experiences and opportunities. It seems, happily, that the positive effects of school may be most evident where home circumstances are difficult (Rutter 1991). Within the school environment there are many contexts which can encourage (or hamper) the child's all-round development: classroom, playground, corridor, sports field, laboratory, art room, kitchen, assembly hall, restaurant, hobby rooms, and more. The school also offers a range of adults who may be responsive to promoting the welfare of children in need. These adults can serve as confidantes, mentors and monitors of the child's progress on the different fronts which school encompasses. Teachers can also serve as guarantors of the child's welfare, since their daily contact and professional perspective allow them to identify children's developmental needs (Gilligan 1998).

Importance of spare-time activities

An important arena for the development of the young person and potential protective factors lies in spare-time activities. Competence and achievement of recognition in activities have been shown to be protective for children with psychiatrically ill parents (Stiffman, Jung and Feldman 1986) or in disharmonious homes (Jenkins and Smith 1990). Such spare-time activities may embrace sport, cultural pursuits (expression and performance), the care of animals, environmental protection and part-time work. Spare-time activities may help to develop instrumental and social skills. A young person may, for example, learn how to relate to peers in a photography club. Social networks may be strengthened. New friends may be found through a shared interest, or a relationship may develop with an adult who, through his or her common enthusiasm, may take on a general mentoring role in the young person's life (Gilligan 1999b). Spare-time activities may enhance a child's sense of self-efficacy and self-esteem. A child may gain from the affirmation of an audience which warms to the quality of his or her musical or dance performances. Spare-time activities may give young people valuable additional role identities as committee member, team player, trainee, or worker. A multiplicity of such role identities is seen to be protective of a person's mental health (Thoits 1983). Spare-time activities can help to promote a sense of belonging and mattering to people who are important to the child, and who count for something in a context that is important to the child. They may help the young person's physical fitness.

Time may be filled and structure provided, and a precious sense of purpose in daily living be acquired.

Promoting resilience in pre-school children: pre-school programmes

Pre-school children need relationships in which they feel valued and are able to achieve if they are to develop a sense of self-efficacy. Protective factors may be found in nursery, playgroup or other pre-school programmes which they may attend. Opportunities for play and socialising with children of the same age may be important for developing social confidence and skills which may improve the prospects for later development of pro-social peer relationships in school.

Support from relatives may be especially important for the primary care-giver of young children (McGlone, Park and Smith 1998). Where the support of parents or other relatives is unavailable or problematic, other sources of help must be called upon. In such circumstances, while a care-giver may value the support of sympathetic professionals, it should be remembered that powerful support may also come from lay helpers, peers or volunteers (Johnson, Howell and Molloy 1993; Gilligan 1999a). Quality pre-school programmes with a strong and appropriately geared educational intent, and which are combined with education and training for the parent, seem very potent in improving the long-term prospects of a child growing up in adverse circumstances (Yoshikawa 1994).

Messages for practice

A resilience-led approach to assessing children in need emphasises a number of points. Focusing on positives and strengths in a child's life may help to improve outcomes. Looking for resources in the child's social network may yield enduring supports for the child. Little things can sometimes make a big difference. While home is very important, so too are school and spare-time activities as possible sources of opportunities for enhancing resilience. It seems likely that children will be more resilient to adverse circumstances if they have:

- supportive relationships with at least one parent
- supportive relationships with siblings and grandparents
- a committed adult other than a parent who takes a strong interest in the young person and serves as an ongoing mentor and role model

- a capacity to develop and reflect on a coherent story about what has happened and is happening to them
- talents and interests
- positive experience in school
- positive friendships
- a capacity to think ahead and plan in their lives.

What are the things that are going well in this child's life?

To whom is this child important?

Who is important to this child?

Who are the people who play a positive part in the child's life (at home, in the neighbourhood, school or further afield)?

In which fields can the child find a sense of achievement?

Is there a concerned adult outside the home who has very regular contact with the child?

Does the child have an adult outside the home whom he or she likes and trusts?

Has the child a realistic way of contacting this adult when necessary?

Has anyone discussed a fallback safety plan for an older child who may occasionally be at risk of harm due to episodes of parental substance misuse or domestic violence?

Do these adults have the confidence and know-how to look for help if they are worried?

Does the child relate fairly easily to peers of his or her own age (check this through adults who know the child well)?

Do there appear to be problems of bullying or being bullied (a possible indicator of other abusive experiences in the child's life)?

Does the child have hobbies and interests which are encouraged and supported?

How does the child get on in school socially as well as academically?

Has the school been briefed adequately on the child's home situation?

Has the school's special knowledge of the child been adequately tapped in assessing the child's developmental progress and vulnerability and strengths?

Does the primary care-giver have people he or she trusts and can rely on for help in moments of stress and crisis?

Does the care-giver have role identities beyond that of care-giver? (Is he or she a club member, employee, volunteer, friend, church member, etc?)

Does the care-giver have a record of using help well or of ambivalence or defensiveness in the face of help?

Has the care-giver had a chance to articulate his/her worries and views as part of the negotiation or formulation of a plan to address child protection and welfare concerns?

Table 11.2 Some key questions to assess sources of resilience as part of an assessment of children in need

Practitioners should be alert to fostering these qualities, opportunities and experiences where they can be found in a young person's life. It is especially important to avoid rupturing key relationships and social ties through placement moves or the like. In many ways the secret lies in nurturing children's sense of belonging and accomplishments, and in preserving positive threads in their lives. In working to build a young person's resilience, a well-rounded assessment is a good place to start. It is suggested that resilience-led questions should help to inform the assessment (see Table 11.2).

Since this chapter began with some wise words quoted from American researchers, perhaps it is good to end with some more wise words, this time from two other Americans on the issue of assessment:

> Assessment should focus not only on the risk factors in the lives of these [vulnerable] children but also on the protective factors. These include competencies and sources of informal support that already exist in the extended family, the neighbourhood, and the community at large and that can be utilized to enlarge a child's repertoire of problem-solving skills and self esteem and self efficacy.
>
> (Werner and Smith 1992, p.208)

Recommended reading

Daniel, B., Wassel, S. and Gilligan, R. (1999) *Promoting Child Development: a Guide for Child Care and Protection Workers*. London: Jessica Kingsley.

Gilligan, R. (1999) 'Working with Social Networks: Key Resources in Helping Children at Risk.' In M. Hill (ed.) *Effective Ways of Helping Children*. London: Jessica Kingsley.

Howe, D., Brandon, M., Hinings, D. and Schofield, G. (1999) *Attachment Theory, Child Maltreatment and Family Support. A Practice and Assessment Model*. Basingstoke: Macmillan.

Saleebey, D (ed.) (1997) *The Strengths Perspective in Social Work Practice*, Second Edition. White Plains, NY: Longmans.

Thompson, R. (1995) *Preventing Child Maltreatment through Social Support – A Critical Analysis*. Thousand Oaks, CA: Sage.

References

Bachay, J. and Cingel, P. (1999) 'Restructuring Resilience: Emerging Voices.' In *Affilia Journal of Women and Social Work, 14*, 2, 162–75.

Barker, G. (1998) 'Non-Violent Males in Violent Settings: An Exploratory Qualitative Study of Prosocial Low-Income Adolescent Males in Two Chicago (USA) Neighbourhoods.' In *Childhood, 5*, 4, pp.437–61.

Bolger, K., Patterson, C. and Kupersmidt, J. (1998) 'Peer Relationships and Self-Esteem among Children Who Have Been Maltreated.' In *Child Development, 69*, 4, pp.1171–97.

Boushel, M. (1994) 'The Protective Environment of Children – Towards a Framework for Anti-oppressive, Cross-cultural and Cross-national Understanding.' *British Journal of Social Work, 24*, 2, pp.173–90.

Bowlby, J. (1988) 'Developmental Psychiatry Comes of Age.' In *American Journal of Psychiatry, 145*, 1, pp.1–10.

Clausen, J. (1995) 'Gender, Contexts and Turning Points in Adult Lives.' In P. Moen, G. Elder and K. Lscher (eds.) *Examining Lives in Context-Perspectives on the Ecology of Human Development.* Washington DC: American Psychological Association.

Department of Health, Department for Education and Employment and Home Office (2000) *Framework for the Assessment of Children in Need and their Families.* London: The Stationery Office.

Gilligan, R. (1998) 'The Importance of Schools and Teachers in Child Welfare.' *Child and Family Social Work 3*, 1, pp.13–25

Gilligan, R. (1999a) 'Children's Own Social Networks and Network Members: Key Resources in Helping Children at Risk.' In M. Hill (ed.) *Effective Ways of Helping Children.* London: Jessica Kingsley.

Gilligan, R. (1999b) 'Enhancing the Resilience of Children and Young People in Public Care by Encouraging their Talents and Interests.' In *Child and Family Social Work, 4*, 3, pp.187–96.

Hartman, A. (1995) 'Diagrammatic Assessment of Family Relationship.' In *Families in Society: The Journal of Contemporary Human Services*, February, pp.111–22.

Jenkins, J. and Smith, M. (1990) 'Factors Protecting Children in Disharmonious Homes: Maternal Reports.' In *Journal of the American Academy of Child and Adolescent Psychiatry, 29*, 1, pp.60–9.

Johnson, Z., Howell, F. and Molloy, B. (1993) 'Community Mothers Programme: Randomised Controlled Trial of Non-professional Intervention in Parenting.' In *British Medical Journal*, 306, pp.1449–52.

Jones, D. and Ramchandani, P. (1999) *Child Sexual Abuse: Informing Practice from Research.* Abingdon: Radcliffe Medical Press.

Kendall-Tackett, K., Williams, L. and Finkelhor, D. (1993) 'Impact of Sexual Abuse on Children: A Review and Synthesis of Recent Empirical Studies.' In *Psychological Bulletin, 113*, 1, pp.164–80.

Kirby, L. and Fraser, M. (1997) 'Risk and Resilience in Childhood.' In M. Fraser (ed.) *Risk and Resilience in Childhood – An Ecological Perspective.* Washington, DC: NASW Press.

Masten, A. and Coatsworth, D. (1998) 'The Development of Competence in Favourable and Unfavourable Environments – Lessons from Research on Successful Children.' In *American Psychologist, 53*, 2, pp.205–20.

McGlone, F., Park, A. and Smith, K. (1998) *Families and Kinship.* London: Family Policy Studies Centre.

Perry, B. and Pollard, R. (1998) 'Homeostasis, Stress, Trauma, and Adaptation. A Neuro-developmental View of Childhood Trauma.' In *Child and Adolescent Psychiatric Clinics of North America, 7*, 1, pp.33–51, viii.

Reder, P., Duncan, S. and Gray. (1993) *Beyond Blame: Child Abuse Tragedies Revisited.* London: Routledge.

Runyan, D., Hunter, W., Socolar, R., Amaya-Jackson, D., English, D., Landsverk, J., Dubowitz, H., Browne, D., Bangdiwala, S. and Mathew, R. (1998) 'Children Who Prosper in Unfavourable Environments: The Relationship to Social Capital.' In *Pediatrics, 101*, 1, pp.12–18.

Rutter, M. (1990) 'Psychosocial Resilience and Protective Mechanisms.' Chapter 9 in J. Rolf, *et al. Risk and Protective Factors in the Development of Psychopathology.* Cambridge: Cambridge University Press, pp.181–214.

Rutter, M. (1991) 'Pathways from Childhood to Adult Life: The Role of Schooling.' In *Pastoral Care in Education,* September.

Sameroff, A., Seifer, R., Baldwin, A. and Baldwin, C. (1993) 'Stability of Intelligence from Preschool to Adolescence: the Influence of Social and Family Risk Factors.' In *Child Development, 64,* 80–97.

Sandler, I., Miller, P., Short, J. and Wolchik, S. (1989) 'Social Support as a Protective Factor for Children in Stress.' Chapter 12 in D. Belle (ed.) *Children's Social Networks and Social Supports.* New York: John Wiley, pp. 277–307.

Stattin, H. and Magnusson, D. (1996) 'Antisocial Development: A Holistic Approach.' In *Development and Psychopathology, 8,* 617–45.

Stiffman, A., Jung, K. and Feldman, R. (1986) 'A Multivariate Risk Model for Childhood Behaviour Problems.' In *American Journal of Orthopsychiatry, 56,* 2, 204–11.

Thiede Call, K. (1996) 'Adolescent Work as an Arena of Comfort Under Conditions of Family Discomfort.' In J. Mortimer and M. Finch (eds.) *Adolescents, Work, and Family – An Intergenerational Developmental Analysis.* Thousand Oaks CA: Sage.

Thoits, P. (1983) 'Multiple Identities and Psychological Well Being: A Reformulation and Test of the Social Isolation Hypothesis.' In *American Sociological Review, 48,* 174–87.

Tracy, E. (1990) 'Identifying Social Support Resources of At-risk Families.' In *Social Work, 35,* 3, 252–8.

Trinke, S. and Bartholomew, K. (1997) 'Hierarchies of Attachment Relationships in Young Adulthood.' In *Journal of Social and Personal Relationships, 14,* 5, 603–25.

Werner, E. and Smith, R. (1992) *Overcoming the Odds – High Risk Children from Birth to Adulthood.* Ithaca: Cornell University Press.

Yoshikawa, H. (1994) 'Prevention as Cumulative Protection: Effects of Early Family Support and Education on Chronic Delinquency and Its Risks.' In *Psychological Bulletin, 115,* 1, 28–54.

CHAPTER 12

Attachment

David Howe

Emotional and behavioural development – concerns the appropriateness of response demonstrated in feelings and actions by a child initially to parents and caregivers and, as the child grows older, to others beyond the family. Includes the nature and quality of early attachments

(From the *Framework for the Assessment of Children in Need and their Families,* p.19)

This chapter considers

- why attachments are important for the developmental wellbeing of the child

- the assessment of the care-giver as attachment figure

- attachment and the developmental needs of children

- assessment issues.

Introduction

Under the creative genius of John Bowlby, insights garnered from evolutionary theory, ethology, systems theory and developmental psychology were fashioned over a number of years into what is today known as attachment theory (Bowlby 1973; 1979; 1980). Attachment theory is a theory of personality development in the context of close relationships. If the quality of close relationships has a bearing on personality, emotional and social development, attachment theory should be of particular relevance and interest to child and family social workers (Howe *et al.* 1999). Relationship difficulties and concerns over social competence are key areas in which welfare agencies are involved when working with children and families. Through their interventions, social workers can improve the quality of family relationships as they seek to promote children's safety and welfare. An objective of intervention, for example, might be to improve parent–child relationships. In extreme cases practitioners might decide such relationships should be severed. Or new relationships, in the form of foster-carers or adopters, might be introduced. In all these family situations the quality and character of children's relationships with their carers and peers is fundamentally important to their developmental wellbeing, physically and psychologically, emotionally and behaviourally.

Different attachment styles and care-seeking behaviours represent different psychological and behavioural strategies developed by children to maximise the care and protection available under particular care-giving regimes. Children increase their chances of survival when they can mentally represent, in the form of an internal working model, the way their interpersonal world appears to work. In particular, they need to understand what increases and reduces the caring and protective responses of their care-givers. Children, including those who are maltreated and neglected, actively seek ways of adapting to their world rather than being victims of it (Crittenden 1996). Understanding children's behaviour as an adaptive strategy, developed in the context of their care giving environment, offers practitioners a powerful conceptual tool that links knowledge of a child's situation to making sense of it. An understanding of attachment theory, which can help practitioners organise what they know about children and carers, plays a key role in the making of judgements about children's welfare.

Attachment behaviour and the attachment bond

The human infant remains vulnerable for a number of years. If children are to survive into adulthood, it is important that they receive care and protection. Evolution therefore favours behaviours that increase young children's chances of survival. Attachment behaviours are a class of behaviours that serve this purpose. They include all those behaviours designed to get distressed infants into close proximity with their care-giver where they might expect to receive care and protection. An attachment bond refers to a tie that a child has to an individual (most often the main care-giver) who is perceived as stronger and wiser. The attachment bond is considered to exist consistently over time, whether or not attachment behaviour is present.

Furthermore, the presence of attachment behaviour does not necessarily indicate the existence of an attachment bond (Belsky and Cassidy 1994). Crying, clinging, following and smiling are among the most common attachment behaviours. Threats to children's wellbeing might come from a number of sources, including those that:

- are internal to the child (hunger, illness, pain)
- are external to the child (danger, threat, fear)
- imply the loss of the care giver, either physically, emotionally or psychologically.

Feeling vulnerable and in danger increases the child's distress and anxiety, which in turn trigger attachment behaviour. When children's attachment behaviour is not activated, their energies can be concentrated on learning about the world and their part in it. This is known as exploratory behaviour and includes play, curiosity, novelty-seeking, conversation and enquiry. Exploratory behaviour is incompatible with attachment behaviour. Care-giving relationships that fail to help children regulate states of arousal and distress, or are instrumental in bringing such states about, therefore inhibit exploratory behaviour. This is why attachment behaviour sustained at the expense of exploratory behaviour has an adverse affect on children's psychosocial development.

A series of observations made by Bowlby and Robertson in the early 1950s noted that young children separated from their mothers appeared to experience a recognisable sequence of highly distressed behaviours (Robertson and Bowlby 1952). The normal reaction shown by children when they are separated from their attachment figure for any length of time comprises three stages. Children's immediate reaction to the loss is to protest with inconsolable crying, sometimes coupled with attempts to find or follow the missing carer. This is followed by a period of despair, apathy and listlessness. And if the separation continues over several days or weeks, children typically enter a third phase of quiet detachment, withdrawal and an apparent lack of interest in the lost care-giver. In this final phase, there is the appearance of recovery, but play and relationships often have a perfunctory quality to them. Upon reunion with care-givers after a long separation, children might show a mixture of anger, crying, clinging and rejection.

Bowlby believed that babies form a strong bond with their primary care-givers which, if broken, causes great upset and distress. The phase of protest seems related to the anxieties children experience when they are separated from their care-giver. The second phase, despair, suggests a period of grief and mourning. And the final phase of detachment and denial is thought to indicate the operation of defence mechanisms as young children attempt to protect themselves against the psychological distress of losing a parent. In this last stage feelings of hurt, upset and anger often appear to be repressed.

Assessing parenting capacity

The responses of care-givers have also been shaped by evolution, although here the adult's experiences over his or her lifetime will modify the final quality and expression of the care-giving response. For example, adults' own experiences of being cared for might affect the way they deal with a distressed infant. Social workers need to understand the relationship history of carers if they are to make sense of their current relationship and care-giving style. To the extent that a parent's own care-giving problems are a product of their own history of being cared for, social workers need to be extra thoughtful about placing children with other family members, including their grandparents. This cautionary note is not meant to exclude such practices, but it does demand that the analysis and assessment of parents and their care-giving is conducted in the light of a full and well-understood family psychosocial history and should form part of the assessment of family history and functioning.

Care-giving responses are generally triggered when adults are faced with infant attachment behaviours. More generally, it is now recognised that even very young babies show a remarkable range of prosocial behaviours, many of which are highly effective in engaging parents and carers. Children's interest in others, indicated by smiles, vocalisation, looks of concentration and overall excitement, normally encourages adults to maintain contact. It is within these interactions that young children learn about themselves and others as emotional, psychological and interpersonal beings. However, if care-givers' interest in their children is either absent or hostile, this has been shown to have damaging developmental consequences.

The carer as attachment figure

An assessment using the *Framework for the Assessment of Children in Need and their Families* (Department of Health, *et al.* 2000), should include, as part of the assessment of emotional warmth, an assessment of the carer/s as attachment figures. There are a number of factors to consider, which are described below.

The formation of selective attachments

Over the first six to seven months, babies move from a general but relatively indiscriminate interest in other people (attachment-in-the-making) to an increasing preference for a limited number of familiar people who become that child's selective attachment figures. These figures are typically mother and father, but can include others such as grandmothers or older sisters if they are involved on a regular basis, and are hierarchically preferred (for example, a distressed child might go to her mother for comfort as a first choice, but be quite happy to approach her father in her mother's absence). By the age of three, children begin to develop a more sophisticated understanding of both their own and their carers' behaviour. They begin to see how things might appear from the other person's point of view. They are able cognitively to represent their carers' goals and plans and distinguish them from their own. This allows children to control and modify their own as well their attachment figures' behaviour. These new mental perspectives allow children to enter into a goal-corrected partnership with their carers. Discussion, sharing and negotiation become the preferred way of pursuing goals and conducting relationships.

However, if the interest and responsiveness of carers is weak, unreliable, hostile or confusing, not only do young children miss out on the stimulation of shared social interaction, they also experience the anxiety and distress associated with the loss of their attachment figure. Loss or separation from the care-giver means that he or she is not available to provide the care and protection that is the goal of the child's attachment behaviour. When children lose their care-giver or experience prolonged separation, their initial reaction is one of great upset and protest. However, such distress is very painful, and children have to defend themselves against the continued hurt. Various forms of withdrawal and detachment represent attempts by children to protect themselves against the pain of the loss or separation.

The loss or unavailability of the carer can be physical, psychological or emotional. The physical unavailability of a carer at key times of distress (when a child is hungry or alone and frightened) means that displays of attachment behaviour are unsuccessful in relieving upset and securing comfort and safety. As a consequence, emotional arousal mounts and remains unregulated. A special dilemma presents itself to children whose carers are physically present but psychologically unpredictable or unavailable. This is often the case where parents are suffering severe depression, are heavy abusers of drugs or alcohol, or are preoccupied with their own anxiety and distress (Lyons-Ruth 1996; Crittenden, Partridge and Claussen 1991). Here, uncertainties about the care-giver's ability or willingness to provide care and protection are the actual cause of the child's anxiety. Anxiety normally leads to an increase in attachment behaviour designed to bring the child into close, protective proximity with the care-giver. But in such cases, the person who causes the emotional distress is also the figure to whom the child would normally expect to turn to gain comfort and understanding. The distress experienced by children who suffer the dilemmas posed by neglect, abuse and emotional maltreatment places them at increased risk of a large number of negative developmental consequences.

Care-giving behaviour

Mary Ainsworth, who worked with Bowlby in the early years of her career, went on to recognise a number of dimensions of care-giving which should be considered as part of an assessment of parenting capacity:

1. Care-giving can be more or less sensitive and attuned to the physical and psychological condition of the baby. For example, insensitive carers might be very poor at reading and responding to children's signals of need and distress.

2. Degrees of acceptance or rejection may also be recognised. For example, some parents accept their babies, whatever the child's mood or behaviour. They also acknowledge that parenthood involves constraints on one's lifestyle. In contrast, rejecting care-givers often resent the demands that children make on them emotionally.

3. Care-giver–child relationships can be mapped in terms of levels of parental cooperation and interference. Carers who recognise, support and respect their babies' autonomy appear able to cooperate with their children's needs and accomplishments. Interfering and rejecting carers are less able to recognise, respect or enjoy the full range of their children's needs and behaviours.

4. Along the accessibility–ignoring scale, accessible carers remain alert and available to their infants. Carers who are prone to ignore their children continue to be absorbed in their own needs and pursuits, only engaging with their children when it suits them as adults.

Parents do not have to perform perfectly along these four care-giving dimensions all of the time. Rather, in Winnicott's neat phrase, they have to be good enough. Parents who provide reasonably warm, sensitive, responsive, interested, flexible, predictable and consistent care have children who develop secure attachments. Children experience their carers as emotionally and psychologically available at times of need. When young children become distressed, more often than not carers are able to soothe and comfort them very quickly. Such responses allow children to see themselves as both loved and effective at eliciting care and protection. Although very young children are not able to tolerate long separations from their attachment figures, with increasing age and cognitive development children can mentally represent their carers' availability and thus cope better with increasingly long absences. They learn to trust their carer as a physical and psychological resource. Language acquisition also helps children to understand that physical absence does not mean permanent abandonment. By the time children start school, they can cope with long periods of separation without anxiety.

Attachment and the developmental needs of the child

Internal working models

Within close relationships young children begin to develop mental representations, or internal working models, of their own worth based on other people's availability and their ability and willingness to provide care and protection (Ainsworth et al. 1978). The ability to model cognitively key aspects of the interpersonal environment increases both social understanding and effectiveness. In terms of achieving emotional and social competence, children need to generate mental representations of (i) the self, (ii) other people, and (iii) the relationship between self and others. It is within close relationships that young children learn about the self and others, feelings and behaviour, emotions and social interaction. Interacting with other people helps children to learn to understand themselves. And by understanding themselves, they can begin to make sense of other people and social relationships. Social empathy and understanding are highly important skills which children need to develop if they are to cope well with life. Children who make poor progress in these areas find the social world hard going.

Children who suffer frequent loss or changes of care-giver, for whatever reasons, are likely to find that their ability to trust and make sense of relationships and understand other people and themselves is upset. In situations of neglect and adversity, many children's most familiar and predictable relationships might have been with their siblings. In emotionally thin environments, children may be both providers and receivers of each other's care. The maintenance of sibling relationships, particularly in the case of looked-after children who are separated from their brothers and sisters, can be an important aspect of case management.

The formation and development of the internal working model explains how the quality of external relationships influences the quality of children's internal psychology. As attachment relationships become psychologically internalised, the quality of a child's social experiences becomes a mental property of the child. Attachment theory explains why close relationships matter, how they are developed, and how their qualities influence psychological experience, cognitive modelling and relationship styles. Over time, internal working models begin to organise experience rather than be organised by it. In this sense, mental modelling produces continuity in the way we behave, relate, feel and respond. Our personality begins to acquire a regular, enduring quality. We begin to expect certain things of ourselves and of others, while others feel that we are becoming more familiar and predictable to them. Fundamental, therefore, to the formation of the internal working model is the quality of the relationship between children and their selective attachment figures. Within each care-giving relationship, the self will be experienced as more or less lovable, interesting, effective, and worthy of care and protection. In short, the self will be experienced either positively or negatively. Similarly, children will experience their attachment figure as more or less emotionally available, responsive, sensitive, interested, and accepting. In short, other people will be viewed either positively or negatively.

Patterns of attachment

Based on empirical findings, four combinations of the way self and others are mentally modelled within the parent–child relationship have been identified:

1. Secure attachment patterns: children experience their care-giver as available, and themselves positively.

2. Ambivalent patterns: children experience their care-giver as inconsistently responsive, and themselves as dependent and poorly valued.

3. Avoidant patterns: children experience their care-givers as consistently rejecting, and themselves as insecure but compulsively self-reliant.

4. Disorganised patterns (often associated with children who have suffered severe maltreatment): children experience their care-givers as either frightening or frightened, and themselves as helpless, angry, and unworthy.

Each pattern is associated with a characteristic set of emotional and relationship behaviours across the lifespan. Recent work on adult attachments and the care-giving behaviour of parents recognises how internal working models and their associated attachment styles continue to affect behaviour, emotions and social relationships, particularly the demands of intimate relationships experienced in romantic partnerships and in parenthood. Insecure attachment styles in themselves are not pathological (indeed in some circumstances they can be highly functional), but most children and adults experiencing social, emotional and behavioural difficulties typically display pronounced insecure attachment behaviours of one kind or another.

Each attachment style is an adaptive response to the care-giving situation in which the child finds himself or herself. The behaviours make sense within the context of the particular care-giving relationship. The behaviours adopted are a defensive strategy developed by children to help them cope with feelings of distress and anxiety. Whatever the quality of the relationship, the attachment system is designed to bring children into proximity with their attachment figure, where ideally they will be comforted and understood. Even when care-givers are rejecting, neglectful or abusive, children have to develop behavioural and psychological strategies that attempt to ward off anxiety or in which they try to seek alternative ways of psychologically securing the attachment figure. It therefore has to be understood that even children whose parents are violent and abusive develop and show attachment behaviour, albeit of a distinctive, insecure kind. It is the type and quality of attachment behaviour that is of interest, and not its perceived presence or absence, strength or weakness. Only in extreme, special cases (institutional nurseries, profound neglect, multiple serial care-giving) might we expect to find children who show no attachment behaviour under conditions of distress and anxiety.

Attachment styles and children's behaviour

Research evidence shows that not only do different attachment styles develop as adaptive responses to particular care-giving regimes, but each style is associated with recognisable patterns of social and emotional behaviour. Although this is a complex field, typical patterns include the aggressive, attention-seeking, dependent and helpless behaviours shown by many children, classified as ambivalent. Their parents tend to be neglectful and inconsistent, both psychologically and physically. Family life is often chaotic, dramatic, crisis-ridden, emotionally competitive and enmeshed. At times of heightened helplessness, parents might threaten to leave their children – 'I'm going and you'll never see me again'; 'I'll kill myself and then you'll be sorry.' Referrals typically suggest that the children are out of control. Parents demand that they should be looked after by foster-carers, only to change their mind once the child has been removed. These cases generally have to be accepted as long-term. They make heavy demands on both the agency and its workers.

Many maltreated children who have suffered abuse and neglect are classified as disorganised in infancy, and avoidant or defended and controlling in later childhood. This category requires a great deal of careful and subtle analysis and includes a wide range of child-care concerns. It includes parentified children who anxiously find themselves compulsively caring for the carer whilst denying their own emotional needs. Children of very depressed parents or children of mothers who are being physically abused by their partner, for example, might show behaviours associated with this pattern.

Other children, who have suffered prolonged physical and sexual abuse, might lose all trust in other people as a source of care or protection. Parents who neglect their children as well as abuse them physically and emotionally are experienced as both unpredictable and dangerous (Crittenden 1995; 1996). They are left warily to defend themselves, psychologically and physically. For them, to be cared for by others represents danger. It is therefore safer to look after oneself; to control rather than be controlled. These are children who, in a sense, have survived danger and violence (they are still alive). They experience themselves as people who can generate anger and violence in others. These experiences produce a self that feels both powerful and bad, invulnerable yet unlovable. As a result disturbed mixtures of low self-esteem, recklessness, hyper-vigilance and aggression can appear (Crittenden 1996). These are children who have difficulty recognising and understanding their own and other people's affective states. They are unpopular with their peers. They easily attribute negative intentions to other people's behaviour. Levels of social understanding and competence are typically low for these children. As a result they show both high levels of aggression and social withdrawal. Many children who attack or sexually abuse other children and animals, who show extreme conduct disorders and perform very poorly educationally, can be understood within the logic and evidence that define these disorganised/controlling patterns of attachment (Cicchetti 1989; Crittenden 1996; Crittenden 1997; Lyons-Ruth 1996).

A developmental attachment perspective, supported by a good deal of international and cross-cultural research, can therefore help social workers to make sense of complex and turbulent cases in which there are concerns about the developmental wellbeing and safety of children (Howe 1995; Howe *et al.* 1999). The approach also sheds a powerful light on adult psychosocial behaviour, particularly in situations where there are emotional and attachment-related issues (Main 1995). These include relationships with sexual partners, one's own children and social workers. The theory also helps social workers to understand their own emotional and psychological behaviours in difficult and demanding situations. This is a reminder that if social workers are to function sensitively, astutely and safely, they need good-quality supervision and case analysis.

Intervention

The increasing stability of the internal working model means that an individual's behavioural and relationship style becomes more predictable, self-confirming and difficult to shift. However, change remains possible at any time across the lifespan. New experiences always have the capacity to alter people's representations and expectations of the worthiness and effectiveness of the self and the availability of others. Support and understanding provided within the context of a confiding relationship has repeatedly been found to promote psychological wellbeing, esteem, confidence and resilience (for example Brown and Harris 1978). Such observations form the basis of most attachment-based interventions (Main 1995; Howe *et al.* 1999). By altering people's experiences of close relationships, insecure internal working models in which the self and others are represented negatively can be changed. For example, parents might improve their care-giving behaviour so that they behave with greater sensitivity, attunement and interest.

The ability of social workers to remain available and consistent provides families with a secure professional relationship within which reflection and understanding might increase. Foster carers, teachers and peer groups might also offer relationships in which children and adults develop more secure and positive views of themselves and others. An attachment perspective recognises that relationships are where things can go wrong in the first place, but equally relationships are generally the place where things are eventually put right.

Summary

Attachment theory offers a compelling set of ideas about how children develop close relationships with their main care-givers, how they attempt to adapt and survive in their particular care-giving environment, and how their behaviours and coping strategies can be understood as functional within the care-giving settings which gave rise to them. However, to the extent that adaptive behaviours require children to distort, deny and omit information, their ability to develop coherent, integrated and balanced mental representations of themselves and others is frustrated. Behaviours which appear functional within the parent/child relationship, therefore, may be dysfunctional in other social contexts such as the nursery, classroom and peer group.

A lifespan approach is now taken to attachment theory. There is great interest in the continuities and discontinuities that affect attachment styles and internal working models from childhood to adulthood. In their attempts to promote children's welfare, social workers seek to disconfirm children's insecure working models, either by improving the quality of their close relationships with parents and peers, or by providing them with new care-giving relationships in substitute families.

Attachment behaviour is triggered by feelings of distress, particularly where attachment-related issues are present. It occurs in most emotionally demanding situations, and it occurs in adults as well as children. Day-in, day-out, social workers (and their agencies) practise in emotionally demanding environments which trigger characteristic coping styles, defensive strategies and adaptive behaviours. Underpinning all practice using an attachment perspective is the provision of relationships in which the other is experienced as available and responsive, consistent and understanding. If social workers are to offer and promote these kinds of relationships, their capacity to reflect on their own functioning has to be maintained (Fonagy et al. 1991). The role of good supervision is essential in this process.

Recommended reading

Atkinson, L. and Zucker, K. (eds.) (1997) *Attachment and Psychopathology.* New York: Guildford Press.

Bowlby, J. (1988) *A Secure Base: Clinical Applications of Attachment Theory.* London: Routledge.

Heard, D. and Lake, B. (1999) *The Challenge of Attachment for Caregiving.* London: Routledge.

Howe, D., Brandon, M., Hinings, D. and Schofield, G. (1999) *Attachment Theory, Child Maltreatment and Family Support: A Practice and Assessment Model.* Basingstoke: Macmillan.

References

Ainsworth, M. D. S., Blehar, M., Aters, E. and Wall, S. (1978) *Patterns of Attachment: A Psychological Study of the Strange Situation.* Hillsdale, NJ: Lawrence Erlbaum.

Belsky, J. and Cassidy, J. (1994) 'Attachment: theory and practice.' In M. Rutter and D. Hay (eds.) *Development Through Life: A Handbook for Clinicians.* Oxford: Blackwell Science, pp. 373–401.

Bowlby, J. (1973) *Attachment and Loss, Volume II: Separation, Anxiety and Anger.* London: Hogarth.

Bowlby, J. (1979) *The Making and Breaking of Affectional Bonds.* London: Tavistock.

Bowlby, J. (1980) *Attachment and Loss, Volume III: Loss, Sadness and Depression.* London: Hogarth Press.

Brown, G. and Harris, T. (1978) *Social Origins of Depression.* London: Tavistock.

Cicchetti, D. (1989) 'How Research on Child Maltreatment has Informed the Study of Child Development.' In D. Cicchetti and V. Carlson (eds.) *Child Maltreatment.* New York: Cambridge University Press, pp.377–431.

Crittenden, P. (1995) 'Attachment and Psychopathology.' In S. Goldberg, R. Muir and J. Kerr (eds.) *Attachment Theory: Social, Developmental and Clinical Perspectives.* Hillsdale NJ: Analytic Press, pp. 367–406.

Crittenden, P. (1996) 'Research on Maltreating Families: Implications for Intervention.' In J. Briere *et al.* (ed.) *The APSAC Handbook on Child Maltreatment.* Thousand Oaks: Sage, pp.158–174.

Crittenden, P. (1997) 'Patterns of Attachment and Sexual Behavior: Risk of Dysfunction versus Opportunity for Creative Integration.' In L. Atkinson and K. Zucker (eds.) *Attachment and Psychopathology.* New York: The Guilford Press, pp.47–93.

Crittenden, P., Partridge, M. and Claussen, A. (1991) 'Family Patterns of Relationship in Normative and Dysfunctional Families.' In *Development and Psychopathology, 3,* pp.491–512.

Department of Health, Department for Education and Employment and Home Office (2000) *Framework for the Assessment of Children in Need and their Families.* London: The Stationery Office.

Fonagy, P, Steele, H., Moran, G, Steele, M. and Higgit, A. (1991) 'The Capacity for Understanding Mental States: The Reflective Self in Parent and Child and its Significance for Security of Attachment.' In *Infant Mental Health Journal, 13,* pp.200–217.

Howe, D. (1995) *Attachment Theory for Social Work Practice.* Basingstoke: Macmillan.

Howe, D., Brandon, M., Hinings, D. and Schofield, G. (1999) *Attachment Theory, Child Maltreatment and Family Support: A Practice and Assessment Model.* Basingstoke: Macmillan.

Lyons-Ruth, K. (1996) 'Attachment Relationships among Children with Aggressive Behavior Problems: The Role of Disorganised Early Attachment Patterns.' In *Journal of Consulting and Clinical Psychology, 64,* pp.64–73.

Main, M. (1995) 'Recent Studies in Attachment: Overview, with Selected Implications for Clinical Work.' In S. Goldberg, R. Muir and J. Kerr (eds.) *Attachment Theory: Social, Developmental and Clinical Perspectives.* Hillsdale, NJ: The Analytic Press, pp.407–474.

Robertson, J. and Bowlby, J. (1952) 'Responses of Young Children to Separation from Their Mothers.' Coumer Centre, Internationale Enfance, Paris, 2, pp.131–140.

CHAPTER 13

The Assessment of Children with Complex Needs

Ruth Marchant

Ensuring equality of opportunity does not mean that all children are treated the same. It does mean understanding and working sensitively and knowledgeably with diversity to identify the particular issues for a child and his or her family, taking account of their experiences and their family context.

(From the *Framework for the Assessment of Children in Need and their Families,* p.12, 1.43)

In this chapter the following are considered:

- what is meant by complex needs
- human rights issues and the social model of disability
- issues in the assessment of children with complex needs
- involving children in the assessment process
- pointers to anti-oppressive practice with disabled children.

Introduction

There's nothing complicated about me.

(13-year-old with multiple impairments and major health care needs, in communication to the author)

This chapter is written from a social model perspective on disability. Definitions of complex needs are briefly explored, and three key issues are considered in relation to assessment work with this group of children: the concept of parenting in terms of responding appropriately to the needs of the child; the use and limits of developmental milestones; and the boundaries between control and maltreatment, or between treatment and abuse. The chapter concludes with some guidance on involving children with complex needs in the assessment process, including the use of advocates. This is a sensitive and controversial area to cover so briefly, and references are given for further reading.

Defining complex needs

The dictionary definition of complex has two sources: 'complicated' and 'compound' (made up of many). There are no absolute criteria for judging which children have complex needs; complexity is about the competence of services or the experience of workers as much as anything inherent in a child. In general the threshold for complexity has shifted downwards over the years.

The boundary that defines complexity is likely to continue to shift as increasing numbers of children live with severe and multiple impairments and as services and communities become more competent at meeting the needs of these children. This shift is illustrated in the development of inclusive mainstream education. Ten years ago the use of a powered wheelchair might have been defined as a complex need; five years ago, it might have been nasogastric or gastrostomy tube-feeding; now, more recently, assisted ventilation. In many areas of the UK children with these needs are now attending mainstream schools. This demonstrates that there is no absolute threshold for complexity. There is also controversy concerning definitions of disability in general (see Robinson and Stalker 1998, for a recent summary of the debate as it relates to children). For the purposes of this chapter 'complex needs' is used to refer to:

- children who have major health care needs in addition to their impairments, including children with life-limiting conditions

- children who have more than one impairment affecting their communication or more than one impairment having other major on their lives

- children whose impairments have been caused by maltreatment, including those children whose disability is a consequence of the parent inducing or fabricating the child's illness.

Most children with complex needs will, then, be disabled, but not all disabled children have complex needs.

Human rights issues and the social model

The social model of disability considers oppressive attitudes to be a major issue for disabled children. As Morris notes: 'Children who have physical, sensory and/or intellectual impairments have (often) been treated as less than human, resulting in segregation, discrimination and sometimes a failure to recognise their right to life' (Morris 1998a, p.54).

A social model approach reframes the problem outside the child and makes clear the barriers that disabled children face in accessing their rights. The social model uses the term 'disability' not to refer to impairment (functional limitations) but rather to describe the effects of prejudice and discrimination: the social factors which create barriers, deny opportunities, and thereby dis-able people. An understanding of the social model of disability suggests that many of the potential problems faced by children with complex needs are not caused by their conditions or impairments, but by societal values and adult behaviour. Shakespeare and Watson note that a major problem for disabled children is that they live in a society which views childhood impairment as problematic. They comment:

> We may no longer follow the traditional route of abandoning or killing disabled children (in most cases), but we are keen to invest immense amounts of money in developing techniques to prevent them being born. If by any chance an impaired child slips through this screen, an array of techniques is available to intervene.

(Shakespeare and Watson 1998, p.20)

Assessments of children with complex needs cannot be value-free on these issues. The values that guide decisions about whether children should live or die also influence our approaches to children's day-to-day experiences. Patterns of care for disabled children are tolerated that would not be accepted for non-disabled children. For example, a child with autism, known to the author, aged six years old, is sleeping regularly in four different places: his family home, a residential school, a link family and a residential respite care unit. He is also admitted to hospital frequently for seizure control. In addition, standards of care or approaches to control are accepted that would not be tolerated for other children. For example, another child aged nine who has dual sensory impairment and learning disabilities spent long periods of time tied to a chair or bed to prevent her injuring herself or others. Parents and school staff felt this was the only way to keep her and others safe.

The *Framework for the Assessment of Children in Need and their Families* (Department of Health, *et al.* 2000) is inclusive of all children. Additional information for assessments where children are disabled is also given in *Assessing Children in Need and their Families: Practice Guidance* (Department of Health 2000a). Part of the challenge for those who assess children with complex needs is the oppressive context in which such assessments take place. Additionally, balancing the needs that a child shares with all children with any particular needs resulting from his or her condition or impairment can be extremely difficult and raise enormous controversy.

Several features of the *Framework for the Assessment of Children in Need and their Families* are particularly helpful for children with complex needs: for example, the emphasis on responding to children's individual needs; the expectation of children's involvement in the process of assessment; the commitment to working with parents and children, and the underlying ecological and empowerment models.

Children with complex needs can be seen to be swimming against many tides. In terms of abuse, disabled children have been rendered particularly vulnerable, facing an increased risk of abuse in most settings (Westcott and Cross 1996; Westcott and Jones 1999). Therefore, they ought to be over-represented amongst children whose names are placed on a child protection register. However, as indicated in Chapter 1, research in the UK and elsewhere suggests that disabled children may be among the least well protected (Westcott 1998) and the least often consulted in routine assessments (Morris 1998b).

The inclusive approach of the new framework for assessment presents an opportunity to challenge and address some of this.

Issues in the assessment of children with complex needs

Where a child's needs are complex, assessments of parenting capacity can be particularly challenging. Some children need more parenting or more skilled parenting than others; some children need intensive parenting for much longer than others. As Statham and Read (1998) note: caring for a disabled child can make demands on parents and carers that go well beyond what is expected of parents of non-disabled children. The task of physically caring for a child with complex needs may be more complicated, more time-consuming, less familiar, more anxiety-provoking, physically harder and emotionally more difficult. An apparently simple expectation of parents, such as ensuring that the child's medical appointments are kept, requires careful consideration, given that many children with complex needs have extensive contact with the medical world. For example, a four-year-old child known to the author has already attended more than 300 medical appointments, including therapy sessions, consultations, clinics, GP visits.

Basics like dental care can also be far more difficult to arrange because of access issues. Knowing just what is involved in a child's day-to-day care, or realising that most parents would be driven to distraction by a child's behaviour, can operate powerfully on professionals' expectations about parenting standards. A clear value base, at both personal and organisational levels, and skilled supervision are essential to ensure that equal assessment standards are applied to all children.

The social model suggests also that practitioners explore more widely the context in which the child lives. Looking at the supports available to the family to meet their child's needs is an important part of the Assessment Framework. Supports available to most parents are often less available to parents of children with complex needs. The risk of family breakdown is higher, and baby-sitting and other informal supports may be much harder to find (Baldwin and Carlisle 1994; Beresford 1994).

The cultural identity of disabled children needs active recognition. The situation of black disabled children requires particular attention, because the effects of racism and disablism can compound each other. Research demonstrates that families from minority ethnic groups caring for a severely disabled child are even more disadvantaged than white families in similar situations (Baxter *et al.* 1990, Chamba *et al.* 1999).

The long-term impact on families of living in a world that relentlessly rejects their children must be considered, and it is crucial to remember the role of professionals in this process. Multiple assessments come with the territory for children with complex needs. Their impact is illustrated in this account by Murray:

> When I first had Kim he was my son. A year later he was epileptic and developmentally delayed. At eighteen months he had special needs and he was a special child. He had a mild to moderate learning difficulty. He was mentally handicapped... I was told not to think about his future... By the time he was four he had special educational needs. He was a statemented child. He was dyspraxic, epileptic, developmentally delayed and he had complex communication

problems... At eight he had severe intractable epilepsy with associated communication problems. He was showing a marked developmental regression. He had severe learning difficulties. At nine he came out of segregated schooling and he slowly became my son again. Never again will he be anything else but Kim – a son, a brother, a friend, a pupil, a teacher, a person.

(Murray and Penman 1996, p.6)

The pressures of parenting a child with complex needs can be very demanding. The more complex the child's needs the higher the risk of skewed expectations and standards. The fragmentation of services can add to the pressures. And yet practitioners need to find ways to assess whether the parent(s) can respond appropriately to the child's developmental needs, and, if not, establish whether services may enable them to do so. One approach is to ask what would be reasonable parenting for a child with these particular needs at this stage in his or her development, as stated in Section 31 of the Children Act 1989.

The use and limits of developmental milestones

Untangling concerns about a child's developmental needs can be particularly challenging where the child has complex needs. Separating out the impact of a child's impairment(s) from his or her experiences can be extremely difficult. Simple assessment standards should be used with great care. The Assessment Framework states that assessments should consider the child developing within expected milestones. This means that professionals should assess whether a child is developing in line with what would be expected of a child with similar impairments at a similar level of development (not necessarily age).

The boundary between control, treatment and abuse

Children with complex needs are more likely to be perceived as having challenging behaviour. Assessments of what constitutes appropriate control for these children can be particularly difficult. Children with learning disabilities, autism, or language delay face an increased risk of developing challenging behaviour, and physical and sensory impairments are also known to increase this risk. However, this increase is not necessarily a direct result of the impairments: these children may also face disrupted relationships; frequent assessments and/or medical investigations; repeated rejection; low expectations and poor social opportunities, which will influence their behaviour. The social model of disability is again helpful in framing the right questions.

Some children presenting with challenging behaviour can get caught up in the child protection system by mistake, with devastating consequences for the child and for the family. For example, a three-year-old girl known to the author had been seen repeatedly at casualty with injuries to her head, arms and eyes. Concerns were raised about emotional abuse or non-accidental injury and an initial child protection conference was held within child protection procedures. As part of the assessment process a second medical opinion was sought and the child was found to have a rare chromosomal abnormality associated with self-injurious behaviour. Although very few conditions directly affect a child's behaviour, this possibility needs to be actively considered. Whatever the cause of a child's behaviour, and sometimes this may never be absolutely clear, assessments must address the appropriateness of responses to that child's behaviour.

If professionals have failed to provide appropriate support and guidance, then assessments of what is reasonable at home are likely to prove particularly difficult. In assessments where there are issues concerning control of a child's behaviour, clear definitions which clarify the boundaries between reasonable control and abuse become essential. The following guidelines are adapted from Lyons (1994):

- the child's welfare must be the paramount consideration

- any response to a child's behaviour must be based on a consideration of what is in that child's best interests and what the child would personally recognise as being in his or her own interests, were he or she of the age and capacity to make such decisions

- restrictive measures should be adopted only to deal with severe challenging behaviour when there is no alternative, and should be used in the least detrimental manner and for the shortest possible time

- any measures of control should always be part of a plan with long-term strategies to meet the child's needs and encourage other behaviours, and should first have been discussed by the parents, professionals and carers involved.

In a similar way, the boundary between treatment and abuse can be difficult to identify. Issues around the withholding of treatment or the application of certain treatments may be part of the focus of an assessment. A social model approach again suggests a wider perspective, and encourages professionals to see treatments from the child's viewpoint: 'All these efforts to make a child normal by stimulating brain waves, hanging them upside down, pushing, pulling and cajoling, mean that the child receives the very clear message that there is something about them that nobody likes. Chances are that they will learn not to like it either' (Middleton 1996).

Sometimes the concerns are not so much about the actual treatment the child receives but the knock-on effect it has on their day-to-day lives, perhaps spending long periods of time away from family and friends or missing out on time to play or relax. A useful guiding principle for assessment is that services should always meet a child's particular or special needs in ways that least disrupt the needs that they share with all children.

The majority of parents want what is best for their children, but the more complex a child's needs, the less likely is there to be consensus on what is best for him or her. Issues of consent become crucial, and ways to assess the validity and risk of new or controversial treatments are helpful.

The following are drawn from a list of questions suggested for evaluating treatments for autism (Howlin 1998), but could be more generally applied in assessments where there is disagreement about appropriate treatments:

- how long has the therapy been used?
- what research is available?
- for whom does this approach work best?
- what alternative interventions might be tried?
- how has the decision been made that this therapy is appropriate for this child?

Howlin urges particular caution where there are no individual assessments and no formal outcome measures for a treatment.

Involving children in the assessment process

Most children with complex needs will have had extensive previous experiences of assessment, as will their families. At least some of these experiences are likely to have been within a pathologising, deficit model where the child was tested against some concept of normality. Some children are very clear about the focus of this kind of assessment: 'its always about what's wrong with me ... they're only interested in the bits of me that don't work. They want to see what I can't do' (11-year-old girl with severe physical impairments; communication to the author).

For children with extensive experience of the medical world, the very word 'assessment' may have difficult connotations. The *Oxford English Dictionary* defines 'assess' as: 'To fix or determine the amount of; to estimate officially the value of'. The social model, again, suggests the importance of the context in which assessments take place, a context in which disabled children are often seen as of less value than other children. Families can also find assessments very stressful:

'I found assessment meetings a nightmare. I felt I was listening to people talk about somebody other than the child I lived with. After the first assessment at the child development centre I went home and cried for four days ...' (Murray and Penman, 1996. P.6).

Given this context, it is crucial that assessments of the child's needs are presented to children in an accessible, honest and fair way that makes clear the different focus of the assessment. For example, the worker can explain:

'I want to spend some time with you and see how things are for you,' and 'It's my job to find out what you think about things; I want to know whether things are OK for you and whether you are safe,' or 'I'd like to talk with you about how your life is and what your views are about your future.' For some children it may be necessary to distinguish very explicitly this type of assessment of need from others:

'This is not about your disability or your illness. I am not trying to find out about what is wrong with you.'

Involving children who have complex needs in meaningful ways requires us to broaden our definition of communication and to be willing to try new approaches. Individualised, responsive ways of working are essential. We often act as if speaking is the only valid way to communicate, and yet we know that this is rarely the case for any child. Total communication means tuning in on all channels. Recent work suggests innovative ways to engage children in research processes (Morris 1998c; Beresford 1997; Marchant *et al.* 1999) and these approaches are relevant for assessment work.

Sometimes being alongside a child is the most potent assessment tool. On other occasions communication with a child will need the help of an appropriately skilled third party. Thought needs to be given to finding this person: independent, objective interpreters are often not available for children with complex needs, whose communication methods may be very idiosyncratic. The ideal is someone who knows the child well, is trusted by the child, and yet is relatively neutral in terms of the assessment process. For example, a 9-year-old boy known to the author communicates using eye pointing on a personalised communication board of words and symbols. It takes time to understand how he indicates 'yes' and 'no'. He is dependent for all his care and spends his time at residential school and in foster care. At the beginning of his assessment his social worker found out who could communicate well with him, and offered the child a choice of three people to help her communicate with him. This gave him control within safe boundaries. (See Marchant and Page 1993, for further discussion on working with communicators.) Sometimes establishing direct communication with a child is far easier than anticipated. For example, a 13-year-old girl, Janice, communicates with gestures, signs and some words, although her speech is difficult to understand. Her social worker spent time with her at home and at school. She and Janice became more confident in each other's presence and by the end of the assessment were able to communicate directly with each other without any help.

Working with advocates

Jenkins (1995) defines child advocacy as the activity of achieving rights for children, whether through the process of acting on their behalf, or of assisting them to act for themselves. Advocacy on behalf of children has a relatively short history; in particular, rights-oriented advocacy with children is in its infancy. Child advocacy has until recently meant adults acting in the best interests of children, as perceived by adults. Parents have traditionally been expected to act as advocates for their disabled children, and it is still often thought that parents are likely to be the child's best advocates. For many children this is undoubtedly the case, and many parents will also take into account the child's own views and feelings. However, informal advocacy usually means the adult acting on their perception of the best interests of the child, rather than representing the child's own view. As Russell notes, parents do not necessarily agree amongst themselves and they certainly do not always agree with their children (Russell 1996). Some recent approaches suggest consulting with disabled adults about what disabled children need, both in terms of individual and collective advocacy (see Westcott and Cross 1996).

Children whose impairments are caused by abuse

In one large study the incidence of impairments caused by or likely to have been caused by abuse was 147 per 1,000 abused children (Crosse et al. 1993). Little is known about the needs of children impaired as a result of maltreatment. Assessment work with a child whose impairments have been caused or exacerbated by abuse requires particular care. The child's knowledge of the cause of his or her impairment should be approached with extreme caution. Experience teaches that such knowledge can be truly unbearable for children, and they may genuinely not know, even when they have apparently been told.

Munchausen Syndrome by Proxy (also known as fabricated or induced illness by proxy), is a very rare form of child abuse, and the links with complex needs are not yet understood. However, one likely consequence of repeatedly inducing illness in a child is long-term impairment (Schreier and Libow 1993). Anecdotal evidence also suggests an increased incidence of fabricated or induced illness by carers among children with complex needs (see Precey 1998). For example, by the age of 10 Matthew, who had multiple complex impairments, had very rarely attended school. He had been removed from six different schools by his mother on the grounds that they could not meet his needs. He was under the care of four different hospitals and nine paediatricians and his medication and care regime changed frequently as his mother dictated. Serious concerns were raised about the possibility of induced illness and a period of residential assessment was sought, but Matthew died before this could take place.

Pointers to anti-oppressive practice with disabled children

Think about your own understanding of disability

Practitioners' perceptions of what it means to be disabled will affect their work. It is helpful actively to explore one's own attitudes and understanding, and to be aware of one's own prejudices, fears and stereotypes. Westcott and Cross (1996) list some questions which might be used to trigger a personal review of our own attitudes. Part of this exploration needs to be a consideration of our own power with disabled children, both as adults and (often) as part of the non-disabled world.

Be clear about the position of your service

If services are aiming to be inclusive of all children, they must ensure that they are appropriate for all children. For example, are children with complex needs made welcome? Is the building fully accessible? Are disabled workers employed? Are toys, books and resources suitable for all children? Are there positive images of disabled children around? It there a policy on anti-discriminatory practice? (For further questions see ABCD 1993; Westcott and Cross 1996).

Take responsibility for communication

Children may have particular needs, especially in relation to communication, which must be addressed to make any assessment meaningful. It is the adult's responsibility to ensure that the child has the best possible chance of communicating. This might mean learning about the child's method; using interpreters or facilitators; tuning in to nonverbal communication, or thinking creatively about ways of listening.

Try to take the child's perspective

Try not to make assumptions about what an impairment means to a child. Aim to understand the impact of the child's impairment from his or her perspective: what it means for this child in this situation and at this stage in his or her development, rather than in the abstract. In direct work with children, do not assume that the child's impairment is of concern unless the child actually brings it into the picture.

Summary

The *Framework for the Assessment of Children in Need and their Families* is designed to be inclusive of all children. Every child has the right to an assessment which is genuinely responsive to their individual needs, however unusual or complex these may be. As a secondary gain, getting things right for children with the most complex needs can potentially improve our practice with all children by strengthening our ability to respond to children as unique individuals.

Recommended reading

Department of Health (2000a) *Assessing Children in Need and their Families, Practice Guidance.* London: The Stationery Office.

Marchant, R. *et al.* (1999) *Listening on all Channels: Consulting with Disabled Children and Young People.* Brighton: Triangle.

Middleton, L. (1999) *Disabled Children: Challenging Social Exclusion.* Blackwell: Oxford.

Morris, J. (1999) *Accessing Human Rights: Disabled Children and the Children Act.* London: Barnados.

Note

In preparation for this chapter we consulted with disabled children and young people through Triangle, and with parents of disabled children through aMaze, a Brighton-based project providing advice, information and support to assist parents to get the best for their disabled children. Quotes in the text referenced as personal communication are from these groups and we are grateful for their consent to use their words.

References

ABCD (1993) *Abuse and Children who are Disabled: A Resource and Training Pack.* Leicester: NSPCC.

Baldwin, S. and Carlisle, J. (1994) *Social Support for Disabled Children and Their Families: A Review of the Literature.* Edinburgh: HMSO.

Baxter, C. *et al.* (1990) *Double Discrimination: Issues and Services for People with Learning Difficulties from Black and Ethnic Minority Communities.* London: Kings Fund Centre.

Beresford, B. (1994) *Positively Parents: Caring for a Severely Disabled Child.* York: Social Policy Research Unit.

Beresford, B. (1997) *Personal Accounts: Involving Disabled Children In Research.* York: Social Policy Research Unit.

Chamba, R., Ahmad, W., Hirst, M., Lawton, D. and Beresford, B. (1999) *On the Edge: Minority Ethnic Families Caring for a Severely Disabled Child.* London: Policy Press.

Crosse, S. B., Kaye, E. and Patnofsky, A.C. (1993) *Report on the Maltreatment of Children with Disabilities.* Washington DC: National Center on Abuse and Neglect.

Davie, R. and Galloway, D. (1996) *Listening to Children in Education.* London: Fulton.

Department of Health, Department for Education and Employment and Home Office (2000) *Framework for The Assessment of Children in Need and their Families.* London: The Stationery Office.

Department of Health (2000a) *Assessing Children in Need and their Families: Practice Guidance.* London: The Stationery Office.

Howlin, P. (1998) *Children with Autism and Aspergers Syndrome: A Guide for Practitioners and Carers.* London: Wiley.

Jenkins, P. (1995) 'Advocacy and the 1989 UN Convention on the Rights of the Child.' In J. Dalrymple and J. Hough (eds.) *Having a Voice: An Exploration of Children's Rights and Advocacy?*

Lyons, C. (1994) *Legal Issues Arising from the Care and Control of Children with Learning Disabilities who also Present Severe Challenging Behaviour: A Guide for Parents and Carers.* London: Mental Health Foundation.

Marchant, R. and Page, M. (1993) *Bridging The Gap: Child Protection Work with Children with Multiple Disabilities.* London: NSPCC.

Marchant, R. and Page, M. (1997) 'Interviewing Disabled Children.' In J. Jones and H. Westcott (eds.) *Perspectives on the Memorandum.* London: Arena.

Marchant, R., Jones, M., Giles, A. and Julyan, A. (1999) *Listening on all Channels: Consulting with Disabled Children.* Brighton: Triangle.

Middleton, L. (1996) *Making a Difference: Social Work with Disabled Children.* Birmingham: Venture Press.

Morris, J. (1998a) *Don't Leave us Out: Involving Disabled Children and Young People with Communication Impairments.* Bristol: JRF.

Morris, J. (1998b) *Still Missing: Disabled Children and the Children Act.* London: Who Cares Trust.

Morris, J. (1998c) *Accessing Human Rights: Disabled Children and the Children Act.* London: Barnados.

Murray, P. and Penman, G. (1996) *Let Our Children Be: A Collection of Stories.* Sheffield: Parents with Attitude.

Precey, G. (1998) 'Assessment Issues in Working with Mothers who Induce Illness in Their Children.' In *Child and Family Social Work, 3*, pp.227–37.

Robinson, C. and Stalker, K. (eds.) (1998) 'Growing Up With Disability, Research Highlights.' In *Social Work, 34*. London: Jessica Kingsley.

Russell, P. (1996) 'Listening to Children with Special Educational Needs.' In Davie and Galloway (1996).

Schreier, H. and Libow, J. (1993) *Hurting for Love – Munchausen by Proxy Syndrome.* London: Guildford Press.

Shakespeare, T. and Watson, N. (1998) 'Theoretical Perspectives on Research with Disabled Children.' In Robinson and Stalker (1998).

Statham, J. and Read, J. (1998) 'The Pre-School Years.' In Robinson and Stalker (1998).

Westcott, H. (1998) 'Disabled children and Child Protection.' In Robinson and Stalker (1998).

Westcott, H. and Cross, M. (1996) *This Far and No Further: Towards Ending the Abuse of Disabled Children.* Birmingham: Venture Press.

Westcott, H. and Jones, D. (1999) 'Annotation: The Abuse of Disabled Children.' In *Journal of Child Psychology and Psychiatry, 40,* 4, pp. 497–506.

CHAPTER 14

Young Carers

Needs, Rights and Assessments

Chris Dearden and Saul Becker

Consideration must be given as to whether a young carer is a child in need under the Children Act 1989. The central issue is whether a child's welfare or development might suffer if support is not provided to the child or family... Services should be provided to promote the health and development of young carers while not undermining the parent.

(From the *Framework for the Assessment of Children in Need and their Families,* p.49, 3.63)

In this chapter we consider the following:

- who are young carers?

- the developmental needs of young carers

- assessing the parenting capacity of parents who are ill or disabled

- assessing family and environmental factors

- using a family approach to assess the developmental needs of young carers

- assessment issues.

Introduction

Young carers are children and young people under the age of 18 who provide care or support to a relative in the home. That relative is usually a parent, but may be a sibling, grandparent or other family member. Young carers have only recently been recognised as children who may need support and services in their own right. This recognition is largely the result of research which initially attempted to ascertain the extent of the problem (O'Neill 1988; Page 1988) and later reported on the identified needs and experiences of young carers (Bilsborrow 1992; Aldridge and Becker 1993). This early research and campaigning by groups such as Carers National Association resulted in considerable interest in what had previously been a hidden social issue.

As interest and recognition has grown, so estimates of the extent of the issue have been formulated. Towards the end of the 1980s it was estimated that there may be 10,000 young carers nationally (O'Neill 1988). Mahon and Higgins (1995), drawing on research in the north of England, suggested that the true figure may be between 15,000 and 40,000. More recently the Department of Health commissioned research which suggests that the national figure is somewhere between 19,000 and 50,000 (Walker 1996). The Department of Health figures are based on young people 'providing, or intending to provide, regular and substantial care' (the terminology used in the Carers Act 1995). Carers National Association, the Young Carers Research Group and others have suggested that consideration of the issues associated with caring should include not only the amount of time children care, but also the impact caring has on them as children. In the UK there are almost three million children under the age of 16 (23 per cent of all children) who live in households where a family member is hampered in daily activities by a chronic physical or mental health problem, illness or disability (Becker, Aldridge and Dearden 1998: xii). While a family member being hampered in this way may not necessarily impact on the child, it would seem to indicate that the figure given by Walker is likely to be an underestimate.

The research literature on young carers indicates that children undertake a range of caring tasks. Broadly, these tasks include domestic chores such as cooking and cleaning; general care such as assisting with mobility, giving medication; intimate care such as bathing and toileting; and emotional support. One in ten young carers provides care to more than one person and many, in addition to caring responsibilities, also provide childcare for their siblings (see for example Bilsborrow 1992; Aldridge and Becker 1993 1994; Frank 1995; Dearden and Becker 1995; 1996; 1998). Caring tasks are influenced by the nature of illness or disability of those receiving support. For example, parents with sensory impairments may depend on the young carer to act as an intermediary between the family and the outside world. Intimate care is more likely to take place when parents have physical health problems or a disability; emotional support is more likely to occur if parents have mental health issues (Dearden and Becker 1998; Becker *et al.* 1998). Furthermore, girls are more heavily involved in all aspects of care, especially domestic and intimate care. These tasks are often associated with gender differences in adult carers (Dearden and Becker 1998).

The *Framework for the Assessment of Children in Need and their Families* (Department of Health, *et al.* 2000) includes three domains which should be considered in terms of assessing and safeguarding children and promoting their welfare: the child's developmental needs; parenting capacity; and family and environmental factors. These will be considered in terms of the needs of young carers.

Young carers' developmental needs

Young carers have needs similar to all children, but may have additional needs (and rights) related to their caring roles. Their developmental needs may be a result of taking on tasks which could be considered inappropriate to their age and development. Personal, intimate care provides a good example of this. In most families children would not be expected to bathe or toilet other family members, particularly their parents.

Young carers may experience educational difficulties. Research indicates that young carers may miss periods of school and may experience difficulty in completing homework, as well as, for example, exhibiting persistent lateness (Aldridge and Becker 1993; Marsden 1995; Frank 1995). These findings are backed up by larger studies of young carers supported by specialist support projects (Dearden and Becker 1995; 1998) which indicate that a third of young carers of secondary-school age are either missing school or experiencing educational difficulties. Young carers may experience isolation and feelings of alienation or difference from their peers if they have domestic and caring responsibilities from an early age (see, for example, Meredith 1991; Bilsborrow 1992; Aldridge and Becker 1993; Dearden and Becker 1995; 1996; 1998; Frank 1995; Newton and Becker 1996; Becker *et al.* 1998). The adoption of tasks and responsibilities can leave young carers with little free time, and so reduce opportunities associated with a healthy psycho-social development, such as spending time with friends, attending clubs and playing sports (Becker *et al.* 1998).

The emotional and psychological impacts on children who care can, in some instances, be severe. While adequate support from professionals and the wider family may mitigate the impacts, some children will inevitably suffer negative consequences. For example, those children whose parents have a terminal, progressive or degenerative illness may live in fear and uncertainty about the future – both their parents' and their own future. Some will inevitably experience the death of a parent. Others may witness a parent in chronic pain and feel powerless to help. Those whose parents have mental health difficulties may witness unpredictable and sometimes irrational behaviour, and can find gauging mood and behaviour and trying to ensure safety (particularly in parents who may be suicidal) particularly stressful (see Dearden and Becker 1995). Providing intimate care can be embarrassing for children and parents alike, and can cause psychological problems for those who feel uncomfortable but have little choice. While many children will not suffer undue psychological and emotional effects from caring, professionals need to be aware of the more negative impacts on others.

Parenting capacity

While parenting capacity may be impeded as a result of illness or disability, this is not necessarily always the case. The majority of ill or disabled parents will be able to provide basic care, emotional warmth, stability, stimulation and adequate guidelines and boundaries for their children. Parenting capacity should not be equated solely with the practical tasks for which some disabled and ill parents may require support and assistance from professionals. Many parents with a physical disability will be healthy and may require only practical support. Others, however, may experience chronic pain, or exacerbations and remission of illness, and others may be facing death from a progressive terminal illness. Thus there are instances where parenting capacity in terms of the dimensions outlined in the framework will be compromised as a result of illness or disability:

> The presence of mental illness can reduce and/or change a parent's responsiveness towards their child. For example, a parent may become less emotionally involved, less interested, less decisive or more irritable with the child. This will affect the quality of the parent–child relationship, parenting capacity and the child's well-being (Falkov 1998, p.64).

However, Falkov also indicates that chronic, unremitting illnesses often have the greatest negative impact on children and that many parents, even those with acute, intermittent psychotic episodes are able to parent their children adequately. Preventive strategies can be adopted to support both parent and child and reduce the likelihood of family separation, which is the major personal concern of children living with a depressed parent (Garley *et al.* cited in Falkov 1998).

Booth and Booth's (1998) pioneering work with adults who grew up with parents with learning difficulties provides a further example of how support can mitigate some of the negative aspects of parental impairment. Booth and Booth's work indicates that the respondents experienced many of the negative external and environmental factors associated with young carers, such as family breakdown, poverty, victimisation, stigma by association, and lack of support. However, they also suggest that such families are often resilient and that the strengths within families and their networks are key when assessing assumptions about parenting, suggesting that negative factors need to be balanced against children's and families' resilience.

Family and environmental factors

Research on young carers indicates that environmental factors such as low income, inadequate housing, lack of community support and alienation from the wider community as a result of prejudice, discrimination and disabling barriers can have negative impacts on disabled parents and their children. Disability and illness are often associated with poverty (Black 1980; Barnes 1992), and many families will be reliant on welfare benefits. The majority of young carers supported by specialist projects are living in low-income families, and many of these are headed by lone parents who are especially vulnerable to poverty (Dearden and Becker 1998). In lone-parent families there is generally no other adult available for support if the parent becomes ill, leaving children to care in the absence of other professional support. Even where there are two parents, one may abdicate responsibility in favour of a child or may have the breadwinner role, again relying on children in the family to provide care and support (Aldridge and Becker 1993; 1994; Dearden and Becker 1995; 1998).

Some families living in inadequate housing may have to rely more on children because the family home is not designed for wheelchair access, or does not have a downstairs bathroom or shower facilities. Much of the social housing for disabled people is designed for one or two people rather than for families, resulting in long waits for rehousing, or expensive adaptations to existing properties. Community care provision has been criticised for failing to meet the needs of people from minority ethnic communities (Dominelli

1989; Atkin 1991; Local Government Information Unit 1991). These environmental factors can also be accompanied by the absence, or lack, of support from the wider family.

In addition some families will face double jeopardy issues, such as being black and having mental health problems, which can result in prejudice and discrimination at two levels. When this is coupled with poverty and social isolation, problems are compounded.

Assessing the developmental needs of young carers

The three domains of the Assessment Framework clearly indicate that many young carers will experience need. If they are assessed and supported as children in need, as defined in section 17 of the Children Act 1989, using a holistic family approach, many of these needs could be met without their worst fears of family separation being realised.

The family approach

The family approach to supporting young carers highlights and promotes the needs of all family members where there is illness or disability present. It recognises that the lack of adequate high-quality services is one of the major reasons why some children become young carers in the first place, and why others have negative experiences of caring, and that this is aggravated by poverty and low family income (Becker *et al.* 1998).

While adequate services (and financial resources) for parents with ill-health or disability will benefit the whole family, many young carers express a need for recognition and services in their own right. Some young people require additional support, often in the form of someone they can talk to about their experiences, worries and concerns (Aldridge and Becker 1993). Many young carers express satisfaction with young carers projects (Department of Health 1996a) which provide not only someone to talk to, but also the opportunity for young carers to meet other children in a similar position – something which often validates their own experiences. In looking at the needs of the whole family, rather than the parent or child in isolation, services can be provided or adapted to reduce the more negative consequences of young caring.

Issues of assessment

Young carers have rights to assessment under the Carers (Recognition and Services) Act 1995. A recent national survey of young carers supported by projects (Dearden and Becker 1998) found that of 2,303 young carers, only 249 had received any formal assessment by social services. Of those who had been assessed, more had been assessed under the Children Act 1989 than the Carers Act 1995. It is not clear whether those assessed under the Children Act 1989 had been assessed as children in need under section 17 only, or also as children at risk of suffering likely or actual significant harm under section 47.

Alarmingly, the likelihood of a young carer getting any assessment is not always increased by factors which one might have thought would be influential, such as the age of the child or the nature of the tasks they perform. So, for example, Dearden and Becker (1998) reveal that it does not matter whether a child is very young or whether they are performing intimate care; these factors (age and caring tasks) are not associated with an increased likelihood of an assessment taking place. This is of concern because, for example, providing intimate care might indicate that a child is providing, or intends to provide, a substantial amount of care on a regular basis – a trigger for assessment under the Carers Act and an indication of need under section 17 of the Children Act.

There are several factors which may explain why so few young carers are assessed as children in need, and it is important to be aware of and acknowledge these factors if families are to be supported. The most important of these are the lack of awareness among social services staff about young carers' needs and rights; families' fear of professional interventions; a lack of consensus regarding which department or section should be responsible for assessing need; and whether young carers should be assessed as children in need, children at risk or as carers. Each of these is discussed in turn below.

Professional awareness

The research indicates that professionals from health and social services often overlook the contribution of children, and the impact on them, in caring and managing the household where a parent or other household member has a chronic illness or disability. Ongoing awareness-raising about the needs and rights of young carers is therefore critical. In addition it is the responsibility of managers in both adult and children's services to ensure that the needs of young carers are identified and met. The *Framework for the Assessment of Children in Need and their Families* (Department of Health *et al.* 2000) has implications for workers in adult services; they have a key role to play in terms of assessing parenting capacity. Local procedures and practice guidance should provide structures enabling professionals from different specialisms to work together to meet the needs of young carers and their families.

Fear of professional interventions

Across the spectrum in literature and research on young carers there is evidence of children's and parents' fear of professional interventions (see, for example, Aldridge and Becker 1993; 1994; Dearden and Becker 1995; 1996) or of the antipathy of families towards professionals, and in particular social workers. Social Services Inspectorate inspections of services to support disabled adults in their parenting role, undertaken in 1999, found that young carers and their parents sometimes underplayed the caring role of the child. The two main reasons for this appear to be fear that the child will be removed from the home, and a difference of view between families and professionals about what was an appropriate level of caring. This negative view of social services is recognised by the Department of Health, which suggests that work needs to be done to promote a more positive profile for social work, based on performance, recognising families' legitimate concerns about delays and child protection (Department of Health 1996a, p.28). Families are unlikely to approach professionals for support if they fear that their children will be removed from the family home. Since parental illness is the third most common reason for children entering the public child care system (Department of Health 1998) and is probably a contributing factor in other admissions where the main reason is 'parents need relief' or abuse or neglect, some of these fears are borne out by practice.

Whose responsibility?

Because young carers are children first and foremost but also fulfil the adult role of carer, they have been victims of debates within social services departments as to whether their assessment and support rightly falls to community care and adult disability services or is the province of children and family services (Department of Health 1996a; Dearden and Becker 1998; Becker et al. 1998). This debate has, in the past, resulted in their falling through the net and their needs not being met by either service. It is important to move forward from such debates and to look at the needs of the whole family. This will mean ill or disabled parents being assessed under the NHS and Community Care Act 1990 and other disability legislation, while their children can be assessed under either the Children Act 1989 or the Carers Act 1995, as children in (potential) need and/or as carers. This is most likely to occur if there are clear protocols within social service departments which promote joint working and encourage close cooperation between staff in adult and children's services.

Children in need, or carers?

There is a strong argument that young carers should be categorised as children in need as defined under section 17 of the Children Act (Family Rights Group 1991; Children's Rights Development Unit 1994; Department of Health 1996a). By categorising carers thus, it becomes possible to assess the child and to provide services to the family, if these services will promote the health and development of the child. It follows that all children in families where there is chronic illness or disability could be viewed as children in potential need and, should specific needs arise, they can be assessed quickly using the *Framework for the Assessment of Children in Need and their Families*.

The Carers (Recognition and Services) Act 1995 offers another route to assessment for some young carers, but using this piece of legislation currently depends on the relative of the young carer also being assessed or reassessed under community care legislation. Use of terms within the Act, such as 'regular' and 'substantial', may also make it difficult for those young people caring for someone with mental health problems to access services under this Act, since it is difficult to quantify the type of support they offer. Nevertheless, the inclusion of young carers in the Carers Act acknowledges their contribution as carers and allows for their views and perspectives to influence the service provision to their relative. It also implicitly acknowledges that there is the potential for conflict between carers and care recipients and allows for separate or joint assessment as appropriate.

The Practice Guide to the Carers Act (Department of Health 1996b) suggests that the Children Act 1989 is the appropriate framework for service provision once young carers have had their needs assessed. A whole-family approach to assessment should ensure that all needs are taken into account and that service provision meets the needs not only of disabled parents, but also of their children.

It is to be hoped that early assessment of young carers' needs, and early interventions to address these needs, should in most cases reduce the likelihood of child protection procedures being initiated. However, there are some cases where concerns that the child is suffering or is likely to suffer significant harm will result in section 47 enquiries. Although there are no statistics available regarding the number of young carers subject to care and supervision orders, anecdotal evidence and the literature on children looked after by the local authority indicate that parental mental health problems may, in some cases, be a significant factor. Research has highlighted how health care professionals' disregard of children's needs in discussions about parental mental health issues (Elliott 1992; Dearden and Becker 1995) may be followed by social work interventions which do not recognise the needs of the child, and which sometimes can result in the child's admission to care. Again, early support and a recognition of the whole family's needs may reduce the occurrence of such interventions. Falkov (1998) cites a former carer who states: 'People tend to protect children and young people. For me, this translated into ignoring my need to be informed and involved' (p.118). Thus assessment must balance children's protection against their needs to remain within the family unit and their needs for support and information. Assessment processes will need to be viewed as a positive way of supporting families and recognising their strengths as well as their weaknesses. Disabled parents must feel that their needs and rights will be taken into account and promoted, and that their parenting abilities will not be questioned inappropriately. Equally, young carers must feel that their abilities as carers are acknowledged and valued and that they are not patronised or ignored in the decision-making process.

Whole-family assessments can identify needs using the three domains by fully including parents and children. Young carers will be empowered if their competencies and experiences are acknowledged and their views sought. One way of gaining the cooperation and confidence of families is to acknowledge their strengths and ask them where the weaknesses lie. The areas covered by the three domains are wide. The assessment is likely to require the sharing of information between several professionals, from adult health and disability, child care, education, and those responsible for providing community care services. Professionals sharing information should follow the guidance on consent and confidentiality outlined in the *Framework for the Assessment of Children in Need and their Families*.

Meetings with the family to complete the assessment should take place at a time appropriate for the whole family, and when all members will be present. An advocate may help the children involved to participate fully and ensure that their views are adequately represented. It is also important that children are offered the opportunity to be assessed separately from their parents, should they so wish. Given that many families are fearful of acknowledging the extent of children's caring roles, no assumptions should be made regarding the distribution of tasks within the family. Equally, parents should not feel judged when disclosing such distributions. It is important to acknowledge that this is how an individual family copes with its situation and circumstances as a result of the lack of viable alternatives.

Summary

Three million children in the UK live in families where a family member is ill or disabled, and in the vast majority of these cases an adequate income, adequate accommodation, good services and the support of family and friends will ensure that children are not drawn into adopting any, or any significant, caring roles. In some cases, however, a lack of resources and support, combined with other factors which include family structure and the gender of care recipients and potential carers, will lead to some children becoming more heavily involved in caring (Becker et al. 1998).

Research indicates that young carers have specific needs which have only recently been identified by policy-makers and practitioners. Recognising and meeting these needs is essential to ensure young carers' healthy psycho-social development and wellbeing.

The inclusion of young carers in children's service plans and community care plans should assist in their identification and can act as a trigger to assessment when required. Families should not be subject to disagreements regarding which department or service is, or should be, responsible for assessing or meeting their needs.

A holistic family approach will ensure that the needs of all family members are taken into account, rather than the needs of either the parent or the child in isolation. Assessment and service provision should reflect family needs, and should support parents in their parenting role and assist them in their parenting responsibilities, while promoting children's rights, welfare, health and development. Services provided under children's legislation, unlike community care, will usually be free of charge – a factor important to families experiencing poverty and inadequate incomes/benefits.

A positive assessment process, leading to positive outcomes for parents and children, will be beneficial not only to the whole family, but also to the wider community. The aim should be to acknowledge, value and respect the reciprocal and interdependent nature of care-giving between young carers and their families, and to support and nurture these relationships through a range of policies, services and procedures. Assessment using the *Framework for the Assessment of Children in Need and their Families* is the way to make this happen.

Recommended reading

Becker, S., Aldridge, J. and Dearden, C. (1998) *Young Carers and their Families.* Oxford: Blackwell.

Dearden, C. and Becker, S. (1998) *Young Carers in the United Kingdom: A Profile.* London: Carers National Association.

Department of Health (1996) *Young Carers: Making a Start.* London: Department of Health.

Department of Health (1996a) *Young Carers: Something to Think About: Report of Four SSI Workshops, May–July 1995.* London: Department of Health.

Walker, A. (1996) *Young Carers and their Families.* London: The Stationery Office.

References

Aldridge, J. and Becker, S. (1993) *Children Who Care: Inside the World of Young Carers.* Loughborough: Young Carers Research Group, Loughborough University.

Aldridge, J. and Becker, S. (1994) *My Child, My Carer: The Parents' Perspective.* Loughborough: Young Carers Research Group, Loughborough University.

Atkin, K. (1991) 'Community Care in a Multi-racial Society: Incorporating User's Views.' In *Policy and Politics, 19,* 3, 159–66.

Barnes, C. (1992) 'Discrimination, Disability Benefits and the 1980s.' In *Benefits, 3,* 3–7.

Becker, S., Aldridge, J. and Dearden, C. (1998) *Young Carers and Their Families.* Oxford: Blackwell.

Bilsborrow, S. (1992) *You Grow up Fast as well... Young Carers on Merseyside.* Liverpool: Carers National Association, Personal Services Society and Barnardos.

Black, Sir D. (1980) *Inequalities in Health: Report of a Research Working Group.* London: DHSS.

Booth, T. and Booth, W. (1998) *Growing up with Parents who have Learning Difficulties.* London: Routledge.

Children's Rights Development Unit (1994) *UK Agenda for Children.* London: CRDU.

Dearden, C. and Becker, S. (1995) *Young Carers – The Facts.* Sutton: Reed Business Publishing.

Dearden, C. and Becker, S. (1996) *Young Carers at the Crossroads: An Evaluation of the Nottingham Young Carers Project.* Loughborough University: Young Carers Research Group.

Dearden, C. and Becker, S. (1998) *Young Carers in the United Kingdom: A Profile.* London: Carers National Association.

Department of Health (1996a) *Young Carers: Making a Start.* London: Department of Health.

Department of Health (1996b) *Carers (Recognition and Services) Act 1995: Practice Guide.* London: Department of Health.

Department of Health (1998) *Children Looked After by Local Authorities, Year Ending 31 March 1997, England.* London: Department of Health.

Department of Health, Department for Education and Employment and Home Office. (2000) *Framework for the Assessment of Children in Need and their Families.* London: The Stationery Office.

Dominelli, L. (1989) 'An Uncaring Profession? An Examination of Racism in Social Work.' In *New Community, 15,* 3, 391–403.

Elliott, A. (1992) *Hidden Children: A Study of Ex-Young Carers of Parents with Mental Health Problems in Leeds.* Leeds: City Council, Mental Health Development Section.

Falkov, A. (ed.) (1998) *Crossing Bridges: Training Resources for Working with Mentally Ill Parents and their Children. Reader for managers, practitioners and trainers.* Brighton: Department of Health/ Pavilion.

Family Rights Group (1991) *The Children Act 1989: Working in Partnership with Families.* London: HMSO.

Frank, J. (1995) *Couldn't Care More: A Study of Young Carers and Their Needs.* London: The Children's Society.

Goodridge, S. (2000) *A Jigsaw of Services: Inspection of Services to Support Disabled Adults in their Parenting Role.* London: Department of Health.

Local Government Information Unit (1991) *Community Care Comment 2: The Black Community and Community Care.* London: LGIU.

Mahon, A. and Higgins, J. (1995) *'…A Life of Our Own.' Young Carers: An Evaluation of Three RHA Funded Projects in Merseyside.* Manchester: Health Services Management Unit, University of Manchester.

Marsden, R. (1995) *Young Carers and Education.* London: Borough of Enfield, Education Department.

Meredith, H. (1991) 'Young Carers: The Unacceptable Face of Community Care.' In *Social Work and Social Sciences Review, 3* (supplement): 47–51.

Newton, B. and Becker, S. (1996) *Young Carers in Southwark: The Hidden Face of Community Care.* Loughborough: Young Carers Research Group, Loughborough University.

O'Neill, A. (1988) *Young Carers: The Tameside Research.* Tameside: Metropolitan Borough Council.

Page, R. (1988) *Report on the Initial Survey Investigating the Number of Young Carers in Sandwell Secondary Schools.* Sandwell: Metropolitan Borough Council.

Walker, A. (1996) *Young Carers and Their Families: A Survey Carried Out by the Social Survey Division of the Office for National Statistics on behalf of the Department of Health.* London: The Stationery Office.

CHAPTER 15

Assessment Prior to Birth

Di Hart

The midwife and health visitor are uniquely placed to identify risk factors to a child during pregnancy, birth and the child's early care.

(From the *Framework for the Assessment of Children in Need and their Families,* p.67, 5.25)

This chapter considers:

- reasons for assessment prior to birth
- current national guidance and implications for practice
- ethical dilemmas
- situations when pre-birth assessment should be considered
- the assessment process
- the assessment task
- analysis and planning.

Introduction: why consider the unborn child?

The justification for statutory intervention into family life is the duty to safeguard and promote the welfare of children. In the case of children as yet unborn, it could be argued that there is little which can be done practically to achieve this goal. Although it may be possible to work in partnership with pregnant women and their partners to increase their chances of having healthy babies by, for example, encouraging good antenatal care or offering treatment for problem substance use, there are no legal means of ensuring that the advice is followed. There have been occasional attempts to enforce compliance through the courts. In 1992 the president of the family division in the High Court ruled that a woman in labour must undergo a Caesarean section in order to prevent her death and that of the baby. This ruling was controversial (Dyer 1994) but not legally challenged. A similar decision taken in 1996 using powers under the Mental Health Act 1983 was challenged and deemed unlawful on appeal. It is likely that there will be further case law but the current position in the UK is that a foetus has no legal status. However, the fact that statutory intervention cannot begin before birth does not preclude assessment taking place with a view to ensuring that the needs of the baby will be met following birth.

Studies have shown that children are at most risk of fatal or severe assaults in the first year of life, usually inflicted by their carers (Creighton 1995; D'Orban 1979). Although firm prediction is not an achievable goal (Dingwall 1989), it is important to try to identify the most vulnerable infants before they are harmed. A small number of babies will not be safe in the care of their parents and may need to be removed at birth. A larger group will not require such drastic action, but will benefit from a protection plan or supportive service that is implemented as soon as they are born.

The inquiry report following the death of Tyra Henry recognised that this opportunity had been missed.

> We think that the seeds of the tragedy had been sown before Tyra was born – not in an abstract or fatalistic sense but in that avoidable errors had by then been made which left the newborn baby exposed to known risk.
>
> (London Borough of Lambeth 1987, p.19)

The panel who considered the death of Doreen Aston expressed a similar view: that she might have been protected had a plan been formulated before her birth (Lambeth, Southwark and Lewisham Area Review Committee 1989).

Current guidance and practice

Following the recommendations of the Doreen Aston Report, *Working Together under the Children Act 1989* (Department of Health 1991a) included a section advocating pre-birth assessment where there is concern regarding a potential risk of harm. The implementation of the 1991 guidance has been inconsistent at a local level, with some Area Child Protection Committees (ACPCs) developing guidelines and procedures, others providing no framework.

The same guidance is included in the updated *Working Together to Safeguard Children* (Department of Health *et al.* 1999):

> Where section 47 enquiries give rise to concern that an unborn child may be at future risk of significant harm, the social services department may need to convene an initial child protection conference prior to the child's birth. Such a conference should have the same status, and proceed in the same way, as other initial child protection conferences, including decisions about registration. (Paragraph 5.98).

Implications for practice

In the absence of clear ACPC guidelines, practice has varied in terms of the nature of assessments undertaken before birth. Social workers are familiar with the task of undertaking enquiries, under section 47 of the Children Act 1989, where there is a specific allegation of likely or actual significant harm to consider. However, they may feel less clear where there is no allegation and, indeed, as yet no baby. They may be unsure whether to approach their task within the context of child protection procedures, to take a supportive stance, or to do nothing other than wait and see.

There have also been different interpretations of the remit to make firm plans before birth. For example, in 1992 the London Borough of Lambeth convened a pre-birth meeting to consider the needs of Mia Gibelli and made decisions that, with hindsight, might have protected her. They did not accord these decisions the formal status of a protection plan and instead allowed Mia to go home with her mother, who then drowned her whilst severely depressed (Cervi 1993).

Unborn children and the child protection register

Although there has been a gradual increase in the overall numbers of unborn children placed on child protection registers, there continues to be wide variation between authorities: some never register unborn children, whilst others frequently do (Barker 1997). What does it actually mean to place an unborn child on the child protection register? The child has no name, no gender, no date of birth, and no action can be taken legally to ensure her or his safety. In the absence of further clarification, local authorities have adopted different approaches to their registration of unborn children. For example, in the author's employing authority, decisions about the register are taken before birth but not implemented until the baby is born, and are not, therefore, evident in the statistical returns to the Department of Health.

Ethical dilemmas

The rights of the unborn child

Child care professionals frequently have to balance the respective rights of parents and children. Although this may be complex, there is clear statutory support for the view that the needs of the child are paramount. There is no such clarity when the child is unborn. The law does not afford an unborn baby the status of personhood, and a pregnant woman is not a human incubator, but retains autonomy over her own body and, as a consequence, that of her baby. There is some tension between this and the fact that the unborn baby can be placed on the child protection register and the mother assessed on the basis of her behaviour during the pregnancy.

Parental rights

Unless the parents have requested support, the prospect of a social worker undertaking an assessment during pregnancy may be alarming. The parents may fear that the baby will be taken from them, particularly if they have a history of previous children being removed. In reality very few babies are removed at birth, and an unpublished study undertaken by the author demonstrated a reluctance to act, rather than over-intrusion. Nevertheless it is wise to keep in mind the fraught and emotional nature of such intervention. Studies have recognised the unique difficulty of considering the removal of a baby at birth, with social workers describing their role as cruel – stealing children (Tredinnick and Fairburn 1980) – or like playing God – against the laws of nature (Corner 1997). The bond between a mother and her baby is universally revered, and professionals may be loath to interfere.

This reverence may be associated with a view that parents must be given a chance to care for their baby. Social workers may lack confidence in the standard of proof required in Children Act proceedings in respect of the likelihood of significant harm, or feel that it is against natural justice to intervene purely on this basis. Finally, the unborn baby is inevitably a shadowy figure, whilst the intrusion into the mother's privacy involved in an unwelcome pre-birth assessment is painfully obvious and uncomfortable. All these factors militate against proactive assessment before birth, but may jeopardise the wellbeing of the baby.

Stereotyping

By definition, a pre-birth assessment is triggered by the characteristics of the parents rather than observations of harm to the baby. This could be seen as persecutory, based on the labelling of deviant behaviour and the slippery slope of 'fitness-to-parent' debates. Some parents are particularly vulnerable to such an approach, and it must be clear that generalisations are inappropriate: for example, that people with learning disabilities cannot parent per se (for further discussion see Chapter 18). Similarly, there is a danger of making negative assumptions about parents from minority groups. There may be differences in parenting style arising from ethnicity, class, religion, age or sexuality, but such cultural difference must be respected. It needs to be acknowledged that stereotyping is a real danger and the principle which must be maintained is that it is the parents' behaviour (violent, intoxicated) that presents a potential risk of significant harm to a child, not the label (schizophrenic, crack user) which has brought them to our attention.

Pre-birth assessment

Advantages and disadvantages of pre-birth assessment

The advantages of such early intervention are that it provides a real opportunity to:

- safeguard the babies most likely to suffer significant harm

- ensure that vulnerable parents are offered support at the start of their parenting career, rather than when difficulties have arisen

- establish a working partnership with parents before the baby is born

- assist parents with any problems that may impair their parenting capacity.

The prospect of a pre-birth assessment will be distressing to parents, but could it actually be damaging? The possible disadvantages of intervention at this time are as follows:

- parents may disappear or a mother may not come to hospital to deliver the baby

- stress may have an adverse effect on the parents' mental or physical health

- there is a risk that a mother could feel pressurised into harming herself and the unborn baby or terminating her pregnancy

- fear of losing the baby may jeopardise the attachment process between parent and child.

When is pre-birth assessment likely to be required?

Some prospective parents are aware of their difficulties and request help from social services departments, but others may be referred because of the concerns they invoke. Given the unwelcome nature of many pre-birth assessments, this level of intrusion can only be justified where there is a likelihood that the needs of the child would not be met without such intervention. There are broadly two situations where this is the case:

- parental problems give rise to concern about the safety of the newborn baby

and/or

- parenting history suggests that the prospect of the baby being adequately cared for throughout childhood is bleak.

The latter is perhaps more complex, in that the newborn baby may not be at immediate risk of suffering harm. Practitioners will be familiar with situations where families have had several children removed and are expecting another child. Do they wait to see whether the pattern is repeated or do they actively consider removing the baby at birth?

Parental issues

These issues are considered in detail in Chapter 17 but those which are most likely to have an adverse impact on the safety of a newborn baby are:

- psychiatric illness, including not only psychosis but conditions such as depression or personality disorder

- substance misuse, including alcohol and legal/illegal drug use

- significant learning disability.

It could be argued that such parental difficulties require a supportive response. Indeed, the first aim of pre-birth assessment and planning is to maximise the chances of parents being able to care for their child, and a range of support should be offered to assist them. This may be successful in enabling parents to respond appropriately to their children's developmental needs. However, recent studies have suggested that there is a correlation between parental mental illness, defined to include substance use, and fatal child abuse (Falkov 1996; Reder and Duncan 1999). This suggests that assessment in these situations is justified. Our wish to respond to the real difficulties of parents and to give them every opportunity to bring up their children must not distract us from the needs of the baby.

Parenting history

Concerns may arise over whether the baby is the first or subsequent child. They are likely to be particularly evident where there has been a history of difficulty in caring for previous children. The importance of history should not be underestimated: the most effective clue to future behaviour may be past behaviour. Some studies have suggested that a history of parental violence or abusive behaviour is an indicator of future risk of harm to children (Hagell 1998; Department of Health 1991b).

Parents may have had children together or in the context of other relationships, and the parenting history of the father/partner is as relevant as that of the mother, although often explored less comprehensively. It is important to consider not only the care that each parent has been able to provide to previous children but the impact of this history on their current situation.

Even where there have been major deficiencies in the care of previous children, there may be evidence of a capacity for change as described in Chapter 5. However, assessment is required to gather and evaluate such evidence.

Fundamental questions for professionals

The fundamental questions when deciding whether a pre-birth assessment is required are:

- Will this newborn baby be safe in the care of these parents?
- Is there a realistic prospect of these parents being able to provide adequate care throughout childhood?

Where there is reason for doubt, a pre-birth assessment is indicated.

The assessment process

An organisational framework for pre-birth assessment

A multidisciplinary framework can assist practitioners and ensure a consistent approach towards pre-birth assessment. The components of such a framework would include:

- the situations where pregnant women and their partners should be referred to social services departments for a pre-birth assessment

- the process for making such referrals

- the nature of the assessment to be undertaken by social services departments

- the contribution of other professionals towards the assessment

- a system for offering family support

- a system for considering and managing child protection concerns

- clarification of the situations where it is appropriate to register unborn children and the process for doing so.

For example, Camden and Islington ACPCs have included a section on pregnant women within their guidance, *Working with Drug and Alcohol Using Parents 1999: Policy, Procedures and Guidelines*. This guidance outlines: the responsibility of all agencies to refer women using drugs in pregnancy to the local obstetric unit and social services department; the social work team responsible for undertaking an assessment; the content of the assessment; the multi-agency meetings which will be convened and the action to be taken if the drug use is not revealed until the baby is born. A leaflet has been written by the multidisciplinary team within the local hospital which explains the policy to expectant parents.

Ensuring that referrals are made

Social service departments cannot undertake an assessment unless they are made aware of the pregnancy and the reasons for concern. Midwives are in a unique position to identify families where a pre-birth assessment is indicated. When giving a medical and obstetric history to a midwife, pregnant women are usually very concerned to provide information that will promote the health of their expected baby and are likely to be honest about issues such as substance use, psychiatric conditions or previous pregnancies.

There will always be families whose problems are so overwhelming or who are so afraid of professional involvement that they will not seek antenatal care, and may therefore slip through the net. Such families are likely to be known to other agencies, however. A drug agency may be aware that a woman using their service is pregnant, or the police may know of a young couple sleeping on the street and expecting a baby. The uncertain territory of pre-birth assessment and the differing priorities of other professionals may make them reluctant to refer. This may be an issue not only between agencies but also within social services departments, where the increasing separation of services for adults and children has led to a degree of fragmentation. Can we be confident that a mental health social worker will refer to a colleague within a child care team if he or she learns that a disturbed client is going to become a father?

It is important that all professionals are aware of their responsibility to consider the needs of unborn children and to refer for an assessment prospective parents who may be unable to care safely for their babies. The development of local guidelines by the ACPC which confirm that such assessments are endorsed by *Working Together to Safeguard Children* (Department of Health *et al.* 1999), and the setting up of systems for joint working would reinforce this message.

Undertaking a multidisciplinary assessment

A range of professionals will have a contribution to make to the assessment. Midwives and obstetricians will be able to monitor antenatal attendance and the extent to which a mother is following medical advice. Specialist workers involved in providing services to parents may have important information, such as the fact that a pregnant woman has relapsed into heroin use. The children's services social worker has a key role in co-ordinating the assessment and has lead responsibility for the child's welfare, as outlined in the *Framework for the Assessment of Children in Need and their Families* (Department of Health *et al.* 2000). The sharing of this information is likely to require specific negotiation by the social worker, as professionals working primarily with adults may be unclear about their responsibility towards unborn children. There may need to be discussion about the fact that normal rules of confidentiality must be breached when a baby's safety is involved.

Where parents are not currently receiving help with identified problems it will be necessary to include this as a component of the process. Again, it will be helpful if a partnership has been established between social services and specialist agencies who can offer this help. For example, it may be desirable to have an up-to-date psychiatric assessment of a father with a history of personality disorder and violence; or to have an agreement with the local drug clinic that they will offer immediate treatment to pregnant women and their partners.

The assessment task

The purpose of the assessment is to establish whether there is a need for intervention to safeguard and promote the welfare of the baby. The first task for the assessing social worker is to engage the parents.

Strategies for engaging parents

Given parents' fears and the lack of clear guidance, pre-birth assessments are a particularly difficult task. Ultimately, parents can refuse to cooperate. If a social worker is feeling uncertain about the assessment task he or she may be only too relieved: 'after all, nothing can be done until the baby is born'. In fact, it will be much more difficult to ensure the safety of a newborn child if there has been no attempt to establish a plan during the pregnancy or if parents feel they have successfully avoided assessment. What strategies can social workers adopt to engage a reluctant family?

- First, it is essential that social workers acknowledge and deal openly with the fear that the baby will be removed.

- Parents need to know whether decisions have been made and, if not, on what basis they will be made. There may be a tendency to want to avoid sharing decisions with parents in case it frightens them off, but the converse is likely to be true. Given honest information about what is happening, parents are more likely to feel empowered to participate in an assessment.

- If parents initially refuse to meet the social worker, it may be necessary to involve other professionals, such as midwives or drug workers. The dialogue with them may encourage the parents to see a social worker.

- Written agreements that clarify the format of the assessment, the concerns about parenting and the measures which parents can take to allay these concerns, are also useful and potentially empowering. Strengths as well as weaknesses should be acknowledged. It is surprising how often parents are unclear exactly what is expected of them, particularly if they have had poor experiences themselves of being cared for.

- Male partners/fathers are often marginalised in assessments although they pose an equal or greater risk of harming children (O'Hagan 1997). This phenomenon is particularly marked in pre-birth intervention – pregnancy and infancy being seen as a women's issue. In fact, prospective fathers are often more involved than they are given credit for and will participate if they are specifically invited to do so.

- The period before a baby is born is usually a time when both mothers and fathers are well motivated. They want to do their best for their child, often seeing her or him as an opportunity for a fresh start and a way of making up for past losses and deprivation; drug-using parents may see the child almost as a cure, the motivating factor to enable them to stop using. Although the unreality of these aspirations may be alarming, they do form the basis for a partnership between the social worker and the parents. The goal is to establish a shared understanding that all those involved want the best for this baby and that the parents will be offered every assistance to provide the best.

The nature of the assessment

Having established that a pre-birth assessment is required, and engaged the parents and other professionals, how does the individual social worker proceed? Unlike a section 47 enquiry, they are not assessing an actual incident or injury but speculating about the likelihood of such events in the future and attempting to do so in the absence of a child. What information is it relevant for the social worker to consider?

Corner (1997) suggests a detailed format for assessing parents with a history of abuse but does not address those situations where this is the first child.

Factors which can be explored by the social worker are:

- the problems facing each parent and the likely impact these will have on their parenting capacity

- the nature of previous abuse or parenting breakdown and each parent's attitudes to these events

- each parent's response to the unborn child

- the relationship between the parents

- support networks.

The meaning which each parent ascribes to the unborn child may usefully be explored: is the child a replacement for a previous child; a means of maintaining the parental relationship; an impediment?

As with all areas of family life, ideas about pregnancy and infancy are subject to cultural variation and these must be recognised during the assessment. For example, Caesarean deliveries and bottle-feeding are disapproved of within many African communities, but strongly advised to HIV-positive women in order to reduce the risk of transmission to their baby. Any plans made must recognise the dilemma faced by a woman who wants to safeguard her baby but is afraid of rejection if her HIV status becomes known to family and friends.

The *Framework for the Assessment of Children in Need and their Families* and the unborn child

The Assessment Framework will facilitate the assessment task in that it is applicable to all families in need of support and not just those where there has been an allegation of abuse or neglect. It provides a structure for gathering and evaluating information. The main focus before birth will be the domains relating to the parents and the context in which they live: the baby is still off-stage and not accessible to an assessment other than in general terms.

The child's needs

Unborn babies clearly do have requirements if they are to be born safe and well, but the main purpose of assessment at this time is to consider whether their needs will be met after the birth. Behaviour during the pregnancy will inform this assessment. For example, a mother's failure to stop using cocaine during pregnancy may provide information about her ability to recognise and prioritise the needs of the baby. Reder and Duncan (1999) suggest that a failure to seek antenatal care is a significant factor in subsequent fatalities, although it must be borne in mind that there may be reasons for failing to attend an antenatal clinic other than indifference to the health of the baby. For example, one mother whose teenager had just been removed from her care on an interim care order assumed that she would not be allowed to care for her expected baby and was too frightened to disclose her pregnancy.

The first task of a pre-birth assessment will be to consider whether the baby's basic needs will be met, that is, will it be fed, kept warm and clean, handled gently and provided with health care? Any special needs of the baby should inform the decision-making: for example, babies affected by opiate withdrawal may be particularly difficult to care for. This is not to say that the baby's other needs, such as the opportunity for a secure attachment, can be ignored; we know that the foundations for the development of emotional wellbeing are laid in infancy, as outlined in Chapter 12.

Parenting capacity

Of the six dimensions of parenting outlined in the Assessment Framework, the most pressing in the context of a pre-birth assessment are those relating to the basic care and safety of the new born baby. The framework provides a vehicle for linking parental problems to parenting capacity. Will a father with a personality disorder be able to tolerate his baby's incessant crying without lashing out, or a mother with severe learning difficulties be able to change her baby's nappy? Assuming parental problems are not so over-whelming as to preclude them responding appropriately to the basic health needs of the baby, there are further considerations in terms of the other dimensions of parenting outlined by the framework. In particular, the parents' capacity to provide warmth, stimulation and consistency in order that the baby will be able to develop and thrive. The social worker will need to consider not only whether parents have the capacity to respond to these needs in the short term, but also whether they are likely to be able to sustain parenting over time. For example, a drug-using mother may be able to care for an immobile baby but be too distracted to keep up with a boisterous toddler.

The Assessment Framework provides a model for considering the capac-ity of each parent. It may be the case that one parent is able to compensate for the difficulties experienced by the other. For example, a depressed mother may have been unavailable emotionally to a previous child but the father/partner has demonstrated an ability to provide emotional security at such times.

Family and environmental factors

The environmental needs of a newborn baby are not complex: the emphasis within a pre-birth assessment will be to ensure that parents have a safe place to live with their baby, basic baby equipment and an income. There may still be instances where the environment will be considered to be unsuitable: drug-using parents may be receiving benefits but spending most of it on heroin, or may be leaving syringes where they will endanger the baby; a mother with a psychotic illness who has lost three tenancies through fire raises serious concern about the risk of harm this poses to her expected baby.

It is essential to focus the assessment not only on both parents but also their wider network. The baby is going to be affected, positively and negatively, by all those with whom he or she comes into contact, and an assessment that excludes significant figures will be flawed. The inevitable challenge of pregnancy and birth will highlight the support structures available to the parents. Given that the situations where a pre-birth assessment is instigated will be those where concerns are serious, families are likely both to have few support networks and to be in particular need of them. Parents with substance use or mental health problems may be isolated or have a peer group who cannot help them because of their own difficulties: one young woman who had been homeless and sleeping out found it impossible to adjust to the isolation of having her own tenancy, and allowed her flat to be taken over by people she had met on the street.

Analysis and planning

Outcome of assessment

Once the social worker has gathered sufficient information, he or she must reach a conclusion as to the best means of promoting the baby's welfare. The initial aim of all assessments should be to explore whether parents can be supported in meeting their baby's needs. The social worker may have been able to establish a partnership with parents which acknowledges potential difficulties and has explored solutions. For example, an assessment of a mother with learning disabilities may establish that she will need additional help in making up feeds, and identify means of providing such support. This will ensure that the baby's needs are met and avoid the need to consider the family within child protection procedures.

There may be other situations where the assessment is less optimistic. A mother may be unable to stabilise her use of drugs; a psychiatric opinion may suggest that a father continues to have delusions about his expected baby; where parents have abused previous children, the social worker may find that there is no evidence of change; or parents may have refused to comply with the assessment, leaving grave doubts about the safety of the baby. It may be that one parent has complied with the assessment and is not thought to pose a risk to the baby, but may be unable to safeguard the baby against a violent partner. In these circumstances a child protection conference should be convened to consider whether a formal protection plan is necessary (Department of Health *et al.* 1999). Such a plan may be able to include sufficient monitoring and support to allow the baby to be discharged home or to another safe setting.

Pre-birth plans

Whatever the conclusion of the assessment, a multidisciplinary meeting, convened either as a child in need meeting or, if appropriate, an initial child protection conference, is likely to be helpful in order to consider the plan. A good pre-birth plan should ensure that everyone is clear about what will happen when the baby is born. Where will the baby live and who will care for her or him? It may be that, although concern is too great to allow the baby to be discharged into the community, a further period of assessment in a supervised setting is indicated. Is such a place available, and how are the arrangements going to be made? Are there going to be legal proceedings or another child protection conference? What further assessment is required and who should undertake it? What is the time-scale for this? The latter is particularly important if the impetus afforded by early intervention is not to be lost by allowing the situation to drift.

Managing non-cooperation

What can be done in the event of non-cooperation, given that there are no statutory steps that can be taken to safeguard the unborn baby? Waiting for a vulnerable baby to be born can lead to feelings of anxiety and power-lessness amongst the professionals, particularly if it is thought that the mother may seek to conceal the birth. In these circumstances, close liaison between the professionals is essential. A plan can be formulated and communicated to the local obstetric units as to the action they should take if the mother presents in labour. Where there is sufficient information to indicate that the baby will be at immediate risk of suffering significant harm, this plan may include legal intervention; where the risks of this occurring are less clear, it may be possible to negotiate that the mother and baby remain in hospital or an alternative place of safety whilst an urgent assessment takes place following the birth.

Removal at birth?

Despite the wish to give parents a chance there will be situations where the decision is taken to seek to remove the baby at birth. This will be the case where there is concern about the immediate safety of the newborn baby or where there is no realistic prospect of the parents ever being able to respond to their child's needs. For example, one mother who suffered from schizophrenia had cared for her first child, but he had failed to thrive despite a high level of support. His mother seemed unable to recognise when he was hungry or distressed, and there was increasing concern, culminating in care proceedings. The second child was born at a time when the mother was acutely psychotic and expressing bizarre ideas about the baby's thoughts and intentions. Midwives were alarmed about her rough handling of the baby on the ward. The baby's father drank heavily and was frequently violent. Neither parent would accept that there was reason for concern, and they threatened the social worker. Although the extended family was interested and involved, they felt powerless to intervene until the baby was effectively abandoned in hospital and they applied for a residence order. When the mother became pregnant for a third time her mental health had stabilised on medication, but she was expressing ambivalence about continuing to take it. She remained in a relationship with the same partner and had been subjected to several assaults by him. A pre-birth conference endorsed the view of social services that there should be an application for an interim care order at birth.

There will be a high level of anxiety amongst professionals as well as parents when such a decision has been taken and it is helpful if the plan is as detailed as possible and recorded in writing. Consider basic questions such as:

- Who should the hospital contact when the mother is admitted?
- Should this contact be when the mother is in labour or after the baby is born?
- What happens if the baby is born out of office hours?
- What level of contact can the parents have with the baby?
- What is the plan in relation to breast-feeding?
- Is there a need to alert other hospitals of the plan?
- What are the arrangements for initiating legal proceedings?
- Are the parents aware of the plan and what is their attitude towards it?

These issues can all provoke a crisis if not clarified in advance and it is important that parents are given as much information as possible.

Further assessment following the birth of the baby

It is uniquely difficult to make decisions about the wellbeing of a baby not yet born and it is rare that final decisions can be taken before birth. The vital component of the actual care given to the baby cannot be assessed until he or she has been born. Midwives will also have valuable information about the parents' attitude to their baby and their ability to provide care. Babies born to women using drugs or alcohol will need specialist monitoring by a paediatrician, and may spend their first few weeks being cared for on a special care baby unit. Again, the staff involved will have extensive information about whether parents can care for the baby over a 24-hour period, whether they can tolerate the stress of their baby's withdrawal symptoms, and whether there is evidence that their substance use is out of control. These are difficult issues for social workers to assess within their more limited contact with families.

Families have the potential to confound our expectations, and the birth of a baby may be the crisis that brings about a change for better or worse. One mother, known to the author, with a history of alcoholism and violence to her sons, had been unable to achieve any change that would enable them to be rehabilitated to her care and they were placed for adoption. In spite of this bleak history, she was able to stop drinking, and an assessment concluded that she should be given the opportunity to look after her next baby. She has continued to provide excellent care to her daughter and there have been no child protection concerns.

The contribution which can be made by a residential assessment for parents and baby is an interesting issue. Perhaps because of the anxiety which professionals feel about the vulnerability of babies, combined with a reluctance to sever the mother/baby relationship, a period of assessment in a residential unit may be suggested. Whilst such assessments may indeed be useful, it is important to ensure that they are purposeful rather than being offered as a safe place for the family to fail. Is there any point, for example, in placing a mother with a chronic psychotic illness, and who has had all her previous children removed, in a residential unit with her baby for assessment? When undertaking pre-birth assessments, we may conclude that no amount of further assessment is going to tell us anything different: this child cannot be cared for by these parents.

Summary

Although targeted at a small minority of families, pre-birth assessment does provide the opportunity to ensure that support and protection are available to the most vulnerable children from the start of their lives. The goal of intervention at this time is compatible with the broader political agenda of maximising the life chances of all children through initiatives such as 'Sure Start' and 'Quality Protects'. The *Framework for the Assessment of Children in Need and their Families* will assist social workers embarking on this sensitive task.

Recommended reading

Howe, D. (1995) *Attachment Theory for Social Work Practice.* Basingstoke: MacMillan.

Morris, N. and Nott, S. (1995) 'The Law's Engagement with Pregnancy.' In J. Bridgeman and S. Millns (eds.) *Law and Body Politics: Regulating the Female Body.* Aldershot: Dartmouth, pp. 53–77.

References

Barker, R. (1997) 'Unborn Children and Child Protection: Legal, Policy and Practice Issues.' In *The Liverpool Law Review*, Vol. XIX (2) pp.219–229.

Cervi, B. (1993) 'Agencies Failed Over Baby Death Case.' In *Community Care*, 25 February p.2.

Corner, R. (1997) 'Pre-Birth Risk Assessment in Child Protection.' In *Social Work Monographs*, Norwich: University of East Anglia.

Creighton, S. (1995) 'Fatal Child Abuse: How Preventable Is It?' In *Child Abuse Review, 4,* pp.318–28.

Department of Health (1991a) *Working Together under the Children Act 1989.* London: HMSO.

Department of Health (1991b) *Child Abuse: A Study of Inquiry Reports 1980–1989.* London: HMSO.

Department of Health, Home Office and Department for Education and Employment (1999) *Working Together to Safeguard Children.* London: The Stationery Office.

Department of Health, Department for Education and Employment and Home Office (2000) *Framework for the Assessment of Children in Need and their Families.* London: The Stationery Office.

Dingwall, R. (1989) 'Predicting Child Abuse and Neglect.' In O. Stevenson (ed.) *Child Abuse: Public Policy and Professional Practice.* Hemel Hempstead: Harvester Wheatsheaf.

D'Orban, P. (1979) 'Women who Kill their Children.' In *British Journal of Psychiatry, 134,* pp.560–71.

Dyer, C. (1994) 'Sharp Practices.' *The Guardian,* 11 January, G2, p.14.

Falkov, A. (1996) *Fatal Child Abuse and Parental Psychiatric Disorder.* London: Department of Health.

Hagell, A. and The Bridge Child Care Development Service (1998) *Dangerous Care: Reviewing the Risks to Children from their Carers.* London: Policy Studies Unit.

Lambeth, Southwark and Lewisham Area Review Committee (1989) *The Doreen Aston Report.*

London Borough of Lambeth (1987) *Whose Child? The Report of the Panel Appointed to Inquire into the Death of Tyra Henry.*

O'Hagan, K. (1997) 'The Problem of Engaging Men in Child Protection Work.' In *British Journal of Social Work, 27*, pp.25–42.

Reder, P. and Duncan, S. (1999) *Lost Innocents: A Follow-Up Study of Fatal Child Abuse.* London: Routledge.

Tredinnick, A. and Fairburn, A. (1980) 'Left Holding the Baby.' In *Community Care*, April 10, pp.22–5.

Part IV

Assessing the Parental Capacity to Respond to the Developmental Needs of the Child

CHAPTER 16

The Assessment
of Parental Capacity

David Jones

Critically important to a child's health and development is the ability of parents or care-givers to ensure that the child's developmental needs are being appropriately and adequately responded to, and to adapt to his or her changing needs over time.

(From the *Framework for the Assessment of Children in Need and their Families,* p.20, 2.9)

Within this chapter the following are considered:

- what is meant by the term 'parenting'
- factors that influence parenting capacity
- dimensions of parenting capacity
- parenting dimensions evolving with the developmental needs of the child
- implications for practice, and examples
- parenting capacity and the assessment process.

Introduction

Thank you very much for your evidence on this child's failure to thrive. Just before you go, Dr. Jones, it would be really helpful if you could help the court with what is meant by parenting, as this is a term

you have used a number of times in your evidence. (Judge Orrelle
Weeks, Denver, Colorado).

In this chapter it will be argued that although practitioners may have to
justify what they mean by 'parenting' within a family justice system, the
most important reason to articulate what we mean by parenting is so that we
have a sound empirical base upon which to enter into a working relationship with families in order to improve a child's welfare. The aim of human
parents is to rear their young to be autonomous individuals who will be
capable of participating fully in the culture in which they live. There is a
remarkable similarity in this fundamental objective but at the same time
there is significant cultural relativity with respect to what is considered
necessary for parents to do in different communities, and also what is
considered to be abuse or neglect (Korbin 1997). Parenting, then, refers to
the activities and behaviours of parents which are necessary to achieve the
objective of enabling children to become autonomous. These activities and
behaviours change as the child develops. Thus, parenting as an activity is
firmly yoked to child outcomes. In this chapter we will consider what are
the minimum requirements and different dimensions of parenting. Before
doing so, parenting behaviours will be placed in a broader context, and
other factors which influence parent and child will be considered.

Factors that influence our understanding
of parenting capacity

If parenting behaviours and salient developmental issues comprised the
whole picture, we would probably be able to list the parenting functions
required without further ado. We could list minimum parenting standards
or requirements, and each dimension would be easily defined and subjected
to measurement and the appropriate validity study. All we would have to do
would be to go down our list and rate the parents' competence on a 1–5
scale. There are a several reasons why such an approach is impossible:

1. Parenting behaviours do not occur within a vacuum. They are
    crucially connected to wider influences which have their impact
    upon individual parents. Notable among these are cultural
    influences and neighbourhood ones (Garbarino and Kostelny
    1992).

2. There are difficulties in defining the dimensions of parenting
    behaviours and demonstrating their individual link with child
    outcomes. However, some progress has been made with measuring

some of the dimensions of parenting. Assessment schemes for measuring the adequacy of safety measures within the home (Barone, Greene and Lutzker 1986), home cleanliness and potential health risks (Watson-Perczel *et al.* 1988), and adequacy of nutrition (Greene *et al.* 1995) have been made, but other dimensions of parenting have proved more elusive: in particular, sufficiency of psychological warmth, and the adequacy of discipline and behaviour-shaping.

3. There can be difficulty in deciding the relative weight which should be ascribed to each dimension. Is one aspect of parenting more important than another, and if so, how much more important? When faced with life-threatening absences of care the question of weight becomes redundant, but with lesser deficits we are not able to weigh the different dimensions accurately. What guidance we do have is described below.

4. The different dimensions of parenting are not isolated factors with no relationships among them. On the contrary, the transactions among different elements are of crucial importance. One aspect of this is the unknown relationship between positive factors, or ameliorating influences, on the one hand, and deficits in parenting behaviours and skills on the other. We do not know whether, and to what extent, highly developed dimensions of parenting have the effect of cancelling out or neutralising the more negative capacities. Similarly, are certain combinations of parenting deficits particularly harmful? Once again, we do not have the empirical base to answer these questions.

5. The relationship between parents and child is not merely a one-way process, but a two-way interaction, with child and adults contributing to the sum effect.

6. There is enormous variability in what we term families. Some families are two-parent, others one-parent, or have step-parents; still others consist of shared parenting arrangements. Other family units in which children receive parenting care involve both parents and grandparents or other relatives or relatively unusual constellations, for instance lesbian parents caring for children.

7. The number of children in families also has an effect on parenting behaviours, as do the particular demands of individual children, e.g. those with disabilities or special needs.

8. Families, and the demands on parenting behaviour, change over time in relation to age, gender issues and disability/difference.

9. There has been particular interest in recent years in widening concepts of parenting beyond examining dyadic relationships such as mother/child or father/child ones. It has been noted that mothers' directly observed parenting behaviours will vary, depending upon whether they are interacting with the child alone, or together with another parent (Belsky, Putnam and Canic 1996; McHale, Kuersten and Lauretti 1996). It is possible to separate influences deriving from a marital conflict, dyadic parenting behaviour and competence and co-parenting. Each of these can be shown to have effects upon the developing child, and this has major implications for how we assess parenting capacity. Mothers and fathers may either support one another in the parenting tasks, or undermine each other's competence through hostility, criticism and aggressive competition (McHale *et al.* 1996).

The net result of these considerations is to place parenting capacity in context. Parenting capacities and behaviour are therefore complex, and subject to influences within the family and from outside. The notion of mere dimensions of parenting can therefore be seen as wanting, unless we are prepared to embed these dimensions of parenting within a broader framework. Once we do so, of course, the implications for assessments become both more complex and at the same time of greater validity.

The ecological framework, as described in Chapter 3, has achieved the greatest consensus among practitioners and researchers as a model within which to place the parent–child relationship, and child abuse and neglect in particular (Belsky *et al.* 1996; National Research Council 1993; Jones 1997). However, although it is a useful model with which to consider the different levels of complexity of social organisation that impact upon parent–child relationships, it does not provide a model for understanding the mechanisms through which different influences operate within the individual case, nor does it help us to ascribe weight to individual factors which might impact upon parent–child relationships. These and similar shortcomings with developmental-ecological models of child abuse have been articulated by Azar *et al.* (1998).

Dimensions of parenting capacity

Having arrived at the position that parenting capacity is subject in itself to a wide range of different influences, both from within and without the immediate family, and may vary according to the particular constellation within the family, does the concept still have any utility left at all? It does, for the following reasons:

1. Careful analysis of parenting behaviours can act as a basis for planning services for a family.

2. Parenting capacity provides a crucial baseline upon which to review change or progress among families in difficulty.

3. Parenting capacity is an equitable basis for state intervention into family life, should this be necessary. A criticism of current assessments is that they are frequently based upon unsystematic evaluations and are subject to bias, prejudice, or simply restricted in their scope by looking at one aspect of parenting while ignoring other important qualities. It would seem preferable that state intervention is based upon a review of minimum parenting requirements, particularly if these are themselves based upon consensus or evidence that the dimensions in question are related to desirable child outcomes.

4. The approach to assessment emphasised here encourages empiricism, even when precise measurement is not available or possible. At least the dimension in question can be described, any deficits or competencies noted, and placed in the appropriate context. Without a framework for conceptualising parenting, the family is at the whim of the individual assessor's bias or prejudice.

With these various considerations in mind and with the above rationale these are the dimensions of parenting which are acknowledged to have a link with desirable child outcomes (Box 16.1). If the standard of parenting competence is markedly low in any one of these areas it may well have a negative impact on the child.

Support for the dimensions of parenting set out in Box 16.1 comes from studies which have explored the link between aspects of parenting behaviour and child outcomes (Loeber and Stouthamer-Loeber 1987; Rutter 1989; Wasserman et al. 1996). The following areas of parenting behaviour and parent–child relationships have been linked with child behavioural and emotional problems: conflict between parent and child; inadequate parental monitoring; lack of parental involvement. Parent–child

Basic Care

Providing for the child's physical needs, and appropriate medical and dental care.

Includes provision of food, drink, warmth, shelter, clean and appropriate clothing and adequate personal hygiene.

Ensuring Safety

Ensuring the child is adequately protected from harm or danger.

Includes protection from significant harm or danger, and from contact with unsafe adults/other children and from self-harm. Recognition of hazards and danger both in the home and elsewhere.

Emotional Warmth

Ensuring the child's emotional needs are met and giving the child a sense of being specially valued and a positive sense of own racial and cultural identity. Includes ensuring the child's requirements for secure, stable and affectionate relationships with significant adults, with appropriate sensitivity and responsiveness to the child's needs. Appropriate physical contact, comfort and cuddling sufficient to demonstrate warm regard, praise and encouragement.

Stimulation

Promoting child's learning and intellectual development through encouragement and cognitive stimulation and promoting social opportunities. Includes facilitating the child's cognitive development and potential through interaction, communication, talking and responding to the child's language and questions, encouraging and joining the child's play, and promoting educational opportunities. Enabling the child to experience success and ensuring school attendance or equivalent opportunity. Facilitating child to meet challenges of life.

Guidance and Boundaries

Enabling the child to regulate his or her own emotions and behaviour. The key parental tasks are demonstrating and modelling appropriate behaviour and control of emotions and interactions with others, and guidance which involves setting boundaries, so that the child is able to develop an internal model of moral values and conscience, and social behaviour appropriate for the society within which he or she will grow up. The aim is to enable children to grow into an autonomous adults, holding their own values, and able to demonstrate appropriate behaviour with others rather than having to be dependent on rules outside themselves. This includes not over-protecting children from exploratory and learning experiences.

Includes social problem-solving, anger management, consideration for others, and effective discipline and shaping of behaviour.

Stability

Providing a sufficiently stable family environment to enable a child to develop and maintain a secure attachment to the primary care-giver(s) in order to ensure optimal development.

Includes ensuring secure attachments are not disrupted, providing consistency of emotional warmth over time and responding in a similar manner to the same behaviour. Parental responses change and develop according to child's developmental progress. In addition, ensuring children keep in contact with important family members and significant others.

Box 16.1 Dimensions of parenting capacity.

conflict includes fighting and arguing as well as overt dislike and rejection of the child. It also includes harsh punishment. These have been linked with behaviour problems and later delinquency. Inadequate parental monitoring involves inadequate supervision and a lack of knowledge of the child's whereabouts or activities. Lack of positive parental involvement in the child concerns cognitive stimulation, as well as lack of emotional support and weak parent–child attachments.

The parenting dimension (Box 16.1) of behaviour guidance links with these qualities. First, excessive parent–child conflict creates a poor model for conflict resolution and teaches the child an unhelpful approach to managing conflict. Similarly, harsh punishments set a precedent for meeting behaviour difficulties with parental violence. Additionally, inadequate parental monitoring means that opportunities to help the child with social problem-solving and emotional regulation are diminished, while lack of positive involvement reduces the opportunity for the child to develop internal controls and to understand his or her own emotional state and impulses. Wasserman *et al.* (1996) found that the three areas of conflict, inadequate monitoring and lack of positive involvement contribute to the child's behaviour problems independently, as well as having a summative effect if all three are present.

Some groups of parents are likely to have these kinds of difficulties to a greater degree than comparison parents. The former would include parents with a history of childhood deprivation (Rutter 1989), particularly when they have histories of abuse or neglect which have not been assimilated or understood in a coherent way prior to becoming a parent (George 1996).

Parenting capacity is also affected by serious disharmony or violence in the adult partnership, or where one or both parent suffers from mental illness or disorder (Garmezy and Masten 1994; Quinton and Rutter 1985), or alcohol or substance abuse (as outlined in Chapter 17). The exact mechanisms through which these forms of parental disorder affect parenting are complex and consist of multiple influences on a number of different levels within the parent–child relationship, family or neighbourhood. For example, the impact of maternal depression on parenting functioning and child behaviour and emotional outcome is unlikely to derive from the influence of depressed mood, per se. It is much more likely that depressed mood affects other aspects of family life and social relationships as well as the availability of social support, and possible subsequent social isolation, and that all of these factors affect parenting.

Furthermore, we have very little research information to help us to unravel the various transactions between different factors which any one family might have to endure, or indeed to unravel the relative influences from positive compared to negative factors. Some helpful evidence has been obtained, however, from the study of the impact of parental mental illness on parenting and the subsequent behaviour of the child. Studies reveal the importance of ameliorative influences, such as having a spouse or partner without mental illness who provides support for an unwell parent, as well as being able positively to parent the child. Equally, the child's temperament and inherent resilience is a factor affecting the degree to which he or she is affected by parental mental disorder (though child factors are unlikely to be as influential as parent ones (Kaufman and Zigler 1989; Rutter 1985). The overall conclusion is that the research base remains a useful guide but, in practice, evaluation and synthesis of a wide number of factors drawn from different levels of social complexity surrounding the child's predicament are the most appropriate feature for practitioners to take on board.

A developmental perspective

Cicchetti (1989) has summarised the key stages of child development from an integrative perspective. These comprise the following:

- attachment (0–12 months)
- autonomy and self-development (1–3 years)
- establishing peer relationships (3–7 years)
- hierarchical integration of attachment, autonomy, and peer relationships (7–12 years).

Cicchetti emphasises the importance of seeing each of these stages in terms of foundations for successive ones, rather than observable stages which come to the forefront and then merely fade over time. The earlier stage is then less prominent, but no less important for future competence. This approach not only emphasises progressive development but also the crucial requirement for integration as the child grows and achieves mastery and competence over the lifespan. A good example is the issue of attachment. Although attachment is considered a key early developmental issue, it remains centrally important in adult life. It will undergo a series of important integrations into other aspects of the child's developing world, for example, during school years, when social integration becomes, in terms of development, the more prominent task. Lack of integration of early attachment can lead to severe, disabling difficulties during later childhood and adult life.

The parents' task in relation to these developmental issues is to bring the necessary elements to bear in order to maximise the child's capacity to achieve these goals. The focus here is on the minimum necessary parenting, rather than an idealised notion of the perfect parent. However, in placing parenting behaviours in direct proximity to the developmental issues of the child it is immediately clear that what is required from the parent will change during the lifespan. Parenting in infancy is significantly different from that required during teenage years.

The development of a secure attachment relationship with a primary care-giver is regarded as the key developmental issue during the first year of life, as described in Chapter 12. This relationship becomes evident through both infant and parent behaviours from age six months on, though its foundations have been laid well before this. The exchange of affection between parent and child, combined with recognition of and absorption with one another and an attendant ability on the part of the infant to cope with stress, are the hallmarks of successful negotiation at this stage. If the parent is unable to provide for this need in the infant, effects can be seen both in terms of the infant's behaviour, the quality of relationship between infant and care-giver, and in the care-giver's own sense of satisfaction and contentment.

Between the ages of approximately one and three years the primary task of the infant is the development of an autonomous self, that is, the beginnings of a development of a sense of self as separate from others. This differentiation is thought to depend upon the earlier consolidation of a secure attachment relationship during infancy. Key issues for parents during this phase include their sensitivity and ability to be flexible enough to respond to the toddler as he or she struggles to discover the limits of personal identity and power within the world. The parent enables the growing toddler to explore her or his environment, while at the same time enabling reliance on a parent or parent-figure for safety and security. This period is also marked by the child's increasing recognition and experience of his or her own emotional state, and the parent is called upon to enable the developing toddler to regulate and begin to be aware of internal feeling states.

This process becomes more sophisticated in the third year of life, as the developing child increasingly differentiates him or herself from others. The rapid development of language and the capacity to represent self, others, and inanimate objects in both play and language marks this period. The parents' sensitivity and availability, both emotionally and to the joys of language, are key parental competencies at this time. Further emotional understanding and regulation also occur during this period.

The period from three to seven years is characterised by establishing friendships and connections with other children. The ability to form friendships and to become integrated into peer groups requires the foundation of the previous stages of development. Self-regulation and the capacity to exhibit empathy and pro-social behaviour, combined with awareness of culturally relevant social mores, are key features. Parents' roles are now significantly different in terms of meeting the developmental needs of the child, despite being based in the dimensions and capacities required for earlier phases of development.

Between seven and twelve years the task for the child becomes one of integration, based upon secure attachment and a capacity to differentiate self from other, as well as extending peer relationships and social networks. Also during this phase the child becomes increasingly aware of his or her own intentions and volition. The sense of right and wrong and development of moral ideas becomes strong at this age, as does the sense of internal thought processes and feeling states. Children's increased capacity to act autonomously and to assume responsibilities becomes clear to the observer.

Finally, during adolescent years, these qualities are further developed, extending the process of integration and increasing the scope and the scale of peer relationships, as well as relationships with other significant adults within the young person's world.

Basic competence in each parenting dimension (see Box 16.1) is required throughout childhood and adolescence in order to meet the developing person's needs. However, in addition to this some parenting qualities become especially salient at different points in development, in order to respond to the particular needs of that child's developmental age and stage. For example, the provision of emotional warmth in infancy revolves around attachment to the primary care-giver, whereas in teenage years it is more likely to comprise emotional warmth and availability to listen and help the young person with his or her everyday problems, and to provide a secure base from which the youngster can establish a network of friends. Examples of these differences in emphasis dependent upon developmental level are found in the Assessment Recording Forms (Department of Health and Cleaver 2000).

Implications for practice

A number of general principles can be derived for practitioners when assessing parenting competence.

1. The parenting concept is not especially helpful unless it is seen as a way of describing parental behaviour and competence set within a broader ecology of the child's world. Thus the emphasis shifts from a consideration of parenting and parent–child relationships to considering these together with adult co-parenting competence, influences of family relationships on parenting, extended family and friendship networks and the influence of neighbourhoods (Garbarino and Sherman 1980; Garbarino and Kostelny 1992) on the capacity of parents to care for their children. Poverty is included (Pelton 1994) and so is the influence of hostile environments. There are broader cultural influences that also impinge on an individual's capacity to parent, for example, cultural attitudes towards violence; sexual relationships; issues of race.

2. The developmental perspective is key when considering parenting capacity.

3. Parenting dimensions are not static but evolve with both the developmental needs of the child and changes in the family's life, for example, the arrival of siblings; changes in family structure; death; illness and other life events.

4. Practitioners cannot assess parenting capacity from one perspective alone, for example, the history taken from one parent, or observations made of one dyad, such as mother–child. A true picture of parenting capacity within the family can only be obtained from multiple perspectives at different times in the life of a family. Nonetheless, the differences between the different times may be important in the overall assessment. For example, the relationship between a mother and her children may be functional when she is on her own with the children, but may become

significantly dysfunctional at times when she is in a hostile or competitive relationship with her partner.

5. A detailed overall description of parenting capacity, incorporating positive or negative qualities of each dimension of parenting, provides an antidote to the biased impression that may derive from observing a striking deficit in one particular dimension.

6. Assessments of parenting capacity need to be linked to the needs of the particular child who is being assessed. For example, taking into account a child's special needs, any disability, or issues of race and culture, temperament, or the special meaning of certain children (for example, those in whom parents invest a special meaning by dint of anniversary of arrival or link with particular life events, deaths or significant relationships).

7. It is necessary to identify who provides parenting and/or who has the potential to do so. How many parents are there available to the particular child in question? From this it is possible to consider not only what each parent provides for the child, but how relationships between different parent figures affect parenting capacity (the co-parenting relationship), and the interaction between an individual's parenting capacity and other contextual factors.

8. It is useful to consider whether the needs of the child can be met by any others if there is significant incapacity in one particular parent, for example, other parents, shared care, respite and/or residential care.

Applying the lessons learnt

Three situations are selected here because they evoke emotional reactions in both professionals and lay public alike, and hence may be considered as particular challenges when it comes to applying the lessons learnt from the understanding of parenting capacity set out above. The first is common and applies to up to a third of all families. The other two are less common: children parented by lesbians; and second, the assessment of parenting competence when one parent has abused a child.

Assessing parenting capacity in stepfamilies

Families with a step-parent highlight several of the above implications. Stepfamilies evolve over several years (Papernow 1993), and are significantly different from traditional ones (Seibt 1996) in several important respects: they challenge and face persisting myths and culturally based expectations; they face particular tasks and have distinguishable characteristics; the new partnership is of primary importance to both adults; stepfamilies are observed to develop over several years into a stable unit (Papernow 1993; Seibt 1996). Assessment of parenting capacity in stepfamilies therefore needs to take these differences into account, because simple transposition of ideas from traditional families would be insufficient. That is not to say that any different standard of evaluation of parenting dimensions is required, but that the roles of individual parent-figures and the context for evaluating competence should be informed by what is known of stepfamily development.

Assessing parenting capacity in lesbian households

The outcomes for children, boys or girls, growing up in a lesbian household have been reviewed (Tasker and Golombok 1991), and a group of children raised by lesbian mothers followed to examine a wide range of outcomes (Golombok, Tasker and Murray 1997). Studies such as this illustrate that there are neither particular influences on the child's relationships with his or her parents and friends, or wider family, nor influences on the child's gender preference that are a consequence of their being raised in a lesbian mother household, per se. The issues facing such children are the same as those facing any other children, that is, the quality of the relationships between the child and significant adults in the context within which those relationships are being enacted. The parenting partnership itself, though less common than the norm, is not the determining factor.

Assessing the parenting capacity of the non-abusive parent

The common assessment task for social workers is to consider the child welfare implications when one parent is known to have abused a child within the family, but an assessment is called for concerning the non-abusive parent. Classically, this occurs to non-abusive mothers in situations where a child has been sexually abused in the family (and is described in Chapters 19 and 20), but also occurs in the less common situation where a mother subjects a child to the form of abuse known as Munchausen Syndrome by Proxy (MSBP) where she fabricates or induces illness in a child (Jones and

Bools 1999), but the father's parenting capacity is in question. In both these situations, one important consideration is whether the non-abusive parent has in fact played a major part in the abuse, either directly, or through collusion with the offending parent. This question may be easier to contemplate with respect to non-offending fathers in MSBP than with non-offending mothers in cases of sexual abuse, presumably because of the preponderance of male violence in families and our reluctance to contemplate the less common female violence. Once this question has been evaluated, the issue of continuing ability to protect the child from further abuse will be a key one. The non-abusive parent's need for understanding and support at a time of significant personal trauma, following the disclosure of abuse within the family, has probably been underestimated to date (Sharland *et al.* 1996). Equally, the non-abusive parent may have significant mental health needs which typically may not be responded to, as treatment plans focus on the abused child or the abusing adult. Nonetheless, the salience of the contribution by the non-abusive care-giver is emphasised in the outcome literature on child sexual abuse (Jones and Ramchandani 1999), and in MSBP (Berg and Jones 1999; Jones and Bools 1999). If a practitioner assesses parenting capacity only in the immediate aftermath of discovery of abuse, the non-offending parent's capacity to provide or their child's needs would be likely to be underestimated, at least in the medium term.

A brief description of these areas illustrates many of the foregoing principles and findings from research. However, there are implications for the process of assessment too.

Summary: implications for the process of assessment

The emphasis on gathering data from all three domains – the developmental needs of the child, parenting capacity and family and environmental factors – has been described in Chapter 2. However, as described by Adcock in Chapter 4, data-gathering alone is insufficient for assessment purposes, and the key task which follows is weighing and balancing these findings and assessing both their combination and transactional effects. At this point a statement of the current situation is useful, listing the various positive and negative factors from the various domains of child, family life and the community. This process involves the judgement of the practitioner concerning salient factors and their relative transactions between one another. Although the research can guide us here, it cannot provide the kind of numerical accuracy which is often sought.

1. Gather data from all domains of risk, including all positive and negative items

2. Weigh relative significance

3. Assess child's current welfare situation, stating assessment of risk of harm

4. Consider future circumstances which may alter child's welfare

5. Identify prospects for change

6. Establish criteria for gauging effectiveness

7. Outline proposed timescale

8. Organise risk management plan

   i Roles and responsibilities for different professionals and agencies

   ii Who will notice and what action will be taken?

   iii Date and time of next review.

Box 16.2 Process of planning intervention

Our formulation of the current situation should also include an assessment of the likelihood of any change (while accepting the limitations on prediction) as described by Horwath and Morrison in Chapter 5. Regarded in this way, assessments of parenting capacity are not ends in themselves, but rather become integral to evaluating the capacity for change. The statement of the child's condition, his or her welfare, and parenting capacity is, however, a crucial tool with which change may be evaluated and decisions made, including legal interventions. Box 16.2 places this initial assessment within a broader process of assessment to be undertaken, wherever possible, in partnership with parents.

The scope of our assessments of parenting are thus incorporated into a much broader framework, designed to promote and facilitate the parents' capacity to meet the needs of their children, rather than being mere free-standing statements of deficit or incapacity.

Using the *Framework for the Assessment of Children in Need and their Families*, professionals can focus on using assessments of parenting capacity as a basis for services to improve children's welfare and, at the same time, gauge change in the future. As a last resort, however, if intervention to prevent significant harm is required in order to protect the child, at least it will have been based on a logical and empirical foundation which places parenting within its proper ecological context, rather than on selected evidence.

Recommended reading

Hoghughi, M. and Speight, A. (1998) 'Good Enough Parenting for all Children – A Strategy for A Healthier Society.' In *Archives of Disease in Childhood, 78*, pp.293–6.

Hoghughi, M. (2000) 'Commentary.' In *Archives of Disease in Childhood, 82*, pp.119–20.

Sturge, C. (2000) 'Commentary.' In *Archives of Disease in Childhood, 82*, pp.117–9.

Taylor, J., Spencer, N. and Baldwin, N. (2000) 'Social, Economic, and Political Context of Parenting.' In *Archives of Disease in Childhood, 82*, pp.113–7.

References

Azar S., Povilaitis, Lauretti A. and Pouquette, C. (1998) 'The Current Status of Aetiological Theories in Intrafamilial Child Maltreatment.' In J. Lutzker (ed.) *Handbook of Child Abuse, Research and Treatment*, pp.3–30. London: Plenum.

Barone, V.J., Greene, B and Lutzker, J. (1986) 'Home Safety with Families being Treated for Child Abuse and Neglect.' In *Behaviour Modification, 10*, pp.93–114.

Belsky, J., Putnam, S. and Crnic, K. (1996) 'Co-parenting, Parenting and Early Emotional Development.' In *New Directions for Child Development, 74*, pp.45–55.

Belsky, J., Hsieh, K. and Crnic, K. (1998) 'Mothering, Fathering and Infancy Negativity as Antecedents of Boys Externalising Problems and Inhibition at Age Three Years: Differential Susceptibility to Rearing Experience?' In *Development and Psychopathology, 10*, pp.301–9.

Berg, B. and Jones, D. P. H. (1999) 'Outcome of Psychiatric Intervention in Factitious Illness by Proxy (Munchausens Syndrome by Proxy).' In *Archives of Disease in Childhood, 81*, pp.465–72.

Cicchetti, D. (1989) 'How Research on Child Maltreatment has Informed the Study of Child Development: Perspectives from Developmental Psychopathology.' In D. Cicchetti and V. Carlson (eds.) *Child Maltreatment: Theory and Research on the Causes and Consequences of Child Abuse and Neglect*, pp.377–431, Cambridge: Cambridge University Press.

Department of Health and Cleaver, H. (2000) *Assessment Recording Forms*. London: The Stationery Office.

Garbarino, J. and Kostelny, K. (1992) 'Child Maltreatment as a Community Problem.' In *Child Abuse and Neglect, 16*, pp.455–64.

Garbarino, J. and Sherman, D. (1980) 'High Risk Neighbourhoods and High Risk Families: The Human Ecology of Child Maltreatment.' In *Child Development, 51*, pp.188–98.

Garmezy, N. and Masten, A. (1994) 'Chronic Adversities.' In M. Rutter, E. Taylor and L. Hersov (eds.) *Child and Adolescent Psychiatry: Modern Approaches*, pp.191–208. Oxford: Blackwell.

George, C. (1996) 'A Representational Perspective of Child Abuse and Prevention: Internal Working Models of Attachment and Caregiving.' In *Child Abuse and Neglect, 20*, pp.411–24.

Golombok, S., Tasker, F. and Murray, C. (1997) 'Children Raised in Fatherless Families from Infancy: Family Relationships and Socioemotional Development of Children of Lesbian and Single Heterosexual Mothers.' In *Journal of Child Psychology and Psychiatry, 38*, pp.783–92.

Greene, B., Norman, K., Searly, M., Daniels, M. and Lubeck, R. (1995) 'Child Abuse and Neglect by Parents with Disabilities: A Tale of Two Families.' In *Journal of Applied Behaviour Analysis, 28*, pp.417–34.

Greene, B. and Kilili, S. (1998) 'How Good Does a Parent Have to Be? Issues and Examples Associated with Empirical Assessments of Parenting Adequacy in Cases of Child Abuse and Neglect.' In J. Lutzker (ed.) *Handbook of Child Research and Treatment*, pp.54–72. London: Plenum.

Jones, D. P. H. (1998) 'The Effectiveness of Intervention.' In M. Adcock and R. White (eds.) *Significant Harm: Its Management and Outcome* (2nd edn.) pp.91–119. Croydon: Significant Publications.

Jones, D. P. H. and Bools, C. N. (1999) 'Factitious Illness by Proxy.' In T. David (ed.) *Recent Advances in Paediatrics, 17*, pp.57–71. Edinburgh: Churchill Livingstone.

Jones, D. P. H. and Ramchandani, P. (1999) *Child Sexual Abuse: Informing Practice from Research.* Oxford: Radcliffe Medical Press.

Kaufman, J. and Zigler, E. (1989) 'The Intergenerational Transmission of Child Abuse.' In D. Cicchetti and V. Carlson (eds.) *Child Maltreatment: Theory and Research on the Causes and Consequences of Child Abuse and Neglect*, pp. 129–50. Cambridge: Cambridge University Press.

Korbin, J. (1997) 'Culture and Child Maltreatment.' In M. Helfer, R. Kempe and R. Krugman (eds.) *The Battered Child*, pp.29–48. London: University of Chicago Press.

Loeber, R. and Stouthamer-Loeber, M. (1987) 'Prediction.' In H. C. Quay (ed.) *Handbook of Juvenile Delinquency.* London: Wiley.

McHale, J., Kuersten, R. and Lauretti, A. (1996) 'New Directions in the Study of Family Level Dynamics During Infancy and Early Childhood.' In *New Directions for Child Development, 74*, pp.5–26.

McHale, J. and Rasmussen, J. (1998) 'Coparental and Family Group-Level Dynamics During Infancy: Early Family Precursors of Child and Family Functioning During Pre-School.' In *Development and Psychopathology, 10*, pp.39–59.

National Research Council (1993) 'Etiology of Child Maltreatment.' In *Understanding Child Abuse and Neglect*, pp. 106–60. Washington DC: National Academy Press.

Papernow, P. (1993) *Becoming a Stepfamily. Patterns of Development in Remarried Families.* San Francisco: Jossey-Bass.

Pelton, L. (1994) 'The Role of Material Factors in Child Abuse and Neglect.' In G. Melton and F. Barry (eds.) *Protecting Children from Abuse and Neglect: Foundations for a New Strategy*, pp.131–81, London: Guildford.

Quinton, D. and Rutter, M. (1985) 'Family Pathology and Child Psychiatric Disorder: A Four-year Prospective Study.' In A. Nicol (ed.) *Longitudinal Studies in Child Psychology and Psychiatry: Practical Lessons from Research Experience*, pp.91–134. Chichester: Wiley.

Rutter, M. (1985) 'Family and School Influences: Meanings, Mechanisms and Implications.' In A. Nicol (ed.) *Longitudinal Studies in Child Psychology: Practical Lessons from Research Experience*, pp.357–403. Chichester: Wiley.

Rutter, M. (1989) 'Intergenerational Continuities and Discontinuities in Serious Parenting Difficulties.' In D. Cicchetti and V. Carlson (eds.) *Child Maltreatment; Theory and Research on the Causes and Consequences of Child Abuse and Neglect*, pp. 317–48. Cambridge: Cambridge University Press.

Seibt, T. (1996) 'Non-traditional Families.' In M. Harway (ed.) *Treating the Changing Family: Handling Normative and Unusual Events*, pp. 39–61. Chichester: Wiley.

Sharland, E., Seal, H., Croucher, M., Aldgate, J. and Jones, D. P. H. (1996) *Professional Intervention in Child Sexual Abuse.* London: HMSO.

Tasker, F. and Golombok, S. (1991) 'Children Raised by Lesbian Mothers: The Empirical Evidence.' In *Family Law, 21,* 184–7.

Wasserman, G., Miller, L., Pinner, E. and Jaramillo, B. (1996) 'Parenting Predictors of Early Conduct Problems in Urban High-Risk Boys.' In *Journal of the American Academy of Child and Adolescent Psychiatry, 35,* pp.1227–36.

Watson-Perczel, M., Lutzker, J., Greene, B. and McGimpsey, B. (1988) 'Assessment and Modification of Home Cleanliness Among Families Adjudicated for Child Neglect.' In *Behaviour Modification, 12,* pp.57–81.

CHAPTER 17

When Parents' Issues Influence their Ability to Respond to Children's Needs

Hedy Cleaver

Parents may be experiencing their own problems which may have an impact through their behaviour on their capacity to respond to their child's needs.

(From the *Framework for the Assessment of Children in Need and their Families,* p.25, 2.20)

The following issues are considered in this chapter:

- research findings on the effects on parenting capacity of mental illness, problem drug and alcohol use and domestic violence

- the social consequences of the above issues

- the impact of parental issues on children at different ages and stages of development

- assessing parents' difficulties and children's needs.

Introduction

This chapter begins with an exploration of the research findings of the impact of mental illness, problem alcohol and drug use, and domestic violence on parents' capacity to respond appropriately to the needs of their children. What follows is a brief description of an assessment record for children in need that is based on this work. The focus is on the above-mentioned parental issues because research shows that they are associated with adverse consequences for children's welfare, which includes abuse and neglect (Cleaver, Unell and Aldgate 1999). Moreover, it has become clear that unless there is evidence of child abuse or neglect, families experiencing such problems may not always receive the services their children would benefit from. For example, the Department of Health's overview of research studies on child abuse, *Child Protection: Messages from Research* (1995), showed that considerable numbers of families drawn into the system had a history of domestic violence, mental illness or problems with alcohol or drugs. However, because child protection enquiries under section 47 of the Children Act 1989 were not usually set within the wider context of promoting children's welfare, these aspects of family functioning were not a prominent feature of the assessment.

Indeed, child protection research has shown that although large numbers of families are drawn into the child protection system, some 75 per cent are filtered out (Department of Health 1995). What many of these families needed and wanted while bringing up their children were services to support them in ways which would ensure that the children remained at home without being at risk of suffering significant harm.

In addition, research shows that assessments tend to be incident-focused and thus fail to take account of either children's developmental needs and parents' capacity to respond to these appropriately, or the wider family and environmental factors. As indicated in the *Framework for the Assessment of Children in Need and their Families* (Department of Health et al. 2000), the assessment should explore how the factors within these domains interact and impact on the current wellbeing of the child. At the same time it is important not to pathologise all children whose parents are experiencing difficulties such as mental illness, substance misuse or domestic violence. Indeed, research suggests that in many such families children suffer no long-term adverse consequences (Cleaver et al. 1999). However, when these issues coexist, particularly if they are linked with domestic violence, the risk of children suffering significant harm does increase considerably.

Research findings on the effects of mental illness, problem alcohol and drug use and domestic violence on parenting capacity

Disorganised lifestyle, inconsistent and ineffective parenting

Mental illness, problem alcohol and drug use and domestic violence all affect parents' emotional and behavioural responses in ways which impact on their parenting capacity. Depression, which may be the result of domestic violence, and the effects of some drugs such as alcohol, tranquillisers, sedatives and solvents, can result in disturbed sleep, a diminished capacity to concentrate, and memory impairment. When parents are thus affected they may have difficulty in organising their lives and fail to provide consistently for their children.

One or more of these negative effects on parents can have adverse consequences for all children regardless of both age and ability. Young children are particularly vulnerable. For example, parental depression or inebriation may result in children missing health checks, or being left either alone or with unsuitable carers. The impact on older children will be different. When parents have difficulty getting up in the morning as a result of disturbed sleep or sedation, children may have to get themselves up and may arrive at school hungry, or late, or not at all. In addition, the parents' condition may result in teenagers assuming the parenting role, not only for themselves but also for the ailing parent and younger siblings. The stresses of coping with parents' problems and the care of younger siblings may mean children are frequently unable to attend school, an issue discussed by Dearden and Becker in Chapter 14.

Helen (10) described how she had to look after her younger brothers and sisters because 'Mummy's often in bed all morning' (Parent with alcohol problems: ChildLine 1997, p.24).

To take on the role of carer will also impact on young people's social lives: 'My mum was depressed, I was unable to be with my friends...I looked after her all the time. I did the cleaning, the tidying, the washing-up and the shopping. If I was out I was worried about her and I would come rushing back' (NSPCC 1997, p.38).

Neglect of basic care

Functional psychoses, although not a common condition, have a profound effect on the sufferer's ability to function. Delusions and feelings of persecution, which are frequent symptoms (and can be brought about from the excessive use of stimulants such as amphetamines, or cocaine), may result in parents' failing to meet even the most basic of their own and their children's needs. In consequence, children may be left without their primary care needs being met; for example, they may be left dirty and hungry.

Domestic violence and depression may also result in such feelings of despair that parents are incapable of caring about themselves or their children: 'At one time I went through a depression that went on for about a year where I didn't bother to do the housework, and I didn't bother to wash myself ... I didn't give a shit about who said what about how the children looked...' (The account of a depressed mother; NCH 1994, p.47).

When parental problems divert monies which would ordinarily be used for essentials such as food and clothes (see 'Reduced standards of living', later in this chapter) children will find it difficult to keep up an acceptable appearance and friendships may be jeopardised: 'They spend all the money on drink. There's no soap in the house and all my clothes are too small. I lost my girlfriend because she said I smell. Others call me names and make fun of me. It hurts' (Paul, aged 14; quoted in ChildLine 1997, p.37).

Difficulty in controlling emotions

The intake of drugs such as cocaine, crack or alcohol, and certain forms of mental illness such as bipolar affective disorder (manic depression) or personality disorder can result in parents exhibiting rapid changes of mood. Parents may swing from one extreme to another, from feelings of apathy and worthlessness to agitation, extreme restlessness and excitability. Similarly, the effect of drugs can change the way the user relates to his or her children: the user may be caring, loving and entertaining at one moment and violent, argumentative and withdrawn at another. Such inconsistent behaviour can be very frightening for children. Many believe that they are responsible for their parents' changing moods: 'When, like, if we'd do something bad, like we didn't take care of our trainers or our clothes that he'd brought us, he'd take it out on her' (13-year-old boy quoted in McGee 1996).

Children might also consider that it is their responsibility to find ways of stopping their parents' negative, hurtful and violent behaviours. This is particularly so for middle-years children who frequently believe in the magical thinking and behaviour so well described by A.A. Milne (1970). For those whose memories need refreshing, his poem advised children to keep to the squares, as walking on the lines would awaken the interest of waiting bears. Children believe that if things are done in the correct way, following a particular ritual, or by saying the right words, the behaviour of their parent(s) will return to normal.

The relationship between parent and child

Attachment between infant and adult is a circular and interactive process, as described in Chapter 12. Insecure attachments have implications for the child's intellectual, emotional, social and psychological functioning. A healthy baby can be a strain for even the most experienced of parents. However, excessive drinking or drug use during pregnancy may result in babies being born with damage to the central nervous system, or with behaviours such as poor feeding, tremors, irritability and occasional seizures. When one or more of these behaviours occur they can have negative consequences for the development of a secure attachment between parent and baby.

Mental illness, problem alcohol and drug use and domestic violence may all affect the ability of parents to maintain a consistent and predictable physical presence in relation to the child. Parents who suffer from these problems are less likely to have bodily contact with the infant, and have a tendency to be insensitive to the infant's signals. Parents' problems may also influence the ways in which they interact with their children. For example, parental mental illness, problem alcohol and drug use and domestic violence are associated with high levels of criticism and rejection of children. Parents who suffer from such difficulties are more likely to respond with irritability and anger, or to fail to respond at all to their children, than parents who are not affected (Davenport et al. 1984).

The development of a good attachment relationship between parents and children may also be disrupted when parents are unable to look after their children (for example, when the resolution of the parents' own problems causes them to leave home). Problem alcohol and drug use may lead to imprisonment if criminal activities have been used to sustain the habit, or otherwise to treatment outside the home. An acute episode of mental illness may result in a parent's hospitalisation. When this happens the care of children may fall to others. If the other parent or a close relative or a member of the family network can provide a stable environment and the time and attention the children require, the negative consequences of separation are much reduced.

Alternatively, separation may be the result of children running away from home to escape their chaotic, violent or abusive families (Faber, McCoard and Falkner 1984). A proportion of children who run away will find refuge and stability in the care of relatives or family friends. Others will need to be looked after by the local authority, with all the well-known concomitant difficulties surrounding placement. For a few, the consequences of parental problems are potentially dangerous: homelessness and a life on the streets (Smith, Gilford and O'Sullivan 1997).

The social consequences associated with parental mental illness, problem alcohol and drug use and domestic violence

The following section explores the interplay between parental problems and family and environmental factors and how these impact on the child. However, we must always keep in mind that mental illness, problem drinking or drug misuse may be understandable reactions to intolerable life circumstances, such as extreme financial need, homelessness or social isolation.

Reduced living standards

To meet the child's needs, families require a standard of living which does not negatively impact on the child's wellbeing. However, parental problems, as we have described above, may have an adverse effect on how the resources that are available to the family are used. For example, a disproportionate amount of the family's income may be used to sustain parental substance misuse.

Living standards may also be affected as jobs are lost due to parents' unpredictable or bizarre behaviour. To sustain the costs of substance use, parents may resort to alternative sources of income such as drug-dealing, theft and prostitution.

The family's accommodation may deteriorate because property is wilfully damaged or destroyed during violent or aggressive outbursts – a common feature of excessive drinking or domestic violence. Alternatively, parents may be so preoccupied by their own problems that the home is neglected and becomes unhygienic and unsafe.

Finally, the family's living standards may be reduced because parents' difficulties mean they disregard essential household bills, and so the supply of basic amenities like water, heating and lighting are discontinued; problems lead parents to forget to buy essentials such as food and clothing.

Isolation from family and friends

Most families rely on relatives and friends for both practical help and emotional support when bringing up their children. But when families include a parent who suffers from mental illness, or from problem alcohol and drug use, or where there is domestic violence, these supports are likely to have been curtailed or lost, thus making parenting a more difficult and stressful experience.

The loss of contact with family and friends can happen in a number of ways. Families are frequently ashamed of their circumstances and restrict contact with friends in order to hide what is happening. Research has shown that few men and only one in three women who are victims of domestic violence tell anyone of their experiences. Feelings of shame and a belief that they would not be believed keeps victims of both sexes silent (Dominy and Radford 1996; Cook 1997): 'I was ashamed; No one would have believed me; I had no friends left I could tell were all reasons given by women for keeping their abuse secret' (NCH 1994, p.79). In some cases secrecy may be imposed on the children: 'He says that if we ever tell anyone he will kill us' (father had an alcohol problem; ChildLine 1997, p.23).

Contact with relatives and friends may also be restricted because drug-users frequently base their social activities and friendships around the procurement and use of the drug. For children this means that the scrutiny and support of non-drug using adults, which is important to ensure that children are not at risk of significant harm, is reduced.

When problem drinking or drug use or mental illness becomes public knowledge, families may be ostracised by neighbours. When this happens it increases the family's sense of isolation and reduces the likelihood of support for the child.

The impact of parental issues on children

Not all children are equally vulnerable to the adverse consequences of parental problems. Research suggests children are less likely to be adversely affected when parental problems are:

- mild and of short duration

- not associated with family violence, conflict and disorganisation

- managed to avoid the family breaking up.

Children may also be protected when other responsible adults are involved in child care, or assume the role of the child's champion or mentor, as described in Chapter 11. The caring adult may be a non-troubled parent, a relative or family friend, a teacher or health-worker. In relation to problem drinking or drug use, children's safety also depends on the adult managing his or her drug or alcohol use safely, for example, storing drugs and alcohol, needles and syringes, out of the child's reach.

Children react differently to adversity depending on their age, gender and individual personality. For example, it is widely accepted that girls are less vulnerable in the short term, but over time are just as likely to exhibit distress as are boys. The child's ability to cope with parental problems and their consequences has been shown to be related to the following:

- a sense of self-esteem and self-confidence

- feeling in control and capable of dealing with change

- having a range of approaches for solving problems.

Such traits are fostered by secure, stable and affectionate relationships and experiences of success and achievement (Rutter 1985).

In assessing the child's needs and the parents' capacity to respond appropriately, it is important that professionals do not assume that all children will be negatively affected by growing up in violent families, or in families where one parent is mentally ill or has a problem with alcohol or drugs. Indeed, a significant proportion of children show no long-term behavioural or emotional disorders. Nonetheless, a considerable number do exhibit symptoms of disturbance which would benefit from services. The challenge facing professionals is to identify which children and families need help, in which areas of their development children are suffering, and what type of services would be most effective. The following section summarises the key issues social workers need to consider when assessing the impact of parental problems on children of different ages and stages of development.

Children of different ages and stages of development: issues for assessment

When assessing the needs of the child it is important that social workers are aware of both the strengths and vulnerabilities relevant to children at different ages. For example, babies and toddlers are vulnerable to intrauterine damage, the impact of post-natal depression, and faulty attachments – issues which are less likely to affect older children. Tables 17.1–17.3 summarise the key research findings for children under 5, from 5 to 9 years, and adolescents (Cleaver et al. 1999).

Vulnerabilities	Strengths
Substance misuse during pregnancy may result in neurological and physical damage and/or symptoms of withdrawal.	Medicines and illicit drugs are safely stored.
Physical and emotional neglect may result in the child's basic needs for food and warmth not being met.	Sufficient income and good physical living standards.
Under-stimulation and neglect (for children aged 3 or more a failure to attend pre-school facilities) may result in cognitive delay.	Regular supportive help from primary health care team and social services departments.
Witnessing unpredictable and frightening parental behaviours may result in symptoms similar to post-traumatic stress disorder. The child may be subjected to physical violence.	Alternative safe and supportive residence for mothers subjected to violence or threats of violence.
Parental unhappiness, tension, irritability or a lack of commitment may lead to a faulty attachment relationship.	The presence of a caring adult who responds appropriately to the childs needs.
Babies and toddlers have difficulty telling anyone of their distress.	

Table 17.1 Strengths and vulnerabilities for children aged from 0 to 5 years in relation to parenting issues

Vulnerabilities	Strengths
The risk of physical injury may lead to symptoms of extreme anxiety and fear. The child may be subject to abuse.	Attendance at school medicals.
School behaviour and academic attainment may be impaired.	Regular attendance at school. Sympathetic, empathetic and vigilant teachers.
Children may blame themselves for their parents' behaviours. Self-blame may result in low self-esteem.	A supportive older sibling. Children who have at least one mutual friend have higher self-worth and are less lonely than those without.
Unplanned separations may cause distress and disrupt education and friendship patterns.	The presence of an alternative, consistent, caring adult who responds appropriately to the child's cognitive and emotional needs.
Embarrassment and fear of parents' unpredictable and disturbing behaviours may lead to the child curtailing friendships.	Social networks outside the family, especially with a sympathetic adult of the same sex. Belonging to organised out-of-school activities.
Children may take on too much responsibility for self, parents and younger siblings.	Being taught different ways of coping and knowing what to do when parents are incapacitated.

Table 17.2 Strengths and vulnerabilities for children aged from 5 to 9 years in relation to parenting issues

Vulnerabilities	Strengths
Coping with puberty without support.	Factual information about puberty, sex and contraception.
Denying own needs and feelings.	A mutual friend. Unstigmatised support of relevant professionals.
An increased risk of psychological problems, behavioural disorders, suicidal behaviours and offending. Low self-esteem.	The ability to separate themselves either psychologically or physically from stressful family situations.
Poor school attainment due to difficulties in concentration, poor attendance in order to look after parents or younger children, unacceptable behaviour resulting in a pattern of school exclusion.	Regular school attendance. Sympathetic, empathetic and vigilant teachers. A champion who acts vigorously on behalf of the child. For those no longer in school, a job.
The fear that revealing family problems will lead to the family being broken up. This may result in increased isolation from friends and adults outside the family.	A mentor or trusted adult with whom the child can discuss sensitive issues. Practical and domestic help.
Increased risk of abuse. Inappropriate role models.	An alternative, safe and supportive residence for children and young people subjected to violence or the threat of violence.

Table 17.3 Strengths and vulnerabilities for children aged from 10 to 14 years and young people of 15 years and older in relation to parenting issues

Middle-year children experience things differently. Although they are still vulnerable to physical abuse and neglect, parental problems can also have an adverse effect on their self-esteem. Children of primary-school age who live in families where these issues occur show greater levels of anxiety, disturbed behaviour, and poorer academic achievement than do children of primary-school age who live in families without these problems.

Adolescents, although vulnerable in similar ways to younger children, also experience additional problems. For example, when parents are absorbed in their own problems adolescents may have little adult guidance and support when going through the hormonal changes and peer-group pressures of puberty. These children are at increased risk of pregnancy or sexually transmitted diseases. Adolescence is also a time for experimentation. But the role models presented by substance-using parents mean that their children are vulnerable to similar behaviours. Parental difficulties may also result in adolescents assuming the role of carer. Although many children are happy to accept a caring role, without support it can be an onerous task and result in poor and erratic school attendance, or isolation from outside social activities, and a denial of the carer's own needs and feelings. But asking for outside help in not easy, because adolescents fear that if they reveal family problems to community or professional agencies it will result in the family being broken up.

Assessment of children's needs and parents' capacity to meet them

Structured assessment records are being developed and evaluated by the Department of Health to accompany the *Framework for the Assessment of Children in Need and their Families*. The assessment records are intended to assist front-line social services staff in the process of assessment, analysis and decision-making. They have not been designed to replace professional skills or to be used as checklists. The records take an approach which acknowledges the interaction between the child's developmental needs (see Chapter 10), parenting capacity (see Chapter 16) and family and environmental factors (see Chapter 3).

The records, when completed, should ensure that: information is recorded in a consistent way; a plan of action is developed; the most effective services are identified; and a child's progress is regularly reviewed. They should act as the basis for reassessment as situations change. In addition, the records will assist local authority social services departments to collect the required information about their performance in achieving the

Government's children's social services objectives (Department of Health 1999).

Summary

Research has shown that the difficulties parents experience may influence their ability to respond appropriately to their children's needs. Although some children will be adversely affected, when families are able to call upon compensatory resources professional support may not be needed. Assessment records have been designed to help social workers identify the strengths within families, as well as the areas where services may be needed in order to safeguard and promote the welfare of the child. The assessment records should ensure consistent information is available to develop plans for children which result in effective services. The records, however cannot replace social workers' professional judgement in assessing children in need.

Recommended reading

Cleaver, H., Unell, I. and Aldgate J. (1999) *Children's Needs. Parenting Capacity: The Impact of Parental Mental Illness, Problem Alcohol and Drug Use, and Domestic Violence on Children's Development.* London: The Stationery Office.

Falkov, A., Hayes K., Diggins, M., Silverdale, N. and Cox, A. (1998) *Crossing Bridges. Training Resources for Working with Mentally Ill Parents and Their Children.* Brighton: Pavillion Publishing.

Velleman, R., (1996) 'Alcohol and Drug Problems in Parents: An Overview of the Impact on Children and the Implications for Practice.' In M. Gopfert, J. Webster and M. U. Seeman (eds.) *Parental Psychiatric Disorder: Distressed Parents and Their Families.* Cambridge: Cambridge University Press.

References

ChildLine (1997) *Beyond the Limit: Children Who Live with Parental Alcohol Misuse.* London: ChildLine.

Cleaver, H., Unell, I. and Aldgate, J. (1999) *Children's Needs. Parenting Capacity. The Impact of Parental Mental Illness, Problem Alcohol and Drug Use, and Domestic Violence on Children's Development.* London: The Stationery Office.

Cook, P. W. (1997) *Abused Men: the Hidden Side of Domestic Violence.* Westport: Praeger.

Davenport, Y. B., Zahn-Waxler, C., Adland, M. C. and Mayfield, A. (1984) 'Early Child-rearing Practices in Families with a Manic-depressive Parent.' In *American Journal of Psychiatry, 141,* pp.230–35.

Department of Health (1995) *Child Protection: Messages from Research.* London: HMSO.

Department of Health (1999) *The Government Objectives for Children's Social Services.* London: Department of Health.

Department of Health, Home Office and Department for Education and Employment (1999) *Working Together to Safeguard Children: A Guide to Inter-agency Working to Safeguard and Promote the Welfare of Children.* London: The Stationery Office.

Department of Health, Department for Education and Employment and Home Office (2000) *Framework for the Assessment of Children in Need and their Families.* London: The Stationery Office.

Department of Health and Cleaver, H. (2000) *Assessment Recording Forms.* London: The Stationery Office.

Dominy, N. and Radford, L. (1996) *Domestic Violence in Surrey: Towards an Effective Inter-Agency Response.* London: Roehampton Institute/Surrey Social Services.

Faber, E., McCoard, W. and Falkner, D. (1984) 'Violence in Families of Adolescent Runaways.' In *Child Abuse and Neglect, 8,* pp.285–99.

McGee, C. (1996) 'Children's and Mothers' Experiences of Child Protection Following Domestic Violence.' A paper given at the Brighton International Conference on Violence, Abuse and Women's Citizenship.

Milne, A. A. (1970) *When We Were Very Young.* London: Methuen.

NCH Action For Children (1994) *The Hidden Victims: Children and Domestic Violence.* London: NCH Action For Children.

NSPCC (1997) *Long-Term Problems, Short-Term Solutions: Parents in Contact with Mental Health Services.* Brent: Brent ACPC.

Rutter, M, (1985) 'Resilience in the Face of Adversity. Protective Factors and Resistance to Psychiatric Disorder.' In *British Journal of Psychiatry, 147,* pp.598–611.

Smith, J., Gilford, S. and O'Sullivan, A. (1997) 'Young Homeless People and their Families: Findings.' In *Housing Research, 229.* York: Joseph Rowntree Foundation.

CHAPTER 18

Implementing the *Framework for the Assessment of Children in Need and their Families* when the Parent has a Learning Disability

*David Cotson, Joanne Friend,
Sheila Hollins and Helen James*

Working with family members is not an end in itself; the objective must always be to safeguard and promote the welfare of the child. The child, therefore, must be kept in focus. It requires sensitivity and understanding of the circumstances of families and their particular needs.

(From the *Framework for Assessing Children in Need and their Families,* p.13, 1.45)

In this chapter we look at the following:

- parenting capacity – the impact of parental learning disability on the child

- longer-term outcomes for children whose parents have a learning difficulty

- planning the assessment and identifying the family's support needs

- engaging parents in the assessment process.

Introduction

Learning disability is usually described as a significant impairment of intelligence and social functioning acquired before adulthood. Approximately 2 per cent of the population – over one million people – can be described in this way. The term 'learning disability' is used in this context in the UK, but elsewhere other terms such as 'mental retardation', 'developmental disability' and 'intellectual disability' are in use. Educational services in the UK use the term 'learning difficulty' and only those children with moderate or severe learning difficulty would usually be regarded as having a learning disability. Many people with a mild learning impairment cope well in society and receive any help they need from family and friends. Most do not need specialist services unless they lack support or have additional needs such as those arising from mental health problems (Department of Health 1998).

The definition of learning disability has been taken from Department of Health good practice guidance, which also makes the following points which necessitate particular consideration during an assessment using the *Framework for the Assessment of Children in Need and their Families* (Department of Health *et al.* 2000):

- people with learning disabilities have the same rights and are entitled to the same expectations and choices as anyone else, regardless of the extent or nature of the disability, their gender or ethnicity

- the foundations of good services for people with learning disabilities are the same as for anyone else. In addition services must be sensitive to the implications of having a learning disability and any associated disabilities

- positive action will sometimes be required to make sure that people with learning disabilities can benefit from the full range of opportunities and choices available

- parents with learning disabilities can in many cases be supported by family and community networks and professionals, enabling them to respond effectively to the needs of their children.

Ultimately, whether a parent has a learning disability or not, it is the quality of care experienced by the child which determines whether parenting capacity can be regarded as sufficient or not. In this chapter consideration is given to those factors, sometimes associated with parental learning disability, which may have a significant effect on the support required by the family.

The chapter refers to parents with learning disabilities and makes no specific reference to race or ethnicity. The reason for this is that, perhaps with the single exception of Henshel's 1972 study of Anglo and Chicano couples in Texas, there has been no research that has taken account of race or ethnicity when examining the topic of parenting by people with learning disabilities. A great deal of the research that has been undertaken in North America has involved mothers who were participating in early intervention programmes or who had been mandated by the courts to attend parenting training classes, and black women are known to be over-represented within this population. But none of this research has treated race as an independent variable in the analysis or presentation of the results, although Koegel and Edgerton (1982) report that black parents with mild learning difficulties appear to be more consistently integrated into social networks than white parents with mild learning difficulties. They appear to be more frequently expected and encouraged to have children and, in general, the fact that they have learning difficulties is not as consistently assumed to interfere with their ability to perform normal social roles. In the UK, the lack of research on this issue (bearing in mind that in any case there has been very little on parenting with learning disabilities) is not unrelated to numbers. Assuming that the incidence of people with learning disabilities and the incidence of parenting within this group is unrelated to race or ethnicity, then the overall prevalence of black parents with learning disabilities in the population is low.

Parenting capacity: the impact of parental learning disability on the child

When assessing the impact of parental learning disabilities on the parents' ability to respond to the needs of their child, professionals should consider both the parents' cognitive functioning and other psychological factors that may impact on their parenting ability.

Cognitive functioning

Research in this area has generally supported the view that intellectual ability is not directly related to parenting capacity, particularly for parents with mild or borderline learning disabilities. However, aspects of the parents' cognitive functioning can have an effect on the child's experience and development. The parents' ability to learn to respond to the needs of their child and the time-scale over which this learning is required to take place will be an important aspect of the assessment. In order to understand the impact of the learning disability itself on parenting capacity, a functional assessment will be of considerably more use than an intellectual assessment on its own. A full-scale intellectual assessment such as the Wechsler Adult Intelligence Scale (WAIS) can be helpful to build a picture of relative strengths and weaknesses in particular areas of cognitive functioning when the subtest scores are analysed. The results of the WAIS can then be used in combination with a functional assessment such as an Activities of Daily Living assessment. This latter type of assessment, typically carried out by occupational therapists, provides information regarding the parents' ability to manage in terms of daily living. It may be helpful to use resources such as *The Parent Assessment Manual* as a guide to what the person already knows, and to what they may learn (McGraw *et al.* 1999). The fairest way to assess an individual's ability to respond to the needs of the child is to observe a real-life situation and assess the parental response, both to the situation itself and to advice regarding the needs of the child.

The work that has been undertaken to evaluate the usefulness of various approaches to teaching parenting skills to this group of parents has shown that intensive, consistent and concrete advice can be beneficial. Many parents with learning disabilities find it difficult to benefit from verbal advice on its own, so words need to be supported by demonstration, and, most usefully, the opportunity provided to apply skills in the setting in which they are to be used. As Feldman (1986) points out, the application of new skills outside the situation in which they were learnt has been shown to be difficult for most parents, and is likely to be even harder for parents with learning disabilities.

One specific aspect of child development on which parental intellect appears to have an impact is language development. Adults with learning disabilities often experience language delay, language disorder and hearing impairment themselves (although frequently undiagnosed), and it is not surprising that this has been consistently identified as an area where parents struggle to provide appropriate stimulation for their child. For example, Peterson, Robinson, and Littman (1983), in a study of verbal interaction between parent and child, found that parents with learning disabilities tended to make fewer descriptive statements to their children compared with other parents. They suggest that the lack of this kind of verbal interaction, which stimulates the child's attention and use of language, may contribute to the language delay which has been observed in some children whose parents have learning disabilities. Thus an important aspect of the assessment would be to consider whether any identified deficits in this area can be overcome, either through improving parental skills by offering specific guidance about talking to the child, or through supplementing the linguistic experience of the child outside the immediate family.

Psychological factors

As well as cognitive difficulties in stimulating a child and gaps in knowledge about parenting, experiential factors may impact on the parenting provided by any parent, including a parent with learning disabilities. For example, some parents with learning disabilities have a history of being themselves looked after by the local authority, and this is a factor which has been shown to affect the quality of parent–child interactions. The experience of emotional deprivation or other abuse as a child, which is regarded as a predictor of parenting difficulties in the non-disabled population, is known to have affected a disproportionate number of people with learning disabilities. There is also a growing body of evidence (Sinason 1992; Brown and Turk 1992) that people with learning disabilities of all ages are particularly vulnerable to physical, emotional and sexual maltreatment. The experience of abuse may have implications for individuals' ability to protect both themselves and their children from future abuse and exploitation.

One important aspect to consider when addressing the complex emotional effects of such childhood experiences is the extent to which the parent is able to evaluate the impact of the experiences on their behaviour, and where appropriate engage in therapeutic work. In the context of the assessment, a significant area of concern is whether the child's emotional needs are able to be met. In our experience there are two areas of particular relevance here. First, it can be the case that parents with learning disabilities anticipate that the child will fulfil their own emotional needs, and this can lead to frustration and difficulty in adjusting when the child's own emotional needs become apparent. Of course this may also be the case for parents who do not have learning disabilities. When parents' emotional needs have not been, or are not being, met elsewhere, as is sometimes the case with this group of parents, their ability to prioritise the child's needs above their own may be limited. Secondly, while practical and concrete parenting skills can be taught, deficits in anticipating and meeting a child's emotional needs are much harder to address effectively.

The importance of early diagnosis and treatment of post-natal depression for the psychological wellbeing of both mother and child has increasingly been recognised. Given that self-report of symptoms, identification of symptoms by partners and loss of adequate functional skills are all important diagnostic indicators, it might be anticipated that detection rates for women with learning disabilities will be lower than for other women. In addition, there is some evidence that women with learning disabilities may be at higher risk of suffering from post-natal depression, given the incidence of chronic untreated depression and poor self-esteem among this group. Perhaps related to this is the finding reported by Seagull and Scheurer (1986) that children of parents with learning disabilities often present as depressed themselves. It is important, therefore, to distinguish potentially treatable psychological difficulties, such as post-natal depression, from those of a more long-standing and pervasive origin, where the potential for change may be considerably less or the issues may require intense intervention.

Relationships with partners

In the authors' experiences the majority of parents with learning disabilities who look after children are women, many of whom do not have stable partners who function in a supportive capacity. Women with mild or borderline learning disabilities are sometimes drawn into relationships with men who do not have learning disabilities, but who do have other difficulties of their own: for example, poor mental health or problems related to alcohol or drug dependence. Because of their vulnerability, mothers with learning disabilities are more often targeted than other mothers by men with a history of offences against children, who see them as providing easy access to children and having a limited ability to protect them from abuse. Research has indicated that where children of mothers with learning disabilities have been abused, the perpetrator is far more likely to be a partner or relative than the mother herself (Tymchuk 1992).

Ability to ensure the safety of the child is an essential aspect of parenting capacity within the Assessment Framework. Women need to be given clear and specific information about the risks of possible maltreatment posed to their children by present or potential partners. Care should be taken by professionals to ensure that this has been explained in a way which the parent can understand, given the learning disabilities. These mothers may need help to develop and implement concrete strategies to keep themselves and their children safe. However, some mothers with learning disabilities will find this information difficult to act on consistently, either because of their limited choice of relationships, poor social networks, or difficulty in grasping the issues.

Assessing family networks and social and community support systems

As part of the assessment, it is important to remember the vital connection between family and environmental factors and parenting capacity for people with learning disabilities. To some extent, the greater the support available, the greater the capacity to parent.

The impact of family and environmental factors on the quality of parenting is identified within the Assessment Framework. Research into the success or otherwise of parenting by people with learning disabilities has shown that success is more likely when the mother has a supportive other to share the responsibility. This term is interpreted quite loosely and may include a partner, grandmother, child or even a health visitor or volunteer. Such supporters in caring should be identified and their actual role understood. With support many adults with learning disabilities can be adequate parents (Tymchuk and Feldman 1991). However, the work of Booth and Booth (1994) and Llewellyn (1995), has demonstrated the paucity of informal support networks available to this group of parents. More than one third of parents in the study by Llewellyn *et al.* (1998) were unable to identify any significant other person in their lives.

Where extended family support exists, it can significantly improve the quality of care offered to the child, both directly and indirectly, through the help and guidance offered to the parent. However, as with any family, not all support from extended family members is positive in its effect; other family members may have learning disabilities themselves, or may have failed to achieve an adequate standard of parenting with their own children, or may pose a risk of abuse to the child. When the parenting ability of the extended family member is responsive to the developmental needs of the child, there is still the possibility that this may undermine the ability of the parent with learning disabilities to meet the child's needs, and may interfere with the development of an appropriate parent–child relationship. Lack of consistency between family members and supporting agencies in the advice given can be a particular source of confusion for some parents with learning disabilities. If the child's wellbeing within the family is dependent on the presence of adults other than the parent with learning disabilities then the likely permanence of this situation needs to be assessed. The level of demand placed on the supporting person may be unsustainable over the longer term, and a breakdown in the child's situation is often related to the loss of a key support figure at a crucial time (Espe-Sherwindt and Kerlin, 1990). If there is relative impermanence of the relationships and friendships formed by a parent with learning disabilities, changes which significantly affect the child can occur quickly and may often be detrimental. One example of this would be a deterioration in the quality of parenting following the establishment of a relationship with a new partner.

Responding to the developmental needs of children whose parents have learning disabilities: long-term outcomes

When assessing parents with learning disabilities, attention tends to be focused on the early years. However, there is evidence that rather than becoming more able to cope over the years, parents encounter increasing difficulties as their child grows older, or another child is added to the family (Accardo and Whitman 1990). The issue of providing guidance and boundaries for the child comes to the fore, and is difficult for many parents with learning disabilities to negotiate successfully. Several authors have suggested that there may be particular difficulties for children who are intellectually more able than their parents, for example McGraw and Sturmey (1993); they may be perceived as challenging and disciplined inappropriately, they may be relied on to carry out too adult a role within the family, they may be unaccepting of parental authority, or they may fail to achieve their intellectual potential. It has been suggested that children with learning disabilities, provided these are not severe enough for them to need complex special care, may fare better, and Booth and Booth (1997) suggest that parents with learning disabilities are more accepting of these children.

Booth and Booth's study, in which they detail interviews with thirty adults who were the children of parents with learning disabilities, provided a mixed picture of experience, but raised concerns about children's emotional welfare even if their physical care was adequate. There was widespread evidence of social isolation and victimisation, and, of those without a learning disability, many described problems at school, including suspension, truancy, frequent punishment, being bullied and having few friends. Although accounts of abuse were frequent, this was rarely perpetrated by the parent with learning disabilities, although often by his or her partner. However, many of those surveyed also described positive aspects to their relationships with their parents, and most had remained close to the parent with learning disabilities. Booth and Booth stress the resilience of some children in surviving difficulties, especially when offered appropriate support from outside the family. Schofield (1996) stresses that although sensitivity to the difficulties experienced by parents with a learning disability is essential, it needs to be balanced by adequate protection for those children who are not receiving appropriate care.

The assessment process

Planning the assessment: a multidisciplinary approach

In order to recognise the needs of both parents and children, combined working between children's services and adult services is required at the assessment stage. This may involve a significant number of professionals, for example adult learning disabilities workers in health and social care, children and family services, child health primary care services and independent or voluntary agencies. While involvement of the learning disability team is vital, it should also be recognised that by having the input of two separate specialist services (learning disabilities and child services) there is the possibility of an unhealthy split occurring, with each service becoming the champion of the rights and needs of their respective service user. It is not uncommon for learning disabilities professionals to be seen exclusively as the advocates for the parent, and, similarly, workers from children's services to be perceived as ignoring parents' needs. Local protocols should exist and outline the roles and responsibilities of those likely to contribute to a multidisciplinary assessment of the needs of the child. This should assist professionals to understand the complementary nature of their respective contributions to the assessment. The importance of involving both learning disabilities professionals and child services right from the start of the assessment is vital.

Initial findings from a Social Services Inspectorate inspection of services to support disabled adults in their parenting role, completed in 1999, found that assessments of parenting skills were often undertaken by staff who did not have the necessary skills. This can lead to the possibility of decisions being made, for example, to place children's names on the child protection register, to leave their names on the register or to remove children from their parents' care, based on inappropriate, inadequate information. It is therefore essential when planning the assessment that the team includes professionals who have the appropriate skills to assess parenting skills.

The first stage of an assessment should be to set up a planning meeting for those involved in the particular assessment. At this meeting the roles or potential roles of various professionals from both adult and children's services can be clarified and agreed. As the assessment progresses, it is equally vital that the network of professionals continues to meet regularly, both to share information and to ensure that any misunderstandings of roles are clarified. In addition, a consistent approach should be agreed by the practitioners carrying out the assessment. Some parents with learning disabilities will not be able to cope if workers do not approach the assessment task in the same way: the parents may become confused as a result.

Assessment: engaging parents

Assessment involving people with a learning disability often requires practitioners to modify their communication style to check for under-standing in an approach which might involve using simpler language, avoiding abstract questions or keeping to one point at a time (Booth and Booth 1994).

It is generally accepted, as outlined earlier, that some people with learning disabilities may not generalise their learning across different settings. For these reasons assessment at home has some advantages over assessment in a venue such as a family resource centre. It will be important to realise that the parents' own needs will be different (and probably greater) if they are assessed in an unfamiliar environment.

Some parents with learning disabilities will have a poor concept of time; this should be taken into account as part of the assessment. If this is not identified prior to the assessment, then a lack of punctuality can be misconstrued as lack of motivation or indifference.

Some people with learning disabilities cope with the demands of everyday living by adhering to a strict routine, and find flexibility within that routine difficult to achieve. Again, when planning the assessment it is necessary for those working with the parent to be aware of this possible inflexibility, as it has implications for how parents will cope with the changing needs of a child. Skills which seem to have been learned appropriately at one stage of the child's development may continue to be applied inappropriately at a later stage. Similarly, some advice may be interpreted too literally, so that, for example, a four-hourly feeding routine may be rigorously adhered to regardless of the child's actual needs. Parents are likely to need specific help to develop and transfer skills to new situations, and the assessment should consider this. Furthermore, it should not be assumed that new skills will be retained indefinitely. There may be a need for reinforcement and repetition. If parents find difficulty with any new task, an alternative way of completing the task should be tried, as part of the assessment process.

Having decided what is to be assessed, and how, it is important to ensure that parents have this information at the outset of the assessment, to avoid misunderstandings. Failure to explain adequately in a way that can be understood may result in parents feeling either unduly pessimistic, or having their expectations raised inappropriately. For example, a decision may be made to carry out parts of the assessment in the parents' home, since this may give a more accurate picture of ability. However, where a child has been looked after by the local authority, parents may assume that seeing the child at home during the assessment means that they will eventually be resuming their care of that child.

Illiteracy is no indication that the parent cannot provide adequate parenting. Some parents will fail to acknowledge and address their lack of literacy skills, as they will worry that this may be taken as an indicator of their inability to parent. This should be taken into account and attempts made to share information in a comprehensible way, for example, supporting any text with visual material can help to clarify the information given. Simple, plain text with clear illustrations, or material presented entirely in pictures or photographs, will have the best chance of being understood. All information should be presented in small amounts and repeated clearly to check for understanding. Showing how to do something is often more effective than an abstract explanation.

An attempt should be made by professionals to build on the positive achievements of the parents. Parents with learning disabilities have usually had previous rejections and failures in their lives, so improving their confidence and self-esteem should be part of the assessment. However, the aspect of bolstering parents' confidence needs to be balanced with their need for honest and realistic feedback, so that their expectations are not raised inappropriately.

The parents' strengths and needs as persons in their own right should be assessed. Parents' own support needs will vary considerably, but may include advice and help with budgeting and managing money, and literacy support. In addition to such practical support with the tasks of everyday living, parents may need advice about making friends with other parents and enjoying close and intimate relationships with their children.

Making decisions and considering choices available to them is an area in which many parents with learning disabilities are at a disadvantage, because of both their limited experience and the abstract thought processes involved.

The decisions which they may need to make in relation to their future as parents will be emotionally difficult and have far-reaching consequences. At all stages of the assessment an identified worker should be available to support them in their decision-making. This should be someone with the time and expertise to help them to consider their options carefully and with understanding before making a choice. Often, this role will be appropriately fulfilled by the social worker from adult services, or a citizen's advocate.

In summary:

- set goals and objectives for the multidisciplinary assessment that are child focused
- show respect for parents' individuality and dignity
- ensure that parents understand the purpose of the assessment
- ensure that parents and children are supported through the assessment process
- evaluate progress regularly.

After assessment: levels of intervention and support

Concerns about the long-term outcomes for children imply that, at the very least, support and reassessment is likely to need to continue over a lengthy period. For many parents, the assessment will indicate the need for significant levels of intervention and support. This raises a number of issues, which need to be considered carefully.

How is professional support perceived by parents with learning disabilities?

How support is perceived by recipients seems to be of crucial importance in determining its usefulness. Llewellyn (1995) talked to parents about how they perceived the professional support being offered to them. Support was seen as unhelpful when it did not take account of the difficulties parents had in understanding and learning new concepts, and when conflicting advice was given by different professionals. Other studies have compared mothers' perceptions of support with that of the professionals working with them and found a significant discrepancy of views (Walton-Allen and Feldman 1991; Llewellyn *et al.* 1998). Professionals perceived the mothers as having more difficulty meeting the needs of their children and therefore needing more intervention than the mothers themselves did. Mothers saw their needs as being different from those indicated by professional assessment, and therefore felt they were being given too much help in some areas and not enough in others. This kind of discrepancy can lead to difficulties in the provision and acceptance of support, particularly in the longer term, with a consequent deterioration in the quality of parenting available to the child.

An essential component of the assessment therefore needs to be an evaluation of the extent to which shared perceptions of the kind of support required can be agreed with the parents.

How much support is required?

Supporting parents with learning disabilities adequately is a complex task, and the number of different professionals and agencies involved can be a daunting prospect and a source of confusion for parents. The issue is further complicated by the fact that while professionals are offering support they necessarily have a monitoring role, so that parents may feel constantly assessed and scrutinised. Added to their fear that their children may be removed if they make mistakes, this level of intervention can seem unacceptably intrusive to many parents. While it may be tolerated during a relatively short assessment period, it may prove unsustainable over a more lengthy period. If parents are unable to respond positively to the level of support they need, then appropriate care for the child cannot be guaranteed.

How long can interventions be maintained?

There is a difference between families where short-term interventions can ensure that parents respond to the needs of the child (albeit with episodic involvement at intervals when crises arise), and those for whom long-term support from services offers the only possibility of children being cared for in an acceptable way. A significant number of parents with learning disabilities is likely to fall into the latter group. In addition to the issues of parents' ability to accept and tolerate this level of support, in most areas resource implications are also likely to be taken into consideration. The effects of the support on the child should be the primary consideration. Offering high levels of support to a family can result in multiple care-givers, which may undermine the attachment to primary care-givers; the latter is an essential feature of healthy emotional development, as described in Chapter 12. Stability of staff support may also be difficult to maintain, which again may have unacceptable consequences for the child.

Following the assessment, some parents with learning disabilities will have to face the loss of the child. In some cases the court, through care proceedings, may decide the child's future at birth. Support for the parents through and after such assessment processes needs careful consideration (see Baum 1994 for a discussion). If a child is to be removed from the parents, even with the parents' consent, the parents' grief will be real, and potentially all the more painful for someone already defined by loss and inability. Failing to recognise and respond to the parents' emotional needs at this time may have negative effects on future relationships.

Summary

Ensuring appropriate outcomes for children whose parents have learning disabilities will be best achieved through the application of the Assessment Framework in an informed way to take account of the particular issues which affect this group of parents. Good practice can be achieved through multidisciplinary working. In particular, practitioners from child and adult services need to be prepared to work cooperatively and creatively to plan and implement the assessment in order to provide an accurate reflection of present and potential parenting capacity. The purpose of the assessment is not only to provide an indication of the level of support that will be necessary to maintain the child appropriately within the family, but also of the parents' ability to accept and tolerate this level of support, probably over a prolonged period of time. Accardo and Whitman (1990) refer to a concern that is expressed by many workers in this field: namely, the parent with learning disabilities may have difficulty in keeping pace with his or her child's development. While the learning of new skills may be possible, a crucial issue is whether the rate of learning can be fast enough. Therefore, when assessing whether or not the child's developmental needs are being responded to, or could be responded to, by parents, it is important to identify whether the parents are learning fast enough to be able to adapt to their child's developmental progress.

Assessment of the ability of parents with learning disabilities to respond to the needs of their children is similar to any other assessment of parenting capacity, although interviewing styles may need modification (Booth and Booth 1994). In general it is not the learning disability itself which brings a parent's ability into question. Causes for concern are far more likely to be associated with the damaging and neglectful experiences that are more common in people with learning disabilities than the general population. In most cases the question then becomes, what support (practical, social, emotional) does this person need to be able to respond appropriately to the needs of his or her child, rather than, will he or she have the capacity to respond appropriately to the child's needs? Parents with learning disabilities may continue to develop their skills and emotional strengths over time, but if they require additional support at the start of the child's life, then they are likely to need continuing support until the child becomes independent.

Such parents are entitled to an assessment which includes a fair representation of their own interests, as it is unlikely that they will be able to represent themselves adequately. The dilemma facing services can be summed up by a reframing of an assessment in the following way. What are the needs of children whose parents have learning disabilities, and of parents with learning disabilities and their children?

Recommended reading

Campion and Hukti (1995) *Who's Fit to be a Parent?* London: Routledge.
Gath, A. (1995) 'Parents with a Learning Disability.' In P. Reder and C. Lucey (eds.) *Assessment of Parenting: Psychiatric and Psychological Contributions.* London: Routledge.
Jackson, C. (1998) 'Listen to Mother.' In *Mental Health Care, 1,* 7, 217–19.

References

Accardo, P. J. and Whitman, B. Y. (1990) 'Children of Mentally Retarded Parents.' In *American Journal of Diseases of Children, 144,* pp.69–70.
Baum, S. (1994) 'Interventions with a Pregnant Woman with Severe Learning Disabilities – A Case example.' In A. Craft (ed.) (1994) *Practice Issues in Sexuality and Learning Disabilities.* London: Routledge.
Booth, W. and Booth, T. (1994) *Parenting under Pressure: Mothers and Fathers with Learning Difficulties.* Buckingham: Open University Press.
Booth, T. and Booth, W. (1997) *Exceptional Childhoods, Unexceptional Children: Growing Up With Parents Who Have Learning Difficulties.* London: Family Policy Studies Centre.
Brown, H. and Turk, J. (1992) 'Defining Sexual Abuse as it Affects Adults with Learning Disabilities.' In *Mental Handicap, 20,* pp.44–55.
Department of Health (1998) *Signposts for Success in Commissioning and Providing Health Services for People with Learning Disabilities.* London: NHS Executive.
Department of Health, Home Office and Department for Education and Employment (2000) *Framework for the Assessment of Children in Need and their Families.* London: The Stationery Office.
Espe-Sherwindt, M. and Kerlin, S. (1990) 'Early Intervention with Parents with Mental Retardation.' In *Infants and Young Children, 2,* pp.21–8.
Feldman, M. A. (1986) 'Research on Parenting by Mentally Retarded Persons.' In *Psychiatric Perspectives on Mental Retardation, 9,* 4, pp.777–97.
Henshel, A-M. (1972) *The Forgotten Ones: A Sociological Study of Anglo and Chicano Retardates.* Austin: University of Texas Press.
Koegel, P. and Edgerton, R. (1982) 'Labelling and the Perception of Handicap among Black Mildly Retarded Adults.' In *American Journal of Mental Deficiency, 87,* 3, pp.266–76.
Llewellyn, G. (1995) 'Relationships and Social Support: Views of Parents with Mental Retardation/Intellectual Disability.' In *Mental Retardation, 33,* 6, pp.349–63.

Llewellyn, G., McConnell, D. and Bye, R. (1998) 'Perception of Service Needs by Parents with Intellectual Disability, their Significant Others, and their Service Workers.' In *Research in Developmental Disabilities, 19*, 3, pp.245–60.

McGraw, S. and Sturmey, P. (1999) 'Identifying the Needs of Parents with Learning Disabilities: A Review.' In *Child Abuse Review, 2*, pp.101–17.

McGraw, S., Beckley, K., Connolly, N and Ball, K. (1999) *Parent Assessment Manual.* Truro Special Parenting Service.

Peterson, S. L., Robinson, E. A. and Littman, I. (1983) 'Parent–child Interaction Training for Parents with a History of Mental Retardation.' In *Applied Research in Mental Retardation, 4*, pp.329–42.

Schofield, G. (1996) 'Parental Competence and the Welfare of the Child: Issues for Those who Work with Parents with Learning Difficulties and their Children: A Response to Booth and Booth.' In *Child and Family Social Work, 1*, pp.87–92.

Seagull, E. A. W. and Scheurer, S. L. (1986) 'Neglected and Abused Children of Mentally Retarded Parents.' In *Child Abuse and Neglect, 10*, pp.493–500.

Sinason, V. (1992) *Mental Handicap and the Human Condition: New Approaches from the Tavistock.* London: Free Association Books.

Tymchuk, A. J. (1992) 'Predicting Adequacy of Parenting by People with Mental Retardation.' In *Child Abuse and Neglect, 16*, pp.165–78.

Tymchuk, A. J. and Feldman, M. A. (1991) 'Parents with Mental Retardation and their Children: A Relevant to Professional Practice.' *Canadian Psychology Psychotic Canadienna, 32*, pp.486–996.

Walton-Allen, N. G. and Feldman, M. A. (1991) 'Perception of Service Needs by Parents who are Mentally Retarded and their Social Service Workers.' In *Comprehensive Mental Health Care, 1*, 2, pp.137–47.

CHAPTER 19

Assessing Parental Capacity when Intrafamilial Sexual Abuse by an Adult is a Concern

Marcus Erooga and Bobbie Print

Studies have found that even in situations where child sexual abuse is alleged, despite early difficulties that may arise because of having to take immediate protective action, it may still be possible to work with children and their families.

(From the *Framework for the Assessment of Children in Need and their Families,* p.13, 1.47)

This chapter considers:

- incidence of sexual abuse
- the trauma-organised system
- the developmental needs of children who have been sexually abused
- assessment of the non-abusing carer/s
- assessment of the family and environmental factors
- assessment of the adult abuser
- issues in assessment of potential to re-abuse, and of adult abusers
- specialist assessments of adult abusers
- measuring change.

Introduction

> Most abuse is committed by the people children have most reason to
> trust … by members of, or individuals known to, their own family or
> by persons otherwise entrusted with their care.

(Utting 1997)

This chapter considers the developmental needs of children who have been sexually abused by an adult family member. Consideration is given to the assessment of the non-abusing carer's ability to protect and meet the child's needs. Issues related to the assessment of the potential of the perpetrator to re-abuse are also discussed.

When a child has been sexually abused or is at risk of being sexually abused, a detailed assessment is required using the *Framework for the Assessment of Children in Need and their Families* (Department of Health *et al.* 2000) and *Working Together to Safeguard and Promote the Welfare of Children* (Department of Health *et al.* 1999). The assessment must consider fully how best to safeguard and promote the welfare of the child, the child's developmental needs and wishes, and the non-abusing carer's ability to safeguard and meet the needs of the child. The assessment should also include an evaluation of the future likelihood of sexual abuse.

Assessments of this nature are complex. They will inevitably require a wide range of professional knowledge and skills, and close multidisciplinary working and cooperation. This should be based on clear agreements about models to be used, tasks to be undertaken and the decision-making process to be followed. Failure to attend to these issues at the outset of the assessment may well lead to inter-agency conflict at a later stage, to the detriment of the interests of all those involved. (For further discussion of high-quality inter-agency working in this context see Hughes 1998.)

The issue of safeguarding children from significant harm from sexual abuse extends beyond protection from those commonly described as Schedule One offenders, as by no means all those who sexually abuse a child are convicted. The attrition rates for convictions for sexual offences are extremely high and it is estimated that less than 10 per cent of all sexual assaults are reported to the police and less than 1 per cent result in the arrest, conviction and imprisonment of the offender (Russell 1984). Indeed, describing the situation in the UK, Gallagher asserts that as matters currently stand, child sex offenders have little reason to fear detection and even less reason to fear conviction. (Gallagher 1998).

Adult female sexual abusers account for only a tiny proportion of recorded sexual offences. *Criminal Statistics for England and Wales* (Home

Office 1997) indicate that between approximately 50 and 100 females were cautioned for sexual offences in each year of 1995 and 1996 (as compared with approximately 2,200 males in each year). This chapter focuses on safeguarding the welfare of children in cases where there is concern about male perpetrators. The reader is referred to Saradjian (1996) for information on the assessment of female perpetrators and child sexual abuse.

The *Framework for the Assessment of Children in Need and their Families* and child sexual abuse

The Assessment Framework consists of three domains:

- the child's developmental needs
- parenting capacity to meet these needs
- the wider family and environmental factors.

Child sexual abuse impacts on all three domains. This can be understood by considering the model developed by Bentovim (1996a and b) to understand child sexual abuse that is based on a trauma-organised system.

Clinical and research evidence indicates that child sexual abuse has traumatic effects on the lives of children and that a process of repeated cumulative traumatic effects causes increasingly severe effects on the emotional life of those involved. Those who traumatise the child are part of a system that allows them to maintain abusive action in secrecy. Other adults in the child's world are also caught in this process and so involved in the system of secrecy, denial and blame.

Trauma-organised systems are essentially action systems. The essential actors in the system are the victimiser, who traumatises, and the victim, who is traumatised. There is either an absence of a protective figure, or potential protectors are neutralised. The victimiser's impulses to act in a physically, sexually or emotionally abusive way emerge from his or her own past experiences. These may feel irresistible or overwhelming and beyond his or her control. The cause is thus attributed to the victim, who, in line with individual, family and cultural expectations, is construed as responsible for the victimiser's feelings and intentions (See also Summit 1983). Any action on the victim's part as a result of abuse, or to avoid abuse, is interpreted as further cause for disinhibition or violent action and justification for further abuse. Any potential protective figure becomes organised or neutralised by the process of 'deletion' and by minimisation of victimising actions or traumatic effects. Deletion and minimisation come to characterise the thinking processes of the victimiser and the victim alike. Potential protective figures, whether inside or outside the family, are also caught within the same belief system. Abusive actions in turn evoke traumatic stress effects in the victim, and these two elements form the core of the trauma-organised system. The repeated nature of such actions comes to organise the reality and perceptions of those involved, including potential protectors and those professionals who attempt to intervene in the family situation.

The developmental needs of children who have been sexually abused

Bentovim's model can be used to understand the effects of child sexual abuse on development. Figure 19.1 describes the traumatic response of a child subject to sexual abuse. The figure illustrates traumatic responses as a systemic, interconnected process with the three effects, re-enactment, avoidance and hyperarousal, at each point of a triangle. Each response can lead to the next, re-enactment to avoidance, to hyperarousal and back again.

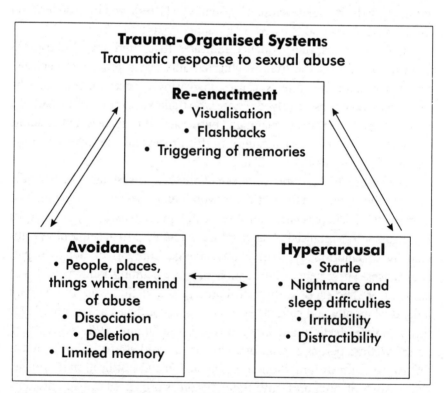

Figure 19.1 The traumatic response of a child subject to sexual abuse

Re-enactment is the intrusion of unwanted, painful and distressing memories of events into the thoughts of a child, reflected in drawing, conversation and play. Avoidance is the attempt to prevent the reminder of abusive experiences, and not wishing to think or speak about events, reinforced by an abuser who demands secrecy or by the disbelief of members of the child's family to whom he or she may have tried to speak. Hyper-arousal, fearfulness, and tension are associated with poor sleeping, poor eating and general problems of concentration. High levels of anxiety, arousal, activity and avoidant behaviour are triggered, and the nature of responses depends very much on the age of the child (Deblinger *et al.* 1989). Intrafamilial sexual abuse is often a repeated rather than a single event, in which case responses accumulate over time. There may be extreme emotional responses and, in a search for meaning for such stressful and uncontrollable events, the child may attribute what is happening to some actions of his or her own. Such beliefs become incorporated both in the response set of the child mediated by biological effects, and in the sense of self which emerges. A stable attributional set may then emerge (Silvester *et al.* 1995).

Browne and Finkelhor (1986) describe these pervasive long-term personality effects as traumagenic dynamic responses:

- powerlessness associated with the invasion and physical discomfort experiences

- stigmatisation linked to the contempt, blaming and denigration so often associated with all forms of abuse

- betrayal through the manipulation of trust, violation of care and lack of protection which occurs.

In addition there is sexualisation, the premature and distressing arousal of sexual responses through inappropriate responses being rewarded, or through induction to a sexual-partner role. Such responses have an incr-easingly powerful effect on self-attributions, and relationship style, and in turn strongly justify the actions of the perpetrator, who misinterprets the child's biological sexual response and compliance as representing true consent. Thus, for the abuser, the responses evoked in the child reinforce and justify his actions.

Thus the process of evoking traumatic effects, and the effects of trauma-genic dynamics, together result in widespread effects on children, young people and adults, on their emotional lives, their attachments and formation of relationships and attachment, their sense of selves and their mental health.

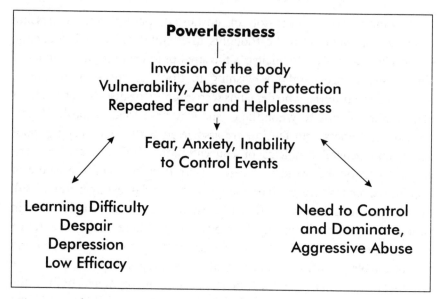

Figure 19.2 The traumagenic dynamics of powerlessness

There are intergenerational effects and various points for intervention, to reduce risk and promote protection. Figure 19.3 illustrates an inter-generational effect in the context of a dysfunctional family and individual which leads to abusive action and the traumatic, traumagenic effects, impact on individual development and relationships. The figure also highlights the types of intervention which can be used to address the issues.

Assessing parental capacity to meet the developmental needs of children who have been sexually abused

In the light of the above, children who have experienced abuse almost always significantly depend on their non-abusing care-givers for protection from future abuse and in overcoming the effects of previous abuse. The need for protection is more than simply protection from physical contact, exposure, voyeurism or other form of sexual exploitation. As outlined above, all abuse has an emotional impact on the victim and sexual abuse has the potential to inflict serious and long-term psychological and emotional damage (Beitchman *et al.* 1992). Even in circumstances where the physical aspects of sexual abuse cease, children may still require protection from the continued psychological damage that can be induced by contact with their abuser. As Salter (1994) observed, the abuse may not end when the touching stops.

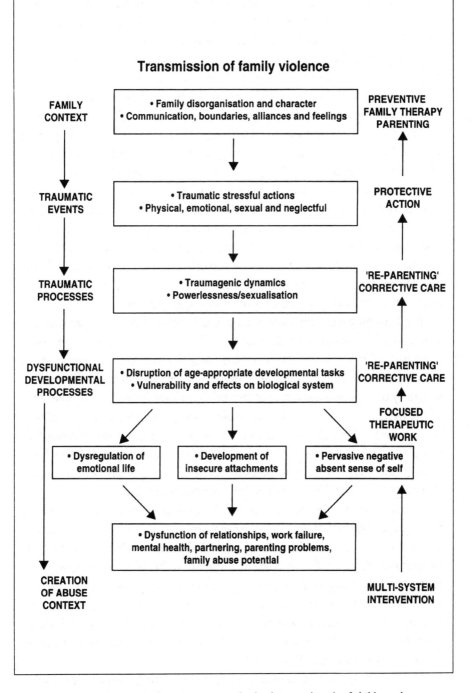

Figure 19.3 Assessing parental capacity to meet the developmental needs of children who have been sexually abused

Non-abusing carers, therefore, should have the motivation, capacity and ability to understand and respond to the psychological and emotional needs of a child who has experienced abuse. In addition, they must understand the ways in which the abuser has coerced the child into compliance, often referred to as 'grooming methods'. Everson *et al.* (1989) identified that incest victims who received the support of their mothers had a far more positive long-term prognosis than those who did not. Without such support the child's recovery and future psychological development are likely to be impaired and even significantly damaged, even if no further abuse occurs (Finkelhor 1986; Salter 1995; Jones and Ramchandani 1999).

Research indicates that in a majority of cases of intrafamilial abuse the non-abusing carer is female (Fisher 1994) and is usually the child's mother or mother-figure. In many cases, therefore, a crucial element in the assessment of parenting capacity is the evaluation of the mother's ability to protect and support children who are considered to be at risk of significant harm. The overriding aim of those conducting assessments of mothers in these circumstances must be that of working in partnership. All too often mothers of children who have been sexually abused by male partners are condemned as secondary abusers or offered little support from pro-fessionals (Farmer and Owen 1995). Many mothers may respond to allegations with shock, confusion, denial, or self-recrimination. Very few will fully understand the issues of risk of significant harm, the complexities of the dynamics of abuse or the possible consequences for victims, and will need considerable help, information and support in acquiring such under-standing. The assessment must therefore pay attention to the mother's strengths and her capacity to meet her children's needs, and the resources that might be available to address any deficits identified.

In assessing the mother it will also be important to consider her own history and issues in order to understand her current functioning or ability to provide what her children need. Jones and Ramchandani (1999) report various studies which found domestic violence to be a feature in 50 per cent of the families studied where sexual abuse was an issue (for example Farmer and Owen 1995; Trowell *et al.* 1998). Up to one-third of parents, par-ticularly mothers, had experienced sexual or physical abuse in childhood (Trowell *et al.* 1998) and one half of the mothers concerned reported depression (Monck and New 1996).

Smith (1994) provides a useful model for assessing a mother's capacity to protect and support a sexually abused child. The model outlines a continuum of possible responses, from optimal to dismal, that can be exhibited by mothers. Smith suggests that whilst fluctuation along the continuum can be expected, it should be possible to determine within a twelve-week assessment period whether a shift towards the optimum is necessary and, if so, achievable. Smith (1994) suggests key areas to be explored when completing an assessment of the non-abusing carer's ability to protect and support which relate to the Assessment Framework in terms of children's needs, as outlined below.

Factors to consider when assessing a mother's capacity to protect and support a sexually abused child

- *Response to disclosure*: does she accept that abuse has occurred, or may occur? If not, what information does she require to help improve her acceptance? Would support assist in making belief a possibility? (Relates to emotional warmth and stability dimensions of parenting capacity.)

- *Certain feelings towards a child who has disclosed*: a range of emotions are initially to be expected, particularly confusion. Time and information may help a mother who blames or scapegoats a child to develop an empathetic understanding of the child's experiences. (Relates to emotional warmth and stability dimensions of parenting capacity.)

- *Role in the disclosing process*: a mother's willingness to report concerns to professionals will depend not only on her understanding of the possible consequences of abuse but on her relationship with the abuser and her expectation of how professionals will respond. (Relates to ensuring safety dimension of parenting capacity.)

- *Position regarding responsibility and blame*: while many mothers may initially blame, at least in part, the children or themselves for the abuse, it is important to help them to recognise that full responsibility lies with the abuser. Without such a shift there must be concern as to whether the child can be adequately protected or supported in the future. (Relates to ensuring safety, emotional warmth and stability dimensions of parenting capacity.)

- *Perceived options*: what protective options does the mother consider she has, how appropriate are they and how likely is she to use them? A mother who believes that any further protective action on her part will result in negative outcomes is unlikely to perceive that she has real options. A mother who has been helped to understand the nature of sexual abuse and its associated risks is more likely to recognise the importance of taking protective action. (Relates to ensuring safety dimension of parenting capacity.)

- *Cooperation with statutory agencies*: a mother's cooperation (rather than rejection of or mere compliance) with professionals is often an important factor in protecting the child. The level of cooperation will be affected by a number of factors, including the approach and attitudes offered by professionals and the mother's ability to recognise the need for professional help. (Relates to ensuring safety dimension of parenting capacity.)

- *Relationship history*: a mother may have demonstrable qualities of independence and strengths that indicate that she would be able to act on concerns and prioritise the needs of the child over the parental relationship. Some may benefit from knowledge that support from their families, community and professionals would be available in such circumstances. In other cases, for example where a mother has a history of significant dependence on a partner or partners, there may be less confidence that she would be able or prepared to take protective actions if necessary, particularly if these were to include or lead to separation from the abuser. (Relates to ensuring safety dimension of parenting capacity.)

- *History of sexual abuse*: research indicates that a significant proportion of the mothers of sexually abused children were themselves victims of childhood sexual abuse (Kelly, Regan and Burton 1991; Jones and Ramchandani 1999). In such cases unresolved memories and feelings may be reactivated in a mother by the knowledge that her children have been or are at risk of abuse. Mothers in these circumstances may require help to resolve issues from their own abuse before they can fully empathise with and support their child. In a small number of cases a mother's abuse may have continued into adulthood or have resulted in the birth of some of her children. In such cases the level of risk of further abuse to the child and the mother must be considered significantly high. (Relates to ensuring safety dimension of parenting capacity.)

- *Other vulnerabilities* such as physical disabilities, mental health problems, drug or alcohol dependency or long-term physical illness may create particular difficulties for some mothers. They may be particularly isolated or require specialised help to gain independence and confidence in their ability to protect their child. (May relate to basic care, ensuring safety dimensions of parenting capacity.)

Assessment of the family and other environmental factors

In the light of the Assessment Framework, broader family and environmental factors should also be included. Print and Dey (1990) suggest, in their model for the assessment of a mother's capacity to protect her children in cases of intrafamilial sexual abuse, that the nature and influence of the mother's support networks – for example, her extended family, religious community and social supports – are also likely to impact on the overall potential to provide appropriate care for the children.

One of the most pervasive dynamics of sexual abuse is its effect on families. The families of children who had been sexually abused were found to have interactional patterns best characterised by less open styles of communication, problems in managing children's behaviour, and expressing less emotional warmth or closeness than is shown in families where children have not been sexually abused (Trowell *et al.* 1998). Commonly, the abuse involves the distortion of usual family features of trust between adult partners and openness with children, care by adults for children and freely negotiated relationships with the extended family and community. How far the distorted relationships can now be ameliorated will form an important element of the assessment.

A multidisciplinary assessment enables information regarding a wide aspect of family functioning, support and monitoring systems to be considered. For example, teachers may provide crucial information regarding the abilities, behaviours and expressed feelings of the children in a family, and thus can have a central role in monitoring any change in these factors if an abuser joins or rejoins the family. Others involved with the family, such as extended family members, health visitors and doctors, may also fulfil similar roles in the assessment.

Assessing the potential of the abuser to re-abuse

A key component of an assessment will be assessing the potential of the abuser to abuse again. To assist with this it is helpful to consider two North

American models: the offending cycle and the four preconditions model developed by Steven Wolf (1984) and David Finkelhor (1984) respectively, which are extremely influential in the UK.

Offending cycle

Practice experience with adult and adolescent males led to the development of the concept of sexual abuse cycles involving dysfunctional responses to problematic situations or interactions. In these models responses are based on distorted perceptions relating to power and control, which then become sexualised. Such models are now regarded as generally applicable irrespective of age or intellectual or developmental functioning.

The sexual abuse cycle for adults, developed by Steven Wolf, is itself part of a more extensive model to explain the development and maintenance of sexually deviant orientations (Wolf 1984), representing cognitive and behavioural progressions prior to, during and after an abusive incident. It is represented cyclically because of the repetitive, compulsive nature of the behaviour sequence, and indicates that previous offence incidents often parallel and reinforce the subsequent offence pattern.

Four preconditions model

Finkelhor (1984) proposes a model which, in summary, suggests four preconditions which must be met before sexual abuse can occur. The potential offender needs to:

1. have some motivation to abuse a child sexually. This may be because the child meets some important emotional need, and/or sexual contact with the child is sexually gratifying, and/or other sources of sexual gratification are not available or are less satisfying.

2. overcome any internal inhibitions against acting on that motivation – commonly this is by way of cognitive distortions, self-serving distortions of attitude and belief, whereby children come to be seen as, in some way, consenting to or responsible for their own abuse.

3. overcome external impediments to committing child sexual abuse – most importantly the supervision the child receives from others.

4. overcome or undermine a child's possible resistance to the abuse. Finkelhor emphasises that this is not an issue to be regarded

simplistically, but may relate to a complex set of factors involving personality traits which inhibit the abuser targeting a particular child, as well as more straightforward resistance to the abuse itself.

It will be apparent that preconditions 3 and 4 are those most relevant to assessment of external factors relating to protection, but an awareness of both models is commended in understanding the process and dynamics of sexual offending.

When considering the models it may be most helpful to consider the Wolf cycle and Finkelhor's preconditions model as complementary, offering different perspectives with which to understand similar processes. A further explanation of both models and a structure for considering them as integrated can be found in Erooga and Masson (1999).

Issues in assessment of the potential to sexually re-abuse

Whilst models which enable an understanding of the process of sexual abuse have been enormously helpful in informing both assessment and treatment, during the 1990s the need for methods to predict likelihood of the potential to abuse became increasingly apparent. A range of models for assisting in this process have therefore been developed (Hanson 1997; Thornton 1997). These are largely based on the understanding that likelihood of sexual offending can be assessed in terms of static or fixed historical factors – for example, previous convictions, history of care, own abuse and dynamic or changing factors such as current circumstances, attitudes and beliefs.

One of the most significant components of the assessment of the person who has previously abused is the evaluation of the risk of significant harm that the individual currently represents to children. This includes the likelihood of re-offending and the nature and impact of any possible further offences. Evaluating this potential to abuse is not an exact process, and there are no measures available for precise prediction. The most accurate indicator of future behaviour is past behaviour, and models that refine the use of an adult's historical or static information in order to predict likelihood of sexual abuse are discussed below. While these models significantly assist this process, it is also important to consider dynamic factors which may increase or diminish risk of significant harm to children. For example, an individual's successful completion of a treatment programme could reduce the perceived level of his or her likelihood of perpetrating significant harm to children, whereas an individual who shows no remorse for abusive behaviour could increase his or her level of likelihood of perpetrating sexual abuse.

It should be emphasised that it is the combination of considering both static and dynamic factors which lends the models their credibility. Predictability of re-offending improves when the predictors used include both types of factor.

Understanding specialist assessments of adults

The Sex Offenders Act 1997 requires those convicted of specified sexual offences to register with the police, and an assessment of their potential to re-abuse to be made. As a result, many police forces and probation services, as well as multi-agency risk panels, have adopted an assessment model developed by David Thornton (1997), the structured anchored clinical judgement (SACJ). This model is based on meta-analysis, that is, analysis of the findings of a number of studies of sex offender re-offence rates (for example, Hanson and Busiere 1998). Although still in the process of refinement, and not intended to be used to replace professional judgement based on available information about a specific situation, it can serve to inform decision-making and suggest measures which might minimise either generalised risk of re-offending or potential risk to specific children. The SACJ risk classification system is designed so that assessments can change over time as more information about the individual becomes available; thus risk status of re-offending will change as the offender's history or current behaviour is better understood. A summary of the model can be found in Grubin (1998).

It is important to note that whilst the outcome of the process is one of three levels of risk – low, medium or high – this represents risk relative to other sex offenders. Those assessed by the model as being low-risk represent a 7 per cent chance of re-offending within a 10-year period. This percentage would be expected to rise over a longer period. Thus 'low-risk' does not indicate low or no risk of re-abusing a specific child or children; each assessment will be dependent on the individual situation.

Given that sexual offending does not just occur but usually will be part of a pattern of behaviour with specific precursors (see for example Wolf 1984), with the offender's participation it is possible to develop relapse prevention plans which identify those precursors. As a further safety measure, behaviour which indicates potentially increasing risk of sexual abuse can be specified, and those around the abuser can have an agreed plan in response to these behavioural signs in order to take preventive action.

A further issue to be considered when assessing the developmental needs of children is potential risk of significant harm from those convicted of sexual assault against adults. In the past, common-sense logic has suggested that this group need not be a concern in child protection terms, as the offence was adult focused. However, closer consideration of the issues has concluded that potential risk of sexual abuse from this group does indeed exist, with Laws (1994) suggesting that from 33 per cent to 50 per cent of all rapists of adults present a risk of sexual violence to children and adolescents. This group should therefore also be the subject of a similar risk assessment process.

Parameters for measurement of change

Given the fundamental problem which sexual abuse of a child by an adult represents, the goals for treatment, and therefore positive indicators for contact or even family reunification, are also relatively demanding. The need for effective interventions with sexual offenders is now well established and the early indicators of effectiveness are positive (Hedderman and Sugg 1997). Thus, in a situation where risk of re-offence is determined as sufficiently low, it is possible to consider situation-specific criteria to be applied to the assessment. In these specific circumstances Fisher and Beech (1998) suggest that the abuser should achieve the following treatment goals:

- admit the full extent of the abuse
- take full responsibility for the offending rather than attempting to place the blame elsewhere
- demonstrate empathy for his victim/s
- demonstrate remorse for the offence (both the above will need to be carefully assessed to take account of the offender's learnt correct responses; see Clark and Erooga 1994)
- recognise and be able to challenge cognitive distortions
- demonstrate an understanding of his motivation to abuse
- be able to admit (sexually) deviant thoughts and fantasies, and to have developed appropriate control strategies
- be able to describe potential risk situations
- have developed appropriate relapse prevention strategies
- acknowledge risk of re-offending
- improve his communication skills with adults

- discuss his offending with appropriate family members as part of marital or family work

- develop a support network in the community of people who will act as monitors (see also Wolf 1984).

Summary

Whilst decision-making about likelihood of re-abuse in the highly charged context of sexual abuse and safeguarding children will always be a difficult and demanding task, there are key elements which can increase effectiveness and minimise the inevitable stress. By using available information and models both concerning the dynamics of sexual abuse and about assessment, by endeavouring to maintain clear and open communication with those involved and affected by the process (family members and professional colleagues), and by a clear focus on the needs and interests of those most vulnerable in the process (children), then rational, explicable and defensible decisions can be made.

Recommended reading

Briggs, D., Doyle, P., Gooch, T. and Kennington, R. (1998) *Assessing Men who Sexually Abuse: A Practice Guide.* London: Jessica Kingsley.

Grubin, D. (1998) *Sex Offending against Children: Understanding the Risk.* Police Research Series, Paper 99. London: Home Office.

Parton, N. and Wattam, C. (eds.) (1999) *Child Sexual Abuse: Responding to the Experiences of Children.* Chichester: John Wiley and Sons.

Smith, G. (1994) 'Parent, Partner, Protector: Conflicting Role Demands for Mothers of Sexually Abused Children.' In T. Morrison, M. Erooga and R. Beckett (eds.) (1994) *Sexual Offending Against Children: Assessment and Treatment of Male Abusers.* London: Routledge.

References

Beitchman, J. H., Zucker, K. J., Hood, J. E., DaCosta, G. A., Akman, D. and Cassana, E. (1992) 'A Review of the Long-Term Effects of Child Sexual Abuse.' In *Child Abuse and Neglect, 16,* pp.101–18.

Bentovim, A. (1996a) *Trauma-Organised Systems.* London: Karnac.

Bentovim, A. (1996b) 'Trauma-organised Systems in Practice: Implications for Work with Abused and Abusing Children and Young People.' In *Clinical Psychology and Psychiatry, 1,* pp.513–24.

Browne, A. and Finkelhor, D. (1986) 'Initial and Long-Term Effects: A Review of the Research.' In D. Finkelhor (ed.) *A Sourcebook on Child Sexual Abuse.* Beverley Hills: Sage.

Clark, P. and Erooga, M. (1994) 'Groupwork with Men who Sexually Abuse Children.' In T. Morrison, M. Erooga and R. C. Beckett (eds.) *Sexual Offending against Children: Assessment and Treatment of Male Abusers.* London: Routledge.

Deblinger, E., McLeer, S. V., Atkins, M. S. D., Ralphe, E. and Foa, E. (1989) 'Post-Traumatic Stress in Sexually Abused, Physically Abused and Non-Abused Children.' In *Child Abuse and Neglect, 13*, pp.403–8.

Department of Health, Home Office and Department for Education and Employment (1999) *Working Together to Safeguard and Promote the Welfare of Children.* London: The Stationery Office.

Department of Health, Department for Education and Employment and Home Office (2000) *Framework for the Assessment of Children in Need and their Families.* London: The Stationery Office.

Erooga, M. and Masson, H. (1999) *Children and Young People who Sexually Abuse Others – Challenges and Responses.* London: Routledge.

Everson, M., Hunter, W., Runyon, D., Edelson, G. and Coulter, J. (1989) 'Maternal Support Following Disclosure of Incest.' In *American Journal of Orthopsychiatry, 59*, pp.197–207.

Farmer, E. and Owen, M. (1995) *Child Protection Practice: Private Risks and Public Remedies. Decision-Making, Intervention and Outcome in Child Protection Work.* London: HMSO.

Finkelhor, D. (1979) *Sexually Victimised Children.* New York: Free Press.

Finkelhor, D. (1984) *Child Sexual Abuse; New Theory and Research.* New York: Free Press.

Finkelhor, D. (1986) *A Sourcebook on Child Sexual Abuse.* Beverley Hills, CA: Sage.

Fisher, D. (1994) 'Adult Sex Offenders: Who Are They? Why and How Do They Do It?' In T. Morrison, M. Erooga and R. C. Beckett (eds.) *Sexual Offending against Children: Assessment and Treatment of Male Abusers.* London: Routledge.

Fisher, D. and Beech, A. (1998) 'Reconstituting Families after Sexual Abuse: The Offenders' Perspective.' In *Child Abuse Review, 7*, 420–34.

Gallagher, B. (1998) *Grappling with Smoke: Investigating and Managing Organised Sexual Abuse.* London: NSPCC.

Grubin, D. (1998) *Sex Offending Against Children: Understanding the Risk.* Police Research Series, Paper 99. London, Home Office.

Hanson, K. (1997) *The Development of a Brief Actuarial Risk Assessment for Sexual Offense Recidivism.* User Report No. 1997–04. Ottawa: Dept. of the Solicitor-General.

Hanson, R. and Busiere, M. (1998) 'Predicting Relapse: A Meta-Analysis of Sexual Offender Recidivism Studies.' In *Journal of Consulting and Clinical Psychology, 66*, 348–62.

Hedderman, C. and Sugg, D. (1997) *Does Treating Sex Offenders Reduce Reoffending?* Home Office Research and Statistics Directorate Research Findings, No. 45. London: Home Office.

Home Office (1997) *Criminal Statistics England and Wales 1996.* London, Government Statistical Service.

Hughes, J. (1998) 'Making inter-agency work.' In *NOTA News, 28*, pp.39–49.

Jones, D. and Ramchandani, P. (1999) *Child Sexual Abuse: Informing Practice from Research.* Oxford: Radcliffe Medical Press.

Kelly, L., Regan, L. and Burton, S. (1991) *An Exploratory Study of the Prevalence of Sexual Abuse in a Sample of 16–21-Year-Olds.* London: Child Abuse Studies Unit, The Polytechnic of North London.

Laws, R. (1994) 'How Dangerous are Rapists to Children?' In *The Journal of Sexual Aggression, 1*, pp.1–14.

Monck, E. and New, M. (1996) *Sexually Abused Children and Adolescents and Young Perpetrators of Sexual Abuse who were Treated in Voluntary Community Facilities.* London: HMSO.

Print, B. and Dey, C. (1990) 'Empowering Mothers of Sexually Abused Children: A Positive Framework.' In A. Bannister (ed.) *From Hearing to Healing: Working with the Aftermath of Child Sexual Abuse.* Chichester: Wiley.

Russell, D. (1984) *Sexual Exploitation, Rape, Child Sexual Abuse and Sexual Harassment.* Beverley Hills: Sage.

Salter, A. (1994) Keynote Address, NOTA Conference, Dundee.

Salter, A. (1995) *Transforming Trauma – A Guide to Understanding and Treating Adult Survivors of Child Sexual Abuse.* Beverly Hills: Sage.

Saradjian, J. (1996) *Women who Sexually Abuse Children: From Research to Clinical Practice.* Chichester: John Wiley and Sons.

Silvester, J., Bentovim, A., Stratton, P. and Hanks, H. (1995) 'Using Spoken Attributions to Clarify Abusive Families.' In *Child Abuse and Neglect, 19,* pp.1221–32.

Smith, G. (1994) 'Parent, Partner, Protector: Conflicting Role Demands for Mothers of Sexually Abused Children.' In T. Morrison, H. Erooga and R. Beckett (eds.) *Sexual Offending Against Children: Assessment and Treatment of Male Abusers.* London: Routledge.

Summit, R. (1983) 'The Child Sexual Abuse Accommodation Syndrome.' In *Child Abuse and Neglect, 7,* pp.177–93.

Thornton, D. (1997) 'Developing Systematic Risk Assessment for Sex Offenders.' Address to NOTA Annual Conference, Southampton, September.

Trowell, J., Kolvin, I., Berelowitz, M., Weeramanthri, T., Sadowski, H., Rushton, A., Miles, G., Glaser, D., Elton, A., Rustin, M. and Hunter, M. (1998) 'Psychotherapy Outcome Study for Sexually Abused Girls.' In Jones and Ramchandani (1999) *Child Sexual Abuse: Informing Practice from Research.* Oxford: Radcliffe Medical Press.

Utting, W. (1997) *People Like Us: The Report of the Review of the Safeguards for Children Living away from Home.* London: Department of Health.

Wolf, S. (1984) 'A Multifactor Model of Deviant Sexuality.' Paper presented at Third International Conference on Victimology, Lisbon.

CHAPTER 20

Young People who Sexually Abuse
Implications for Assessment
Bobbie Print and Marcus Erooga

For a small number of children the causes for concern will be serious and complex and the relationship between their needs, their parents' responses and the circumstances in which they are living, less straight-forward. In these situations, further, more detailed specialist assessment will be required.

(From the *Framework for Assessing Children in Need and their Families,* p.26, 2.25)

In this chapter we consider:

- distinctions between adolescents and adults who sexually abuse
- using the *Framework for the Assessment of Children in Need and their Families* with young people who sexually abuse
- the developmental needs of young people who sexually abuse
- structuring an assessment
- the key components of an assessment
- assessing whether a young person who has abused a family member should remain in, or return to live in, the family home.

Introduction

The professional response to adult sex offenders is based on a consensus that sexually abusive behaviours are habitual and require a lifelong management strategy using relapse prevention techniques (Pithers 1990, George and Marlatt 1989). Such an approach may also be necessary for some adolescents, particularly those who have developed highly compulsive, impulsive or habituated, abusive behaviour patterns. The aim of early intervention in many cases, however, is to prevent or inhibit the onset of such patterns.

Whilst the understanding gained from work with adults provides a useful background for work with adolescents there are a number of distinctions between adults and adolescents who sexually abuse. These differences include:

- the lack of research on adolescents who abuse, compared to the research on adults

- research which suggests that most adolescents who sexually abuse will cease their sexually abusive behaviour by the time they reach adulthood, particularly if they receive appropriate therapeutic help and supervision (Weinrott 1996)

- inappropriate behaviours in adolescents are often less deeply ingrained than in adults and are therefore easier to change

- adolescents are still developing patterns of sexual behaviour and are therefore more open to alternatives to consistently abusive patterns

- distorted thoughts, beliefs and attitudes are also less deeply entrenched in adolescents, and more susceptible to change

- adolescents are more accustomed to education and open to learning new and acceptable skills.

Young people who abuse others are generally compensating for overwhelming negative feelings such as helplessness, vulnerability, loss of control or low self-image (Ryan 1998; Skuse et al. 1998). These feelings, together with other factors such as lack of empathy, distorted thoughts and attributions of responsibility can combine to produce abusive behaviour. Furthermore, research has identified that most young people who sexually abuse others have themselves been subjected to some form of physical, emotional or sexual maltreatment (Lewis, Shanok and Pincus 1981; Smith and Monastersky 1986). These are all indicators of a young person who is in need of help and support. In a number of cases, the absence of intervention to meet the needs of the young person can lead to further abusive behaviour, which in turn can produce significant damage to the psychological health and development of the young person concerned, as well as to his or her victims.

There is increasing consensus that interventions with young people who are sexually aggressive need to be multi-systemic (Bourke and Donohue 1996). As indicated in Section 6.33 of *Working Together to Safeguard Children* (Department of Health *et al.* 1999), three key principles should guide work with children and young people who abuse others. These are: a coordinated approach between youth justice and child welfare agencies; recognition that the needs of young people who abuse should be considered separately from those of their victims; and the assessment should seek not only to identify issues of victim and community safety but the overall needs of the young person. In addition, consideration should be given to the personal, familial, professional and environmental strengths and resources that can be harnessed and utilised in order to formulate a comprehensive intervention and protection strategy. Any intervention should therefore include an assessment of the developmental needs of the child, under section 17 of the Children Act 1989, using the *Framework for the Assessment of Children in Need and their Families* (Department of Health *et al.* 2000). This approach should ensure a holistic assessment rather than focusing exclusively on the sexually inappropriate behaviour.

The *Framework for the Assessment of Children in Need and their Families* applied to young people who sexually abuse

An assessment of the developmental needs of any young person should be based on the Assessment Framework outlined in Chapter 2. For those who have sexually abused others, however, additional consideration needs to be given to particular areas, with some aspects of the work likely to require the involvement of those with expertise in work with young people who sexually abuse. Each of the domains of the framework are considered below in terms of the specific factors that should be considered when assessing the developmental needs of young people who sexually abuse.

The developmental needs of the young person who has sexually abused others

Work on sexually abusive behaviour cannot be undertaken in a vacuum, and any assessment should be set in the context of the young person's whole social and emotional development, as reflected in the dimensions of a child's developmental needs set out in the Assessment Framework. Relevant areas may be:

- significant personal/familial history details
- confusion over personal history
- therapeutic needs other than offence related, e.g. young person's own experiences of abuse
- health issues
- education issues
- accommodation
- employment
- social skills
- activities, hobbies, social interests
- peer relationships and friendships with others (adults, peers and younger children)
- social inclusion and the individual's desire for social acceptability
- young person's goals and plans.

A full personal and developmental history of the young person is likely to inform views on his or her developmental needs. Additionally, an assessment that considers emotional and behavioural development and identity can provide indicators to the problem formation needs of the young person. Relevant research and clinical experience should be used to hypothesise how past experiences may have impacted on the young person to produce the abusive behaviour; what needs they were attempting to meet by the behaviour; why and in what circumstances the behaviour may continue, escalate or diminish in the future. The following are examples of models and research findings that link a young person's developmental experiences to the occurrence of abusive behaviour.

EARLY LIFE EXPERIENCES

Barbaree, Marshall and McCormick (1998) propose that the development of sexual deviance is due in large part to experiences the child has in his early family life. The suggestion is that parental neglect, lack of positive attachments with care-givers and parental coercive controlling behaviours are fundamental factors of early care that can significantly inhibit a young person's ability to form successful friendships and intimate relationships in a way that is mutually satisfying and respectful. The resulting lack of social skills and interpersonal competence prevents the young person from gaining access to appropriate sexual relationships, and the learned coercive responses lead him or her to resort to committing abuse. The young people feel no remorse for their behaviour, as their own experiences have resulted in a lack of empathy and distorted thinking, and the gratification gained from the abusive behaviour serves to reinforce their inappropriate sexual thoughts and arousal.

The model suggests that certain developmental areas in particular should be considered during assessment in order to gain an understanding of why the sexually abusive behaviour has developed and what therapeutic needs may be present such as:

1. problems with the development of attachment bonds and intimacy

Ward *et al.* 1995 suggest that poor attachments in early childhood are particularly influential in the development of intimacy deficits and severe emotional loneliness. Both of these characteristics have been found to be significant factors in adult sex offenders (Garlick, Marshall and Thornton 1996; Smallbone and Dadds 1996).

2. problems in the development of self-esteem

Low self-esteem can result from a variety of experiences including problematic early attachments, own abuse, being bullied, neglect, rejection and loss. Poor self-esteem has consistently been found to be a characteristic of those who sexually abuse children (Marshall 1997; White and Humphrey 1990).

3. development of antisocial behaviour

Those young people diagnosed as conduct disordered, or who have a history of persistent aggressive or criminal behaviours, are considered to present antisocial behaviours. A number of young people who sexually abuse others have such behaviours in their histories (Becker, Cunningham-Rathner and Kaplan 1986; Awad and Saunders 1989) and many exhibit two particular antisocial behaviour characteristics, poor empathy and cognitive distortions or thinking errors. Patterson, DeBaryshe and Ramsey (1989) identified that amongst those who exhibited the most severe forms of antisocial behaviour, early onset of problematic behaviours was frequent. Early symptomatic behaviours can include a difficult temperament in infancy, coercive or disruptive behaviours in school and home, poor relationships, aggressive behaviours, academic failure and truancy. Research has shown that a number of family variables are linked to the development of antisocial behaviours. These include: poor parental attachments (Cadoret and Cain 1980); family break-up during the child's first five years of life (Behar and Stewart 1982); harsh and inconsistent discipline (Loeber and Dishion 1983); poor supervision (Patterson *et al.* 1989).

4. problems leading to development of abusive sexual arousal and behaviour

A significant proportion of young people who sexually abuse others have been victims themselves (Hanson and Slater 1988) and it has been suggested that deviant fantasies may have their origins in a process of learning or conditioning developed from abuse experiences (Marshall, Barbaree and Eccles 1993). Similar effects could also result from indirect experiences of sexually abusive behaviours, such as witnessing abuse, or from early exposure to pornographic material.

FACTORS ASSOCIATED WITH THE ONSET OF SEXUALLY
ABUSIVE BEHAVIOUR IN YOUNG PEOPLE

Studies completed by Watkins and Bentovim (1992) and Skuse *et al.* (1998) found the following to be factors which placed adolescent boys at risk of sexually aggressive behaviour, irrespective of early childhood experience of sexual victimisation:

- witnessing physical violence
- experiencing physical violence or abuse
- discontinuity of care
- rejection by the family.

Parenting capacity

Parents of a young person who has sexually abused others are likely to have a complex array of feelings about the situation, including shame, guilt, anger, confusion and fear. They may find it easier to cope with the situation if they deny, minimise or try to justify their child's behaviour. Whilst such attitudes are not conducive to offering their child appropriate help, support or protection from re-offending, they must be recognised by practitioners as possible parental defence mechanisms. The task for professionals is to assess whether parents can change their attitudes to adopt more helpful views in light of information, advice and support. Parents who are, or can be, motivated to support their child in engaging positively with professionals, and who are willing to involve themselves in the process, can make a significant positive difference in the outcome for the young person.

As stated in Chapter 19, research is beginning to identify the significance of early life and developmental factors in the lives of those who commit sexual offences. For example Prentky et al. (1989) identified inconsistent care as a significant static factor, whilst Ryan et al. (1996) found that a significant number (34 per cent) of those young people referred to sex offender treatment programmes in the United States had spent periods of time in out-of-home placements. It would seem, therefore, that parents' ability to offer stable and consistent care is a particularly important consideration in an assessment. Gilgun (1988) suggested that parents who modelled an environment of openness and were able to communicate comfortably with their children about sexual matters offered a positive protective factor to young people who exhibited sexually abusive behaviours. Parents who find it very difficult to discuss such matters or who hold highly restrictive or inappropriate attitudes towards sexual behaviour and sexuality are unlikely to be able to support their child, and may even inhibit the young person's progress.

Steele and Ryan (1997) suggest that the development of victim empathy in a young person is only possible if the young person has experienced empathetic care from a trusted care-giver. If a young person lives in an environment of neglect or parental lack of interest he is likely to struggle to recognise self-empathy, let alone empathy for others.

The following should be considered as part of the assessment of parenting capacity.

THE PARENT'S/CARER'S PATTERN OF SUPERVISION/CARE

The level of supervision a young person requires will be guided by the judgement as to the risk of further abusive behaviour identified within the assessment. Relevant issues may range from parents' attitudes and abilities to supervise, to their acceptance of the need for an identified supervising officer to monitor and support the young person in the community, or, in extreme cases, the need for a secure residential setting. In respect of everyday care, relevant issues may be: sleeping arrangements; routines (for example, not allowing the young abuser to be involved in bedtime/bath-time activities); restrictions on out-of-home activities; monitoring of the young person's moods, behaviour and relationships; communication/record-keeping.

RESPONSE TO FURTHER INCIDENTS OR COMPLAINTS

Incidents or suspected incidents of sexual abuse should be managed within the guidance *Working Together to Safeguard Children* (Department of Health *et al.* 1999). Parents should be aware of the process and be prepared to cooperate by, for example, reporting suspected abuse, agreeing to participate in planning/strategy meetings and considering alternative placements.

CARERS' OWN NEEDS

This should include identifying and meeting the carers' needs, enabling them to meet the developmental needs of the young person and provide the supervision outlined above.

Family and environmental factors

Adolescents usually have a significant network of people who have influence in their lives. For example, parents, other relatives, carers, teachers, and social workers. The role and involvement of families, in particular, is likely to be significant, as shown by the Dublin based Northside inter-agency project (Sheridan *et al.* 1998), who found a correlation between positive treatment outcomes for young people who had sexually abused and the degree of familial participation and support offered.

Relapse prevention (Pithers 1990; Richardson and Graham 1997) has become the primary treatment model for sex-offenders' programmes across the UK and North America, and is predicated on the individual being able to transfer knowledge and skills from the therapeutic setting to external community situations. Barber (1992), writing more generally on relapse prevention, has suggested that the quality of an individual's social network is the primary factor influencing whether skills and knowledge are maintained post-treatment. The existence of, or potential for, establishing a medium/long-term support network for a young person should therefore be examined as part of an assessment, so that strengths and deficits can be identified. Intervention plans for the young person can then include the development, maintenance and involvement of a support network.

Bentovim (1998) has produced a model that identifies characteristics of young people, victims, families and environments, which indicate whether the prognosis for positive change is hopeful, doubtful or hopeless. Bentovim suggests that where the outcome falls into the 'hopeless' category and there is no possibility of engaging any member of the family network in meaningful therapeutic work, containment may be the only viable response.

In addition to assessing the characteristics of the young person, his family network and his environment, the following should be included in this part of an assessment.

Community safety: the protection of victims and potential victims

The specific indicators of risk of a young person sexually abusing a child should be outlined. Should certain dynamic factors lessen or heighten the degree of perceived risk, these should be identified with a clear statement that the construct of risk of harm may change (in either direction), should these features alter subsequently. The level of perceived risk that the young person represents, together with his or her needs and the resources available to meet those needs, may lead to a view as to the general nature of an appropriate placement for the young person, and any specific conditions or requirements that may be required within the placement.

Vulnerability of victims and/or specific individuals

Most young people will have offended against someone known to them, typically an immediate or extended family member, foster sibling, fellow care resident, neighbour or fellow school pupil. It is important to identify the vulnerability of victims to further abuse. Where the young person is resident with the victims, or there is actual or likely contact, the possible impact on the victim of such contact should be taken into account. The victim's views and wishes should be considered where possible, together with the views of those caring for and working with him or her.

The needs of substitute carers

Many young people will already be, or due to their behaviour need to be, cared for outside their family of origin. Foster-carers should be given guidance on supervision, responding to sexual issues and supporting the young person's work in any programme of treatment. Residential carers face particular complexities in caring for abusive young people in a group care setting. It may be relevant to highlight them at the assessment stage. Most frequently these relate to:

- the need for unified staff approaches to child protection/ supervision issues

- ability to promote alternatives to dysfunctional, control-based behaviours

- understanding of sexuality and consent
- staff group culture concerning issues such as secrecy; responsibility; decision-making
- staff approaches to manipulative/coercive features in young people's relationships
- supervision, support and training
- access to consultancy.

The core assessment: key components

O'Callaghan and Corran (1999) suggest that the main aims of a core assessment for a young person who has abused are to address the following:

1. problem formation: what factors appear to have been influential in the development and maintenance of the abusive behaviour
2. care and developmental needs
3. risk analysis and management strategy
4. the individual's motivation to participate in a therapeutic process
5. identified goals and targets
6. a clearly defined intervention strategy.

Components 1 and 2 have been considered earlier in the chapter. The third component, risk analysis and management strategy, is often the most difficult and contentious aspect of an assessment. The statistical risk prediction models employed with adults (see previous chapter) are not considered applicable for use with adolescents, as the data on which they are based is largely adult-specific. There are comparatively very few similar studies on adolescents. Consequently an assessment of risk of sexually abusing a child and appropriate management strategies, regarding young people who sexually abuse, requires a detailed understanding of the relevant research and theory together with specific skills in interviewing the young people involved. Without such knowledge and skills there is a danger that assessments will be based on inaccurate understanding and inappropriate assumptions derived from knowledge of adult sex offenders. The outcome in such situations has often led to serious misjudgements of risk and the implementation of unsuitable management strategies (Lab, Shields and Schondel 1993). The complexity of this aspect of an assessment usually requires the clinical skills and knowledge of specialist workers who are trained and experienced in conducting this work. It is therefore essential that specialist assessments are commissioned when necessary by the local authority, in order to identify both the potential risk of the young person's sexually abusing children, and strategies for managing the situation.

The fourth component of the core assessment is the young person's motivation to participate in a therapeutic process. A young person's motivation to receive help with his or her sexually abusive behaviour is rarely based primarily on a wish to protect others. Some will be motivated by external factors, such as the consequences for them if they do not accept help, the influence of their parents or other significant individuals, or the possibility of returning to live at home. In some cases it may be that a legal mandate is considered necessary to ensure cooperation. An assessment of a young person's level of motivation should include identification of: internal motivation; external motivation; any factors that may impede participation, for example, substance misuse, lack of family support, repeated absconding. Motivation to work on problem behaviours is important to include as part of an assessment, as those with little or no motivation are unlikely to enter into or complete therapeutic programmes of work. Research has identified that those individuals who fail to complete therapy programmes are at significantly higher risk of committing further abuse than those who complete the programmes (Hanson and Busiere 1998).

The final component is the identified goals and targets and a clearly defined intervention strategy. The collection, collation and analysis of the information provided by the assessment are complex and skilled tasks and will often require the participation of specialist workers. It is, however, important that each of those involved in the assessment process, including the young person, his or her family, carers and significant others, as well as the professional, are given the opportunity to comment on conclusions and recommendations, even if their views are not in the majority.

Assessing whether the young person should remain in or return to the family

When young people have abused others in the family the initial issue to address can be whether the young person should remain in or return to the family. Hackett, Print and Dey (1998) identified that further issues should be considered, that is, resolution and/or reconciliation. They define resolution as work with the victim, carers and the young person who has abused, to address and, if possible, resolve the array of feelings that so often accompanies the discovery of abuse and subsequent professional intervention. Resolution does not require all parties to forgive, or to feel that an ongoing relationship of any kind is appropriate. It may involve reconciliation, or sometimes reunification, although these are not always necessary. Reconciliation is defined as the process of seeking balance, post-abuse, in family relationships. Once again it is not necessary for the young person to be re-united with the family, nor for the young person to be forgiven by the victim or parents.

Hackett and colleagues also identified the following as criteria for considering whether a young person who has abused a sibling should remain in or return to the family:

The victim should:

- be able to acknowledge and discuss the sexual abuse

- not blame him or herself for the abuse

- be willing for the sibling who abused to be united with the whole family

- be confident about her of his own ability to report any further abuse

- feel safe and protected in the home if the sibling who abused is to be returned.

The young person who sexually abused should:

- accept full responsibility for the sexual abuse

- be able to demonstrate empathy for the victim and awareness of the impact of his or her behaviour on other family members

- show remorse for the abuse

- be willing to talk with the victim, and other family members, at their request about the abuse, making appropriate apologies, but without overwhelming (flooding) the victim or family members with unrequested and self-serving apologies

- demonstrate understanding about his or her motivation for the abuse

- be able to acknowledge ongoing risk factors and communicate these to those inside and outside the family, as appropriate, in order to seek help to prevent relapse.

The parents should:

- be able to put the victim's needs for protection first
- be able to confront the young person who abused and express feelings about the abuse
- be able to discuss the impact of the abuse upon themselves as carers
- hold the young person who has abused responsible, and not blame the victim
- be able to accept the differing needs of the victim and the young person who abused, and yet accommodate these within their schema of the family
- be able to make any necessary changes in parenting style and skills, in order to manage risk and facilitate openness.

The wider family should:

- have made an informed choice for reunification
- accept therapeutic intervention
- share potential risk situations where the young person may sexually abuse a child, and have a holistic protection plan involving external supports or checks as appropriate, which are agreed and in operation to manage the situation
- be open about family dynamics whilst maintaining appropriate boundaries
- demonstrate healthy family interactions
- ensure that physical issues in the home requiring attention have been addressed (for example, location of bedrooms, etc.).

Summary

Whilst assessment of a young person who has sexually abused others is never an exact science, a well conducted and thorough assessment along the lines described above can increase the effectiveness and minimise the risks and difficulties involved in the intervention process. The involvement of a multidisciplinary team, including specialist workers who between them are skilled and knowledgeable in gathering relevant information and using relevant research, theories and models about young people who abuse, their victims and families, can help to increase the accuracy of assessments and appropriateness of decision-making. A commitment to inform and involve those who are involved or affected by the process of intervention, including the young person, family members, professionals and, if appropriate, the victim, can help to promote a consensus of opinion and cooperation with the assessment process and outcomes. Remaining focused on the young person who has abused others as a child in need can help an assessment to identify what intervention is required to help the young person develop skills and control behaviours that would otherwise lead to further abusive behaviour.

Assessment is the cornerstone of effective intervention. Without it we cannot accurately identify what changes are needed, what intervention is required, what progress is made, or when necessary change is achieved. In cases where young people have sexually abused others, assessments may be complex and resource-demanding. They offer, however, an opportunity to identify needs and potentially effective interventions that, if successfully implemented, could reduce the future incidence of sexual abuse. Such interventions have enormous potential in reducing the likelihood of significant harm not only to potential victims, but also to the young person who may otherwise demonstrate further sexually abusive behaviours.

Recommended reading

Barbaree, H. E., Marshall, W. L. and Husin, S. M. (eds.) (1993) *The Juvenile Sex Offender.* New York: Guilford Press.

Calder, M. (ed.) (1998) *Working with Young People Who Sexually Abuse.* Dorset: Russell House Publishing.

Erooga, M. and Masson, H. (eds.) (1999) *Children and Young People who Sexually Abuse Others.* London: Routledge.

Ryan G. D. and Lane, S. L. (eds.) (1991) *Juvenile Sexual Offending: Causes, Consequences, and Correction.* Lexington: Lexington Books.

References

Awad, G. A. and Saunders, E. B. (1989) 'Adolescent Child Molesters: Clinical Observations.' In *Child Psychiatry and Human Development, 19,* pp.195–206.

Barber, J. G. (1992) 'Relapse Prevention and the Need for Brief Social Interventions.' In *Journal of Substance Abuse Treatment, 9,* pp.157–68.

Barbaree, H. E., Marshall, W. L. and McCormick, J. (1998) 'The Development of Deviant Sexual Behaviour among Adolescents and its Implications for Prevention and Treatment.' In *Irish Journal of Psychology, 19,* pp.1–31.

Becker, J. V., Cunningham-Rathner, J. and Kaplan, M. S. (1986) 'Adolescent Sexual Offenders: Demographics, Criminal and Sexual Histories, and Recommendations for Reducing Future

Offences. Special Issue: The Prediction and Control of Violent Behaviour: II.' In *Journal of Interpersonal Violence, 1*, pp.431–45.

Behar, D. and Stewart, M. A. (1982) 'Aggressive Conduct Disorder of Children: The Clinical History and Direct Observation.' In *Acta Psychiatrica Scandanavia, 65*, pp.210–20.

Bentovim, A. (1998) 'Family Systemic Approach to Work with Young Sex Offenders.' In *The Irish Journal of Psychology, 19*, pp.19–135.

Bourke, M. L. and Donohue, B. (1996) 'Assessment and Treatment of Juvenile Sex Offenders: An Empirical Review.' In *Journal of Child Sexual Abuse, 5*, pp.47–70.

Cadoret, R. J. and Cain, C. (1980) 'Sex Differences in Predictors of Antisocial Behaviour in Adoptees.' In *Archives of General Psychiatry, 37*, pp.1171–5.

Department of Health, Home Office, and Department for Education and Employment (1999) *Working Together to Safeguard Children.* London: The Stationery Office.

Department of Health, Department for Employment and Education and Home Office (2000) *Framework for the Assessment of Children in Need and their Families.* London: The Stationery Office.

Garlick, Y., Marshall, W. L. and Thornton, D. (1996) 'Intimacy Deficits and Attribution of Blame among Sexual Offenders.' In *Legal and Criminological Psychology, 1*, 251–8.

George, W. H. and Marlatt, G. A. (1989) 'Introduction.' In D. R. Laws. *Relapse Prevention with Sex Offenders.* New York, Guilford Press.

Gilgun, J. (1988) 'Factors which Block the Development of Sexually Abusive Behaviour in Adults Abused as Children.' Paper presented at the National Conference on Male Victims and Offenders, Minneapolis, Mn.

Hackett, S., Print, B. and Dey, C. (1998) 'Brother Nature? Therapeutic Intervention with Young Men who Sexually Abuse their Siblings.' In A. Bannister (ed.) *From Hearing to Healing: Working with the Aftermath of Child Sexual Abuse* (second edition). Chichester: John Wiley.

Hanson, R. and Busiere, M. (1998) 'Predicting Relapse: A Meta-Analysis of Sexual Offender Recidivism Studies.' In *Journal of Consulting and Clinical Psychology, 66*, pp.348–62.

Hanson, R. K. and Slater, S. (1988) 'Sexual Victimization in the History of Sexual Abusers: A Review.' In *Annals of Sex Research, 1*, pp.485–99.

Lab, S., Shields, G. and Schondel, C. (1993) 'Research Note: An Evaluation of Juvenile Sex Offender Treatment.' In *Crime and Delinquency, 39*, pp.543–53.

Lewis, D., Shanok, S. and Pincus, J. (1981) 'Juvenile Male Assaulters.' In D. Lewis (ed.) *Vulnerabilities to Delinquency.* Jamaica, NY: Spectrum Pubs.

Loeber, R. and Dishion, T. J. (1983) 'Early Predictors of Male Delinquency: A Review.' In *Psychological Bulletin, 94*, pp.68–99.

Marshall, P. (1997) *The Prevalence of Convictions for Sexual Offending.* Research Findings, No. 55. London: Home Office.

Marshall W. L., Barbaree, H. and Eccles, A. (1993) 'Pavlovian Conditioning Processes in Adolescent Sex Offenders.' In H. E. Barbaree, W. L. Marshall and S. M. Hudson (eds.) *The Juvenile Sex Offender.* New York: Guilford Press.

O'Callaghan, D. and Corran, M. (1999) 'The Inter-agency Management of Children and Young People who Sexually Abuse.' In S. Bailey and M. Dolan, *Handbook of Adolescent Psychiatry.* London: Blackstone Scientific Press.

Patterson, G. R., DeBaryshe, B. D. and Ramsey, E. (1989) 'A Developmental Perspective on Antisocial Behaviour.' In *American Psychologist, 44*, pp.329–35.

Pithers, W. (1990) 'Relapse Prevention with Sexual Aggressors.' In W. Marshall, D. R. Laws and H. Barbaree (eds.) *Handbook of Sexual Aggression.* New York: Plenum.

Prentky, R., Knight, R., Straus, H., Rokou, F., Cerce, D. and Sims-Knight, J. (1989) 'Developmental Antecedents of Sexual Aggression.' In *Development and Psychopathology, 1,* pp.153–69.

Prentky, R. and Knight, R. (1993) 'Age of Onset of Sexual Assault: Criminal and Life History Correlates.' In G. Nagayama Hall, R. Hirschman, J. Graham and M. Zaragoza (eds.) *Sexual Aggression: Issues in Etiology, Assessment and Treatment.* Washington DC: Taylor and Francis.

Pithers, W., Marques, J., Gibat, C. and Marlatt, G. (1983) 'Relapse prevention with sexual aggressives.' In I. Stuart and J. Greer (eds.) *The Sexual Aggressor.* New York: Van Nostrand Reinhold.

Richardson, G. and Graham, F. (1997) 'Relapse Prevention.' In M. S. Hoghughi, S. R. Bhate and F. Graham, *Working with Sexually Abusive Adolescents.* Guilford: Sage.

Ryan, G. (1998) 'The Relevance of Early Life Experiences to the Behaviour of Sexually Abusive Youth.' In *The Irish Journal of Psychology, 19,* pp.32–48.

Ryan, G., Miyoshi, T., Metzner, J., Krugman, R. and Fryer, G. (1996) 'Trends in a National Sample of Sexually Abusive Youths.' In *Journal of the American Academy of Child and Adolescent Psychiatry, 35,* pp.17–25.

Sheridan, A., McKeown, K., Cherry, J., Donohoe, E., McGrath, C., Phelan, S., Tallon, M. and O'Reilly, K. (1998) 'Perspectives on Treatment Outcome in Adolescent Sexual Offending: A Study of Community-based Treatment Programmes.' In *The Irish Journal of Psychology, 19,* pp.168–80.

Skuse, D., Bentovim, A., Hodges, J., Stevenson, J., Andreou, C., Lanyado, M., New, M., Watkins, B. and McMillan, D. (1998) 'Risk Factors for the Development of Sexually Abusive Behaviour in Sexually Victimised Adolescent Males.' In *British Medical Journal, 317,* pp.175–9.

Smallbone, S. W. and Dadds, M. R. (1996) 'Childhood Attachment and Adult Attachment in Incarcerated Adult Male Sex offenders.' Submitted.

Smith, W, and Monastersky, C. (1986) 'Assessing Juvenile Sex Offenders Risk for Reoffending.' In *Criminal Justice and Behaviour, 13,* pp.115–40.

Steele, B. F. and Ryan, G. (1997) 'Deviancy: Development Gone Wrong.' In G. Ryan and S. Lane (eds.) *Juvenile Sex Offending: Causes, Consequences and Correction* (second edition). San Francisco, CA: Jossey-Bass.

Ward, T., Hudson, S. M., Marshall, W. L. and Steigert, T. (1995) 'Attachment Style and Intimacy Deficits in Sex Offenders: A Theoretical Framework.' In *Sexual Abuse: A Journal of Research and Treatment, 7,* pp.317–35.

Watkins, B. and Bentovim, A. (1992) 'The Sexual Abuse of Male Children and Adolescents: A Review of Current Research.' In *Journal of Child Psychology and Psychiatry, 33,* pp.197–248.

Weinrott, M. (1996) *Juvenile Sexual Aggression: A Critical Review.* Institute of Behavioural Science: University of Colorado.

White, J. W. and Humphrey, J. A. (1990) 'A Theoretical Model of Sexual Assault: An Empirical Test.' Paper presented at Symposium on Sexual Assault: Research, Treatment and Education, Southeastern Psychology Association, Atlanta.

The Contributors

Margaret Adcock is a social work consultant and trainer. She is a member of the Institute of Family Therapy. She works in the Child Care Consultation Team in the Department of Psychological Medicine at Great Ormond Street Hospital, London, and is also a consultant to three adoption agencies. Margaret has worked in a local authority social services department, a hospital setting and a voluntary agency, holding both practitioner and senior managerial positions. She is also engaged in social work post-qualifying education. Her publications include Good Enough Parenting (1985) and two editions of Significant Harm (1998) both co-edited with Richard White.

Dr Nick Banks (PhD) is a chartered psychologist and lecturer in social work at the University of Birmingham. He has research interests and publications in direct work with black families, sociopsychological assessment, child development, fostering and adoption, counselling and therapy. He is active as an expert witness in the courts and has expertise in abuse and parenting issues.

Anne Bannister qualified as a social worker and as a psychotherapist. She is presently a research fellow in the Centre for Childhood Studies at the University of Huddersfield. She was employed by NSPCC for 15 years, pioneering therapeutic work with young people who had been sexually abused. She has published widely on the subjects of child protection and therapy.

Dr Saul Becker (PhD) is the director of the Young Carers Research Group and a senior lecturer in social policy at Loughborough University. He has a professional background in social work and welfare rights. He has researched and published extensively on issues concerned with informal care, community care, social security, poverty and social work.

Hedy Cleaver is a senior research fellow at Royal Holloway College, University of London. She has been involved in the development of structured assessment records to accompany the *Framework for the Assessment of Children in Need and their Families* and together with I. Unell and J. Aldgate wrote *Children's Needs – Parenting Capacity* (1999).

David Cotson qualified as clinical psychologist in 1992. He is currently the senior practitioner in the Wandsworth locality of the South West London NHS Trust Services for Adults with Learning Disabilities. Since 1994 he has also been a trustee director of Access for Living, a charity providing supported housing for adults with learning disabilities in South East London.

Chris Dearden is a senior research fellow in the Young Carers Research Group at Loughborough University. She has a professional background in nursing. She has researched and published extensively on carers' and young carers' issues and is co-author, with Saul Becker and Jo Aldridge, of *Young Carers and their Families* (1998).

Marcus Erooga is an NSPCC area children's service manager in the North West and a visiting research fellow at Huddersfield University. He has experience of practice and management of services relating to sexual abuse and sexual offending. He is author of a number of publications on child protection issues, and is co-editor of *The Journal of Sexual Aggression* (NOTA, Whiting and Birch) and *Children and Young People Who Sexually Abuse Others: Challenges and Responses* (1999).

Joanne Friend is a social worker in the community team for adults with a learning disability in Derby City. She has a special interest in developing resources for parents with a learning disability.

Robbie Gilligan is a senior lecturer in social work and academic co-director of The Children's Research Centre at Trinity College, Dublin. He has recently co-authored with Brigid Daniel and Sally Wassell *Promoting Child Development: A Guide for Child Care and Protection Workers* (1999). He is a member of the editorial board of the journal *Child and Family Social Work* and of the advisory boards of the journals *Children and Society, Adoption and Fostering, Irish Journal of Social Work Research* and *Child Care in Practice*.

Rosemary Gordon works as a national training manager for the NSPCC Child Protection Training Group. Her lead area is developing and producing training and resource materials for an external market. These have included *Train and Protect, ABCD (Abuse and Children who are Disabled)* and *Turning Points* – a resource pack for communicating with children. She also provides consultancy on the production of training packs to other organisations and individuals. Ro has produced *The Child's World: Assessing Children in Need*, in partnership with the University of Sheffield and the Department of Health.

Jenny Gray trained as a social worker in New Zealand but has spent most of her professional career working in England. She has a child care background and joined the Social Services Inspectorate in 1990. Her current responsibility is to provide professional advice on child protection policy within the Department of Health. She has lead responsibility for the *Framework for the Assessment of Children in Need and their Families*.

Di Hart is employed by Camden Social Services. Whilst managing a children and families social work team in a hospital, she developed an interest in pre-birth assessment, particularly in relation to drug-using parents, and has undertaken a research project on this topic. Di is currently seconded to develop a service for children infected or affected by HIV, and to implement the *Framework for the Assessment of Children in Need and their Families*.

Enid Hendry is head of Child Protection Training for the NSPCC. Enid manages the NSPCC's National Training Group and in that role has been responsible for managing the development, production and dissemination of a number of training packs, most recently *Making an Impact: Children and Domestic Violence* and the pack accompanying the Assessment Framework. She is currently co-editing a book on inter-agency training, drawing on the work of PIAT (Promoting Inter-Agency Training), of which she is a founder member. She is Associate Editor of *Child Abuse Review*.

Professor Sheila Hollins is head of the Department of Psychiatry of Disability and professor of psychiatry of learning disability at St George's Hospital Medical School in the University of London and consultant psychiatrist in learning disability in South West London Community NHS Trust. She is a Fellow of the Royal College of Psychiatrists. In 1993 she was seconded to the Department of Health as senior policy adviser on learning disability. In 1994 she served a four-year term as chair of the Executive Committee of the Faculty of Psychiatry of Learning Disability at the Royal College of Psychiatrists. She is currently a member of the Minister's Advisory Committee on Learning Disability at the Department of Health. She has published widely in the area of learning disability and mental health and is also the editor of the 'Books Beyond Words' series of counselling books for people with learning disabilities on subjects such as bereavement.

Jan Horwath is a lecturer in social work studies at the University of Sheffield. Her professional and research interests focus on training and professional development, child care practice and the management of child welfare services. Her recent publications include *Effective Training in Social Care: From Theory to Practice* (1999), written with Tony Morrison, and *Working Together for Children on the Child Protection Register* (1999), co-edited with Martin Calder. She has been responsible, in partnership with the NSPCC and the Department of Health, for the production of the training pack *The Child's World: Assessing Children in Need.*

Professor David Howe is professor of social work at the University of East Anglia, Norwich, where he teaches and carries out research. His writing and research interests include adoption, attachment theory, and child abuse and neglect. He is the author of a number of books including most recently *Patterns of Adoption: Nature, Nurture and Psychosocial Development* (1998), and, with colleagues at the School of Social Work in Norwich, *Attachment Theory, Child Maltreatment and Family Support* (1999). He is also the editor of the journal *Child and Family Social Work.*

Gordon Jack qualified in social work from Oxford University in 1978 and spent the early part of his career working with children and families in social services departments in the North of England. He has been teaching child care social work on the MA/Dip.SW programme at Exeter University since 1991, where he is now head of the Department of Social Work and Probation Studies.

Helen James is a principal clinical psychologist with the Community Health Services Trust in Derby. Her job involves the assessment and support of parents with a learning disability.

Dr David P.H. Jones is a consultant child and family psychiatrist and senior lecturer at the Park Hospital for Children, Oxford. He leads a multidisciplinary child psychiatric clinical team providing services for abused children and their families. He has researched and published widely in the fields of child abuse and neglect, and consent to treatment among children.

Ruth Marchant works directly with disabled children and young people, and has particular interests in communication, consultation, children's rights and child protection. Ruth is a director of Triangle Services for children, an organisation providing national consultation and training in relation to disabled children, and direct support to children and young people in Sussex.

Tony Morrison is an independent social care trainer and consultant working widely in the areas of inter-agency development, supervision and interviewing skills. He retains a practice base at the G-MAP programme in Greater Manchester, where he runs a programme for parents whose children commit sexual assaults. His publications include *Staff Supervision in Social Care* (1993) and *Effective Staff Training in Social Care: From Theory to Practice* (1999), written with Jan Horwath.

Bobbie Print is a social worker and a director of the G-MAP programme, an independent therapeutic service to sexually aggressive young people based in Greater Manchester. The programme undertakes assessments, group, individual and family work with young people who sexually abuse others. Bobbie has specialised in this field of work for the past ten years. She has authored a number of publications and has trained extensively in this area of work. She was a founding member of NOTA and a member of the organisation's National Executive Committee until 1998.

Wendy Rose is a senior research fellow at the Open University. She worked for eleven years in the Department of Health as Assistant Chief Inspector (Children's Services) advising on the development and implementation of child care policy. Wendy has a background in social services practice, policy and management in local authority and National Health Service settings. She has been working with the Department of Health to develop guidance and associated resources, publications and research on assessing children in need and their families.

David Shemmings is a senior lecturer in social work at the University of East Anglia, Norwich. He is the author of a number of articles and chapters on involving family members in family support and child protection processes. He is the author of the Department of Health sponsored training pack *In On The Act*, concerning the involvement of children in decision-making processes, and is editor of the accompanying reader. Currently he is undertaking research into adult attachment theory and its implications for social work.

Yvonne Shemmings works as an independent consultant and social researcher, providing training and evaluation to social services and health organisations. Previously she was a social work practitioner in family support and child protection services and a manager responsible for planning and reviewing for 'looked after' children. She is the author of a number of chapters and articles on the empowerment of family members and was a member of the advisory group which produced the Department of Health sponsored training pack *In On The Act*, concerning the involvement of children in decision-making processes.

Dr Harriet Ward is senior research fellow in the Department of Social Services at Loughborough University. Since 1987 she has been involved in the Department of Health programme for assessing outcome for children looked after away from home (the 'Looked After Children' project). She has directed the research and development on this initiative since 1992. With Wendy Rose she is editing *Approaches to the Assessment of Need in Children's Services* (forthcoming 2001) which explores issues involving assessment of need at service and strategic levels.

Subject Index

Author Index